TypeScript 2.x By Example

Build engaging applications with TypeScript, Angular, and
NativeScript on the Azure platform

Sachin Ohri

BIRMINGHAM - MUMBAI

TypeScript 2.x By Example

First published: December 2017

Production reference: 1191217

Published by Packt Publishing Ltd.
Livery Place
35 Livery Street
Birmingham
B3 2PB, UK.

ISBN 978-1-78728-003-8

www.packtpub.com

Credits

Author
Sachin Ohri

Reviewer
Sandeep Singh

Commissioning Editor
Richa Tripathi

Acquisition Editor
Denim Pinto

Content Development Editor
Nikhil Borkar

Technical Editor
Madhunikita Sunil Chindarkar

Copy Editor
Safis Editing

Project Coordinator
Ulhas Kambali

Proofreader
Safis Editing

Indexer
Rekha Nair

Graphics Coordinator
Tom Scaria

Production Coordinator
Nilesh Mohite

About the Author

Sachin Ohri is a Technology Architect with a keen interest in web-based technologies. He has been writing web applications for more than a decade, with technologies such as .NET, JavaScript, Durandal, Angular, and TypeScript.

He works on providing technical solutions, including architectural design, technical support, and development expertise, to Fortune 500 companies.

He considers himself a polygot developer willing to learn new languages and technology. Recently, he has been focusing on cloud-based web application development with Microsoft Azure. He holds various Microsoft certifications, such as Microsoft Azure Architect, Microsoft ASP.NET MVC web application, and Microsoft Programming with C#.

Acknowledgments

It would not have been possible to write this book without the complete support of my family and friends. They have been there, inspiring and motivating me along the way. Thanks to my friends who provided technical support and guidance during the course of this project.

Special thanks to the Packt team, Anurag, Nikhil, and Denim, who have been very encouraging and made the entire process smooth.

About the Reviewer

Sandeep Singh has over 15 years of experience in web application development. He currently works as a senior solution architect at one of the Fortune 100 companies. He specializes in JavaScript, Angular, and React.

I would like to thank my family for supporting me through this endeavor.

www.PacktPub.com

For support files and downloads related to your book, please visit www.PacktPub.com. Did you know that Packt offers eBook versions of every book published, with PDF and ePub files available? You can upgrade to the eBook version at www.PacktPub.com and as a print book customer, you are entitled to a discount on the eBook copy. Get in touch with us at service@packtpub.com for more details.

At www.PacktPub.com, you can also read a collection of free technical articles, sign up for a range of free newsletters and receive exclusive discounts and offers on Packt books and eBooks.

https://www.packtpub.com/mapt

Get the most in-demand software skills with Mapt. Mapt gives you full access to all Packt books and video courses, as well as industry-leading tools to help you plan your personal development and advance your career.

Why subscribe?

- Fully searchable across every book published by Packt
- Copy and paste, print, and bookmark content
- On demand and accessible via a web browser

Customer Feedback

Thanks for purchasing this Packt book. At Packt, quality is at the heart of our editorial process. To help us improve, please leave us an honest review on this book's Amazon page at https://www.amazon.com/dp/1787280039. If you'd like to join our team of regular reviewers, you can email us at customerreviews@packtpub.com. We award our regular reviewers with free eBooks and videos in exchange for their valuable feedback. Help us be relentless in improving our products!

This book is dedicated to Shaurya and Inaya.

Table of Contents

Preface

TypeScript has been a revolution in client-side development. It has taken mainstream concepts, such as types, classes, interfaces, generics, and decorators, and introduced them to the JavaScript world. The best part is that TypeScript does not introduce any new language but provides features that are currently in TC39 discussions for JavaScript.

All JavaScript code is valid TypeScript code, which allows developers to migrate and use TypeScript in the existing application. In this book, we will comprehensively cover TypeScript features, from basic features to advanced ones. We will introduce the features along with hands-on application development to aid better understanding.

Along with TypeScript, we will also look at Angular and learn the intricacies of the framework. We will be developing two applications along the way and both these applications will use Angular as their frontend framework.

By end of this book, we will look at the NativeScript framework, which will help us convert our Angular/TypeScript applications to native mobile platform applications. We will also look at Microsoft Azure as our cloud platform to deploy our web applications.

The purpose of this book is to provide readers with the knowledge of TypeScript and Angular so that they can build real-world applications effectively and efficiently.

What this book covers

Chapter 1, *Getting Started with TypeScript*, provides us with an introduction to TypeScript and its features. We will create a small ToDo application, which provides insights into basic TypeScript features.

Chapter 2, *Our First Application – Sports News Combinator*, introduces us to the basic concepts of TypeScript and Angular. We'll take a look at types in TypeScript and how to set up an Angular application, along with the concept of components.

Chapter 3, *Sports News Combinator – Adding Features*, covers important concepts of TypeScript, such as interfaces, classes, and object-oriented programming. In Angular, we look at data binding, directives, and templates.

Chapter 4, *Sports News Combinator – the Final Version*, adds final features to the application and, in doing so, covers decorators, dependency injection, routing, and HTTP using RxJS observables in Angular.

Chapter 5, *Application 2 – Trello,* is our second application. With this application, we'll look at generics, namespaces, and modules in TypeScript. We'll also look at some of the advanced features of Angular, such as communication between components and life cycle hooks.

Chapter 6, *Trello – Adding Features*, takes us deeper into the feature set of TypeScript and Angular. We cover iterators and async programming using callbacks, promises, and observables. In Angular, we'll look at pipes and dependency injection.

Chapter 7, *Testing the Trello Application*, introduces us to the testing features provided in Angular. We look at the unit testing of services, pipes, and components.

Chapter 8, *Trello – Using Angular CLI*, provides us with the details of the Angular CLI and its feature set. We look at creating new applications, generating components, services, pipes, classes, and interfaces. Then, we shift our focus to features such as building, serving, and linting any Angular-based web application.

Chapter 9, *Trello Mobile – Using NativeScript*, allows us to convert our web application into a native mobile application. In this chapter, we will look at the NativeScript framework and see how we can use its features to create Android and iOS applications from our web application.

Chapter 10, *Deploying Sample Trello on the Cloud Using Microsoft Azure*, explains cloud as our deployment platform. We will look at Azure as *Platform as a Service* and deploy our application using FTP and GitHub. We will also look at how Azure enables us to perform continuous deployment for our application.

What you need for this book

All our examples and code snippets use TypeScript and Angular, which can be developed in any IDE. We prefer to use Visual Studio Code but you can use any IDE that you are comfortable with, such as Sublime, Atom, and WebStorm, among others.

Who this book is for

This book does not assume any prerequisite knowledge of TypeScript or Angular from its readers. We cover all the concepts of TypeScript and Angular, starting from the basic ones and moving towards the advanced concepts.

We do cover the concepts of JavaScript with respect to TypeScript, but it would be helpful if you have some basic understanding of JavaScript.

All our applications use basic HTML and CSS; although not necessary, having a basic knowledge of these can help readers design applications more easily. We do provide the entire code base, including all the HTML and CSS for the readers to refer.

Conventions

In this book, you will find a number of text styles that distinguish between different kinds of information. Here are some examples of these styles and an explanation of their meaning. Code words in text, database table names, folder names, filenames, file extensions, pathnames, dummy URLs, user input, and Twitter handles are shown as follows: "The next lines of code read the link and assign it to the to the `BeautifulSoup` function." A block of code is set as follows:

```
#import packages into the project
from bs4 import BeautifulSoup
from urllib.request import urlopen
import pandas as pd
```

When we wish to draw your attention to a particular part of a code block, the relevant lines or items are set in bold: [default] exten => s,1,Dial(Zap/1|30) exten => s,2,Voicemail(u100) exten => s,102,Voicemail(b100) exten => i,1,Voicemail(s0) Any command-line input or output is written as follows:

```
C:\Python34\Scripts> pip install –upgrade pip
C:\Python34\Scripts> pip install pandas
```

New terms and **important words** are shown in bold. Words that you see on the screen, for example, in menus or dialog boxes, appear in the text like this: "In order to download new modules, we will go to **Files** | **Settings** | **Project Name** | **Project Interpreter**."

Warnings or important notes appear like this.

Tips and tricks appear like this.

Reader feedback

Feedback from our readers is always welcome. Let us know what you think about this book-what you liked or disliked. Reader feedback is important for us as it helps us develop titles that you will really get the most out of. To send us general feedback, simply email feedback@packtpub.com, and mention the book's title in the subject of your message. If there is a topic that you have expertise in and you are interested in either writing or contributing to a book, see our author guide at www.packtpub.com/authors.

Customer support

Now that you are the proud owner of a Packt book, we have a number of things to help you to get the most from your purchase.

Downloading the example code

You can download the example code files for this book from your account at http://www.packtpub.com. If you purchased this book elsewhere, you can visit http://www.packtpub.com/support and register to have the files emailed directly to you. You can download the code files by following these steps:

1. Log in or register to our website using your email address and password.
2. Hover the mouse pointer on the **SUPPORT** tab at the top.
3. Click on **Code Downloads & Errata**.
4. Enter the name of the book in the **Search** box.

5. Select the book for which you're looking to download the code files.
6. Choose from the drop-down menu where you purchased this book from.
7. Click on **Code Download**.

Once the file is downloaded, please make sure that you unzip or extract the folder using the latest version of:

- WinRAR / 7-Zip for Windows
- Zipeg / iZip / UnRarX for Mac
- 7-Zip / PeaZip for Linux

The code bundle for the book is also hosted on GitHub at `https://github.com/PacktPublishing/TypeScript-2x-By-Example`. We also have other code bundles from our rich catalog of books and videos available at `https://github.com/PacktPublishing/`. Check them out!

Errata

Although we have taken every care to ensure the accuracy of our content, mistakes do happen. If you find a mistake in one of our books-maybe a mistake in the text or the code-we would be grateful if you could report this to us. By doing so, you can save other readers from frustration and help us improve subsequent versions of this book. If you find any errata, please report them by visiting `http://www.packtpub.com/submit-errata`, selecting your book, clicking on the **Errata Submission Form** link, and entering the details of your errata. Once your errata are verified, your submission will be accepted and the errata will be uploaded to our website or added to any list of existing errata under the Errata section of that title. To view the previously submitted errata, go to `https://www.packtpub.com/books/content/support` and enter the name of the book in the search field. The required information will appear under the **Errata** section.

Piracy

Piracy of copyrighted material on the internet is an ongoing problem across all media. At Packt, we take the protection of our copyright and licenses very seriously. If you come across any illegal copies of our works in any form on the internet, please provide us with the location address or website name immediately so that we can pursue a remedy. Please contact us at `copyright@packtpub.com` with a link to the suspected pirated material. We appreciate your help in protecting our authors and our ability to bring you valuable content.

Questions

If you have a problem with any aspect of this book, you can contact us at `questions@packtpub.com`, and we will do our best to address the problem.

Getting Started with TypeScript

"JavaScript that scales."

"TypeScript is a typed superset of JavaScript that compiles to plain JavaScript."

"Any browser, any host, any OS, and open source."

These are official statements by the TypeScript team.

"Surprisingly simple, extraordinarily powerful."

This is how I describe TypeScript.

The purpose of this book is to provide readers with an opportunity to see and understand the preceding quotes and appreciate TypeScript for its power and elegance.

In this chapter, we will introduce TypeScript and take a brief look at its features that help us write client- and server-side (Node.js) applications that are scalable, maintainable, reusable, and future-proof.

The fundamental principle of TypeScript is that it's a *superset of JavaScript* and *all valid JavaScript is a valid TypeScript*. This allows developers to start using TypeScript with their existing knowledge of JavaScript and be productive.

We will be covering the following topics in this chapter:

- We will start by looking at what the common issues/pitfalls of JavaScript are, the so-called *not-so-good parts*.
- Then we will move on to take a look at how TypeScript tries to solve those.
- We will then dive deeper and explore the features of TypeScript that stand out from its competitors and are the most appealing.
- We will also look at TypeScript architecture and its features.
- TypeScript provides support for the wide array of editors; we will look at configuring Visual Studio and Visual Studio Code for TypeScript development.
- We will get familiar with the TypeScript compiler and how TypeScript allows the configuration of compiler options. TypeScript is amazingly flexible for equipping developers with the power to configure the settings when compiling their code.
- At the end of this chapter, we will look at some of TypeScript's widely used syntax and keywords. Post that, to kick-start our journey, we will create a small application. We will develop a to-do list in TypeScript where a user can create a new to-do item and its description and view the list. This example will not use any other frameworks such as jQuery but will be purely developed in TypeScript. We will demonstrate how plain TypeScript can work and help us develop web applications.

So, let's get going!

The current state of JavaScript

If you have developed any web applications and written more than a few lines of code in JavaScript, you will have encountered one of the many quirks of JavaScript. Web application development has gone through some major changes in the last decade or so. We have been writing more and more complex applications that need to have a highly interactive user interface. There have been libraries which have helped us along the way, such as jQuery, Knockout, and so on, but they can only go so far to manage an ever-expanding code base.

Applications written in JavaScript tend to become cluttered and difficult to maintain after a few hundred lines of code if we do not follow best practices and patterns. To solve this problem, many JavaScript frameworks have come along, such as Durandal, Backbone, React, and Angular, which have helped manage these complexities. They did succeed to some extent, but we were still writing in JavaScript and were still susceptible to its nature.

JavaScript is a very flexible language with features such as dynamic typing, hoisting, and closures. Flexibility comes with a price and if you are building medium- to large-scale applications, this price of writing and managing JavaScript code is very steep. If we don't follow recommended design patterns such as the revealing module pattern or the prototype pattern, we quickly end up with code that is difficult to manage.

The not-so-good parts of JavaScript

JavaScript, for all its flexibility and features which make it suitable for web-based applications, has some quirks which, if not understood and implemented correctly, cause applications to have unintended behaviors. If you have done development in JavaScript, you will have read or heard about the *good parts of JavaScript*, a term made famous by Douglas Crockford, but let's look at the *not-so-good parts* as well.

Features

The following are the features of JavaScript which should be understood before you can write an effective large-scale application:

- Type inference
- Arrays
- Equality comparison
- Null and undefined

Type inference

One of the main features of JavaScript is that it's a dynamically typed language. This means a type of a variable is determined at runtime and the compiler does not generate any errors if there is a type mismatch until it fails. We can have the same variable hold a string, a number, an array, or an object and JavaScript will not complain, but it can cause errors at runtime if not handled. JavaScript uses type inference to identify the type of data stored in a variable, based on which it operates on the variable. The following is an example where type inference fails between a number and a string.

In the following code, when num is assigned a value of 1, JavaScript infers it as a number and performs addition when we try to add a value to num. Later, when we assign a string to num, JavaScript infers it as a string and performs concatenation when we try to add a value:

```
var num = 1;
num += 1;
console.log(typeof(num)); // returns: number
console.log(num);   // returns: 2
num = 'str';
Console.log(typeof(num));   // returns: string
num += 1; // retun: str1
```

Arrays

Arrays are a very common example of where JavaScript dynamic typing fails. We define an array variable, score, which has the list of scores in it. To fetch the selected elements from an array, we use the slice function. Till the time score is an array, this works, but imagine if someone wanted to assign a single element in an array and instead they assigned a number. Now the same slice function will fail:

```
var score = [1,2,3,4,5,6];
console.log(score.slice(2, 4)); // returns: [3,4]
score = 10;
console.log(score.slice(2, 4)); // Uncaught TypeError: score.slice is not a
function
```

Equality comparison

If you have a number in quotes, JavaScript will determine it as a string but, if you do a comparison in an if statement to a literal number, then JavaScript will automatically try to convert the string into a number and perform the comparison:

```
var result = '1';
console.log(result == 1); // returns true
console.log(result === 1); // returns false
```

Now, this can be something which you may or may not have expected to happen, because sometimes we may not want JavaScript to do these type of comparisons. For small applications, you can make sure that you are passing proper types, but that's not so easy in the case of large-scale applications. One solution would be to use === rather than ==, which makes JavaScript not coerce the type of a variable. These solutions are not intuitive and we have seen many developers making this mistake.

Null or undefined

Like dynamic type, JavaScript allows variables to be assigned null or undefined. Unless proper validations are done every time a variable is accessed, we get to see errors such as **undefined is not a function** or **cannot read property x of undefined**. This happens because there are no specific checks in JavaScript by the language to make sure we are not accessing or assigning any variable or function as undefined or null. TypeScript, with its type declaration, reduces the probability of having such issues and, in addition to that, TypeScript has a compiler flag, `strictNullChecks`, which allows the compiler to flag any instance where the application is assigning any null or undefined type. The TypeScript compiler also does control flow analysis to keep track of whether a variable can be null or undefined.

The control flow analysis means that TypeScript is able to scan through the code and identify whether a specific variable or property can be null or undefined.

<h2>Soft skill

Another challenge can be for the developer with the non-JavaScript background. A lot of developers move from server-side languages such as Java or C# and are accustomed to writing an object-oriented style of code. JavaScript, with its keywords of *prototype*, does provide a mechanism to achieve most of the object-oriented concepts but these concepts are not easy to understand and use.

TypeScript solves these problems by adding types to the variables, to parameters, and to the return value of functions. Having types defined helps TypeScript to identify and flag such scenarios. TypeScript maintains the flexibility of JavaScript with respect to types by not making it mandatory to define them. TypeScript, similar to JavaScript, infers the type based on the initial value assigned to the variable. If, at a later point in time, the same variable is assigned a conflicting type, TypeScript flags it at design time as well as at compile time.

 TypeScript has a special type, `any`, to handle situations where you are not sure what type value a variable can hold. This comes in especially handy when we want to start using TypeScript in our existing JavaScript project and don't want to migrate the existing code base. If we copy our existing JavaScript code to a TypeScript file (valid JavaScript is a valid TypeScript), TypeScript will try to infer data types for all the variables and parameters and where it's not able to infer, it will assign `any` as a data type.

TypeScript to the rescue

TypeScript is cross-platform language and works on Windows, Linux, and macOS. You can create TypeScript applications on any platform and an IDE of your choice. Modern web application frameworks also support TypeScript, with Angular one of the prominent ones. In fact, Angular 2 has been written in TypeScript by Google.

While developing any large-scale web applications, there is a lot of JavaScript that is involved for things such as validations, navigation, the workflow of the application, UI rendering, API calls, and so on. In my experience, any time JavaScript reaches a few thousand lines of code, it becomes overly complex, which causes unintended behavior and runtime errors. TypeScript provides features which help manage these complexities, such as static typing, encapsulation using modules and classes, custom types, interfaces, and much more.

Benefits of TypeScript

There are many benefits of TypeScript over JavaScript and we will cover a few of them here:

- TypeScript is a superset of JavaScript. This means any JavaScript code you have is already a valid TypeScript code. You can take your existing JavaScript code, copy it into a TypeScript file, and it will be compiled successfully. This helps developers who have some familiarity with JavaScript to transition to TypeScript. The following figure shows where TypeScript resides in the JavaScript ecosystem:

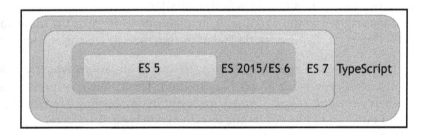

As the preceding figure shows, TypeScript contains all the existing features of ES5 and ES6, and the proposed features of ES7, along with some features which are specific to TypeScript, such as interfaces.

- The JavaScript language has a handful of types, for example, *String, Number,* and *Boolean,* but TypeScript adds in few more primitive types to the list, such as *Tuple, Enum,* and *Never.* TypeScript also allows you to create your own custom types in an object-oriented fashion. These types help make your code safer, more manageable, and easier to refactor with fewer bugs, and increases developer productivity. The TypeScript compiler uses all these types to check the code for errors and helps to resolve the issues long before the code is deployed in the production environment. Having types helps create a faster development cycle.

- TypeScript, with all its types, compiles into vanilla JavaScript so that it can run on any web browser, on any platform, or even on the server side using Node.js. The syntax of TypeScript is not specific to Microsoft technologies but follows the JavaScript ECMA standards. TypeScript follows ES6 (ECMAScript 2015) syntax where possible and for features that are currently not available in ES6, uses the proposed ES7 feature set. TypeScript, under its compiler option, allows you to compile the code to either the ES3, ES5, or ES6 version of JavaScript. The following figure shows the process of compiling TypeScript to plain old JavaScript:

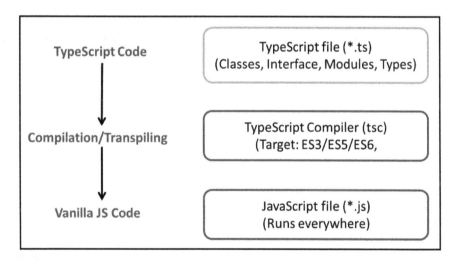

- There are a rich set of editors that can be used to program with TypeScript, such as Visual Studio, Visual Studio Code, Sublime, Atom, and so on. If you are using such an editor, it provides you with features such as IntelliSense, design-time error checks, navigation between code paths, renaming, and refactoring options. We will explore editors in the upcoming section.

TypeScript comparison with JavaScript

Let's look at an example of how TypeScript makes life easy with types and error checking. Take a look at the following JavaScript code. It's perfectly legal code, though it is not following the recommended best practices:

```
function getLargestNumber(arr){
    result=0;
    for( index =0; index < arr.length; index++){
        if(result < arr[index]){
            result =  arr[index];
        }
    }
    if(result > 0) {
       result = true;
    }
    else result = false;
    return result;
}
score = [1,2,3,4,5,6,];
highestScore= getLargestNumber(score);
```

The preceding code, when executed, will return `true` from `getLargestNumber`, something which you would not have expected.

This code has multiple potential bugs in it:

- The `result`, `index`, `score`, and `highestscore` variables are not declared with a `var` or `let` keyword so they end up leaking into the global namespace
- We are using `result` to store the largest number and then assign a Boolean value to it based on what is stored in `result`

Now, let's copy this code to the TypeScript file. It immediately shows these errors with a red squiggly line. If you hover over any of these variables, you will see the message `Cannot find name 'result'`. TypeScript does not allow declaration without a `var` or `let` keyword (the `let` keyword was introduced in ES6). The following screenshot shows the code when copied to a TypeScript file:

```
1    function getLargestNumber(arr){
2        result=0;
3        for(index =0; index < arr.length; index++){
4            if(result < arr[index]){
5                result =  arr[index];
6            }
7            if(result > 0) {
8                result = true;
9            }
10           else{
11               result = false;
12           }
13       }
14       return result;
15   }
16
17
18   score = [1,2,3,4,5,6,];
19   highestScore= getLargestNumber(score);
```

Let's add the `let` keyword before all the variable declarations; this will help us get rid of the first error. For the second issue, where we are assigning two different types of values, *number* and *boolean*, to the `result` variable, TypeScript does not allow that. At line **2**, TypeScript implicitly inferred *number* as a type for the `result` and when we try to assign *boolean* on lines **8** and **10**, TypeScript alerts us to the error. The following screenshot shows the code after we have added the `let` keyword for all variable declarations:

```
1    function getLargestNumber(arr){
2        let result=0;
3        for(let index =0; index < arr.length; index++){
4            if(result < arr[index]){
5                result =  arr[index];
6            }
7            /* if(result > 0) {
8                result = true; // TypeScript warns that type 'true' is not assignable to type number
9            }
10           else{
11               result = false; // TypeScript warns that type 'false' is not assignable to type number
12           }*/
13       }
14       return result;
15   }
16
17
18   let score = [1,2,3,4,5,6,];
19   let highestScore= getLargestNumber(score);
```

There is one more error reported by TypeScript in the preceding code, for input parameter to the function. The error states that **Parameter 'arr' implicitly has an 'any' type**. This is because we have not defined the type of the input variable. In TypeScript, we can configure our compiler options to enable/disable certain types of errors. This allows teams to create their own rules of what should be termed as an error and what should not. In our application, I have enabled a compiler flag, noImplicitAny, as true. This option informs the compiler to flag variables whose data type is *any*.

In our example, TypeScript is not able to identify the data type of the variable arr, and hence assigns the any type, which is then flagged as an error. So, let's assign the data type to our variable as shown in the following screenshot:

```
1    function getLargestNumber(arr:number[]){
2        let result=0;
3        for(let index =0; index < arr.length; index++){
4            if(result < arr[index]){
5                result =  arr[index];
6            }
7            /* if(result > 0) {
8                result = true; // TypeScript warns that type 'true' is not assignable to type number
9            }
10           else{
11               result = false; // TypeScript warns that type 'false' is not assignable to type number
12           }*/
13       }
14       return result;
15   }
16
17
18   let score = [1,2,3,4,5,6,];
19   let highestScore= getLargestNumber(score);
```

Now, if we try calling getLargestNumber by passing data other than an array of numbers, TypeScript will flag that as well. The following code will fail because we are trying to call getLargestNumber by assigning an array of strings:

```
let names=['john,','jane','scott'];
let sortedNames= getLargestNumber(names);
```

We saw in these examples the benefits of having a strongly-typed language. If we try to assign a number to a variable with the type string, TypeScript will flag it as an error, and if you are using one of the editors which have TypeScript integrated into them, you may end up seeing these errors as you type. If not, then these will be caught by the TypeScript compiler. These benefits help us churn out high-quality code with minimal possible bugs and increased productivity.

With pure JavaScript, you will have to do type checking at every possible point. Never assume that your function will receive the right set of parameters; always check the output returned by a function which may be a number or Boolean as in our case above. TypeScript helps solve all these problems.

 TypeScript will compile the code and produce JavaScript even if there are any design-/compile-time errors.

Alternatives to TypeScript

To overcome the flaws and limitations of base JavaScript, many alternate programming languages mushroomed, including CoffeeScript, TypeScript, Dart, and recently Flow, that compile to JavaScript, in the end. All these languages are trying to solve challenges such as encapsulation, scoping, and type inference, among others. Some of them have been there for a while and some are pretty new. CoffeeScript is very similar to Python and relies on concise syntax and lambda expressions. Both CoffeeScript and Dart try to encapsulate JavaScript by introducing a new language which would then convert to JavaScript. The primary difference between these languages and TypeScript is that TypeScript does not introduce new syntax but builds on top of JavaScript. If you are a JavaScript developer, it's very easy to start with TypeScript but that's not the same case with these languages.

Flow was introduced by Facebook in 2016 as a way to provide type checking to JavaScript. It is very similar to TypeScript in the sense that the primary purpose is to provide a way to solve the problem of static types. Flow also enjoys significant support, primarily in the Facebook domain of applications such as **React** and **React Native**. Both Flow and TypeScript are very good choices to help write robust JavaScript code. One primary difference between Flow and TypeScript is that Flow only does type checking and relies on tools such as **Babel** to do the transpiling, whereas TypeScript has a very exhaustive set of tools to provide type checking and transpiling.

Another option is to write JavaScript in ES6 (ES2015) format; the advantage of this is that you are writing pure JavaScript and there is no need to do any transpiling or learn a new framework. But, currently, not all browsers support all the features of ES6 and you would have to make use of frameworks such as Babel to convert your ES6 to ES5. TypeScript uses most of the existing ES6 features and adds some features such as types to make the code more robust and error-free.

TypeScript features

The TypeScript architecture can be divided into five main components:

- **Core TypeScript compiler**: This is the base of the TypeScript language; it manages all the low-level tasks which allow TypeScript to expose its rich set of features and compile the code into JavaScript. The core compiler consists of modules such as **type resolver**, which is responsible for resolving types, checking semantic operations, and providing error or warning conditions where appropriate, and preprocessor, which manages references between files using `import` or `/// <reference path=.../>`.

- **Language service**: The language service is a layer on top of the core compiler which exposes features that are required by editors, such as IntelliSense, debugging, statement completion, refactoring using symbols, and formatting. The language service is also responsible for incremental build configuration using the `watch` flag. This configuration allows the TypeScript compiler to keep watching for any changes to your files and if it detects any changes, the compiler automatically initiates the build.

- **Standalone compiler**: The standalone compiler is the high-level compiler exposed by TypeScript. In TypeScript, to compile the code, we use this standalone compiler (`tsc`) which runs through the TypeScript file (`*.ts`) and spits out a JavaScript (`*.js`) file.

- **TypeScript features**: The TypeScript features which are exposed to use are provided at this layer. This layer is an abstraction of the language service and the core compiler.

- **Editor plugins**: TypeScript supports a wide variety of editors through plugins. Editors such as Visual Studio Code, Visual Studio, Sublime, and Atom are the most popular ones. TypeScript plugins help you write code in these editors by providing support for auto build, IntelliSense, design-time error checking, and so on.

The following diagram shows the high-level architecture of TypeScript:

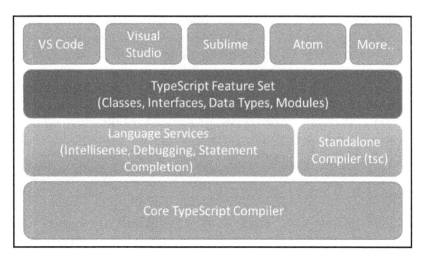

Features

TypeScript has a rich feature set which creates a very compelling reason for its use. These features provide a platform to write large-scale web applications, all the while keeping code manageable, robust, error-free, and modular. The following list shows the main features provided by TypeScript as listed here:

- Data types
- Control flow analysis
- Encapsulation
- Inheritance
- Interface
- Shapes
- Decorators

Now, let's take a look at the features in detail.

Data types

Duck typing is the ability of a language to determine types at runtime. JavaScript follows the duck typing paradigm; it has types but they are determined dynamically and developers don't declare them. TypeScript goes one step further and adds types to the language. Having data types has been proven to increase productivity and code quality, and reduce errors at runtime. It's better to catch errors at compile time rather than have programs fail at runtime. TypeScript provides the feature of inferring types, thus allowing developers to only optionally define types. As seen in the following code, projectStatus is assigned the type number:

```
let projectStatus = 1;
projectStatus = 'Success';// Error: Type 'Success' is not assignable to
type 'number'
```

TypeScript determined the type as number and then alerted us when we were trying to assign a string. TypeScript also provides features such as union types (we can assign multiple types to a variable) and intersection types. We will be discussing these in detail in the next chapter.

Control flow analysis

TypeScript provides type analysis based on the code flow. Types can be narrowed or broadened based on the code flow. This helps to reduce logical errors when we have multiple types of a variable and logic varies with type as shown in the following code:

```
function projectStatus (x: string | number) {
    if (typeof x === 'string') { // x is string | number
        x = 10;
    }
    return x; // type of `number
}
```

TypeScript by code flow analysis determined that the type of x returned from the function is a number.

Encapsulation

Encapsulation is one of the key pillars of object-oriented programming, which states that objects of a function should only expose required members to external code and hide the implementation details. With encapsulation, we provide a flexibility to the system to change its implementation without changing the contract. TypeScript provides encapsulation through the concept of classes, modules, and access modifiers. Classes are like containers which contain common features. Classes expose only the required fields using access modifiers such as `private/public/protected`. Modules are the containers of classes and provide another level of encapsulation for the group of classes achieving specific functionality:

```
class News{
    public channelNumber : number;
    public newsTitle: string;
    private url: string;
}
let espn = new News();
espn.channelNumber = 1;
espn.newsTitle = 'NFL Today';
espn.url = 'http://go.espn.com'; // url is private and only accessible
inside the class
```

The `espn.url` will throw an error because the URL property is private to the class.

Inheritance

In object-oriented programming, inheritance allows us to extend the functionality of a class from a parent class. In TypeScript, we use a keyword, `extends`, in a child class and refer the parent class. By extending the functionality in the child class, we can have access to all the public members of the parent class:

```
class Editor {
  constructor(public name: string,public isTypeScriptCompatible : Boolean)
{}

  details() {
    console.log('Editor: ' + this.name + ', TypeScript installed: ' +
this.isTypeScriptCompatible);
  }
}

class VisualStudio extends Editor{
    public OSType: string
```

```
    constructor(name: string,isTypeScriptCompatible : Boolean, OSType:
string) {
        super(name,isTypeScriptCompatible);
        this.OSType = OSType;
    }
}

let VS = new VisualStudio('VSCode', true, 'all');
VS.details();
```

The `VisualStudio` class extends the `Editor` class and hence the instance of `VisualStudio` inherits the `details` method.

Interface

The primary purpose of an interface is to drive code consistency. An interface is a contract defined and any class that *implements* the interface needs to implement all the properties of that interface. The interface is a pure TypeScript concept and is not part of ECMAScript; this means that when TypeScript code is converted to JavaScript, interfaces are not converted:

```
interface Planet{
    name: string;
    weather: string;
}

class Earth implements Planet {
    name: string;
    weather: string;
}

let planet: Planet= new Earth();
```

Shapes

TypeScript allows the flexibility to assign objects with different identifiers if they have the same attributes. This means that if two objects have the same set of attributes then they are considered to be of the same type and we can assign one object to another:

```
interface Planet{
    name: string;
    weather: string;
}

class Earth implements Planet {
    name: string;
    weather: string;
}

let planet: Planet;

class Pluto{
    name: string;
    weather: string;
}

planet = new Pluto()
```

Here, we assigned an instance of `Pluto` to `planet` even though `Pluto` does not implement `Planet`. This happens because the attributes and their type in the `Pluto` class are same as interface .

Decorators

Decorators are a TypeScript-specific concept at the moment, although they are in a stage two proposal for JavaScript (`https://github.com/tc39/proposal-decorators`). The decorator is one of the structural design patterns from the *Gang of Four*, which implies adding additional responsibility to an object. In TypeScript, they are experimental features and we need to enable them in the compiler configuration (`tsconig.json`). TypeScript allows the use of decorators on classes, properties, methods, and accessors. Decorators are commonly used in Angular and we will see the examples in the upcoming chapters.

TypeScript syntax and keywords

The TypeScript program is organized into modules, which contain classes, functions, and variables. Each of these features are achieved using specific keywords, such as `export` for exposing a class or function to an outside module, and `import` for accessing a class or function from a different module. The following figure shows the high-level structure of typical TypeScript code. The module is the outermost container which will be composed of multiple classes. Each class will contain variables and functions to provide a specific functionality:

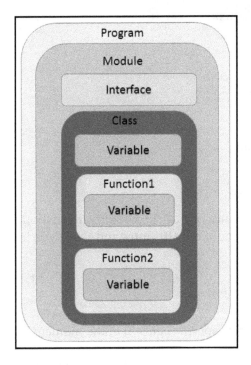

The following table provides an overview of some of the keywords available in TypeScript:

Keyword	Description
Basic types	TypeScript has many basic types, such as Boolean, Number, String, Array, Any, Never, Null, and Undefined.
Classes	These are containers for properties and functions. Classes compile into JavaScript functions.

Constructor	Similar to the OOP concept, providing a method which is called when an object of a class is created. It can be used to initialize properties in a class.
Interface	Defines a contract which is then implemented by a class. It can have properties and function declaration.
Implements	Keyword used to inform the compiler which interface is implemented by a class.
...	Rest parameter, which allows a function to accept multiple parameters and receive them as an array.
=>	Fat arrow function, which provides alternate syntax for defining functions.
Module	Container for classes.
Import/export	Keywords used to define which members of a module are exported or imported.
Generics	Generics allow you to write functions which may accept different data types. This allows us to write functions which are reusable.
Enum	Enum allows us to define a set of constants which have numeric values associated with it.
Iterators	Any object which implements `System.iterator` is iterable. This means that object will return a list of values which can be iterated upon.

There are many more keywords and features provided by TypeScript and we will go through them and use them in our examples in subsequent chapters.

Installation and setup

In this section, we will look at the installation process of TypeScript and the editor setup for TypeScript development. Microsoft does well in providing easy-to-perform steps to install TypeScript on all platforms, namely Windows, macOS, and Linux.

Installation of TypeScript

TypeScript's official website (`https://www.typescriptlang.org`) is the best resource to install the latest version of TypeScript. On the website, go to the **Download** section; there, you will find details on how to install TypeScript. Node.js and Visual Studio are the two most common ways to get TypeScript. TypeScript supports a host of other editors and has plugins available for them in the same link. We will be installing TypeScript using Node.js and using Visual Studio Code as our primary editor. You can use any editor of your choice and be able to run the applications seamlessly. If you use full-blown Visual Studio as your primary development IDE, then you can use either of the links, Visual Studio 2017 or Visual Studio 2013, to download the TypeScript SDK. Visual Studio does come with a TypeScript compiler but it's better to install it from this link so as to get the latest version.

To install TypeScript using Node.js, we will use **npm** (**node package manager**), which comes with Node.js. Node.js is a popular JavaScript runtime for building and running server-side JavaScript applications. As TypeScript compiles into JavaScript, Node is an ideal fit for developing server-side applications with the TypeScript language. As mentioned on the TypeScript website, just running the following command in the Terminal (on macOS) / Command Prompt (on Windows) window will install the latest version of TypeScript:

```
npm install -g typescript
```

To load any package from Node.js, the `npm` command starts with `npm install`; the `-g` flag identifies that we are installing the package globally. The last parameter is the name of the package that we are installing. Once it is installed, you can check the version of TypeScript by running the following command in the Terminal window:

```
tsc -v
```

You can use the following command to get the help for all the other options that are available with `tsc`:

```
tsc -h
```

TypeScript editors

One of the outstanding features of TypeScript is its support for editors. All the editors provide support for TypeScript language services, thereby providing features such as IntelliSense, statement completion, and error highlighting. If you are coming from a .NET background, then Visual Studio 2013/2015/2017 is a good option for you. Visual Studio does not require any configuration and it's easy to start using TypeScript. As we discussed earlier, just install the SDK and you are good to go. If you are from a Java background, TypeScript supports Eclipse as well. TypeScript also supports plugins for Sublime, WebStorm, and Atom, and each of these provides all the rich feature sets.

Visual Studio Code (**VS Code**) is another good option for an IDE. It's a smaller, lighter version of Visual Studio and primarily used for web application development. VS Code is lightweight and cross-platform, capable of running on Windows, Linux, and macOS. It has an ever-increasing set of plugins to help you write better code, such as TSLint, a static analysis tool to help TypeScript code for readability, maintainability, and error checking. VS Code has a compelling case to be the default IDE for all sorts of web application development. In this section, we will briefly look at the Visual Studio and VS Code setup for TypeScript.

Visual Studio

Visual Studio is a full-blown IDE provided by Microsoft for all .NET based development, but now Visual Studio also has excellent support for TypeScript with built-in project templates. A TypeScript compiler is integrated into Visual Studio to allow automatic transpiling of code to JavaScript. Visual Studio also has the TypeScript language service integrated to provide IntelliSense and design-time error checking, among other things.

With Visual Studio, creating a project with a TypeScript file is as simple as adding a new file with a `.ts` extension. Visual Studio will provide all the features of TypeScript out of the box.

VS Code

VS Code is a lightweight IDE from Microsoft used for web application development. VS Code can be installed on Windows, macOS, and Linux-based systems. VS Code can recognize the different type of code files and comes with a huge set of extensions to help in development. You can install VS Code from `https://code.visualstudio.com/download`.

VS Code comes with an integrated TypeScript compiler, so we can start creating a TypeScript project directly. The following screenshot shows a TypeScript file opened in VS Code:

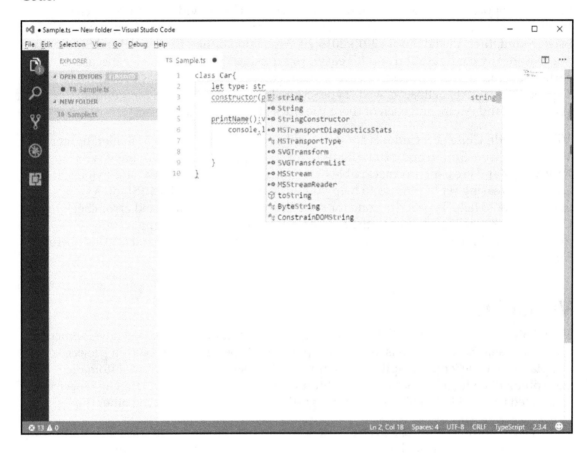

To run the project in VS Code, we need a task runner. VS Code includes multiple task runners which can be configured for the project, such as Gulp, Grunt, and TypeScript. We will be using the TypeScript task runner for our build.

VS Code has a Command Palette which allows you to access various different features, such as **Build Task**, **Themes**, **Debug** options, and so on. To open the Command Palette, use *Ctrl + Shift + P* on a Windows machine or *Cmd + Shift + P* on a macOS. In the Command Palette, type `Build`, as shown in the following screenshot, which will show the command to build the project:

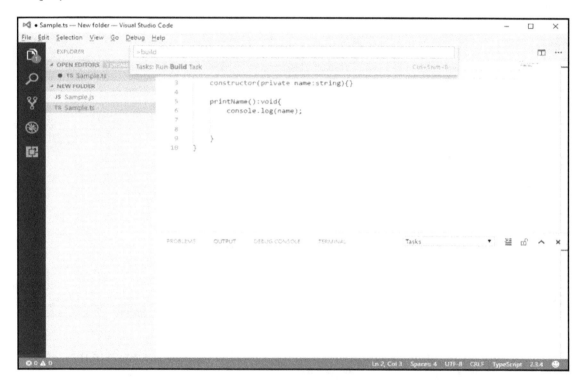

When the command is selected, VS Code shows an alert, **No built task defined...**, as follows:

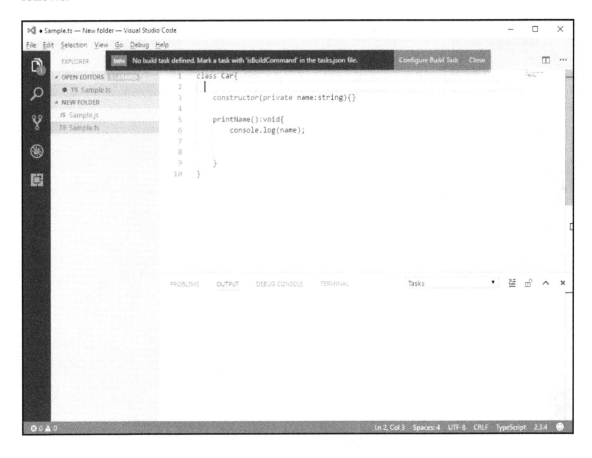

We select **Configure Build Task** and, from all the available options as shown in the following screenshot, choose **TypeScript build**:

This creates a new folder in your project, `.vscode` and a new file, `task.json`. This JSON file is used to create the task that will be responsible for compiling TypeScript code in VS Code.

TypeScript needs another JSON file (`tsconfig.json`) to be able to configure compiler options. Every time we run the code, `tsc` will look for a file with this name and use this file to configure itself. TypeScript is extremely flexible in transpiling the code to JavaScript as per developer requirements, and this is achieved by configuring the compiler options of TypeScript.

TypeScript compiler

The **TypeScript compiler** is called **tsc** and is responsible for transpiling the TypeScript code to JavaScript. The TypeScript compiler is also cross-platform and supported on Windows, macOS, and Linux.

To run the TypeScript compiler, there are a couple of options. One is to integrate the compiler in your editor of choice, which we explained in the previous section. In the previous section, we also integrated the TypeScript compiler with VS Code, which allowed us to build our code from the editor itself. All the compiler configurations that we would want to use are added to the tsconfig.json file.

Another option is to use tsc directly from the command line / Terminal window. TypeScript's tsc command takes compiler configuration options as parameters and compiles code into JavaScript. For example, create a simple TypeScript file in Notepad and add the following lines of code to it. To create a file as a TypeScript file, we just need to make sure we have the file extension as *.ts:

```
class Editor {
  constructor(public name: string, public isTypeScriptCompatible : Boolean)
{}
  details() {
    console.log('Editor: ' +  this.name + ',
                TypeScript installed: ' +
                this.isTypeScriptCompatible);
  }
}

class VisualStudioCode extends Editor{
    public OSType: string
    constructor(name: string, isTypeScriptCompatible : Boolean,
            OSType: string) {
        super(name, isTypeScriptCompatible);
        this.OSType = OSType;
    }
}

let VS = new VisualStudioCode('VSCode', true, 'all');
VS.details();
```

This is the same code example we used in the *TypeScript features* section of this chapter. Save this file as `app.ts` (you can give it any name you want, as long as the extension of the file is `*.ts`). In the command line / Terminal window, navigate to the path where you have saved this file and run the following command:

```
tsc app.ts
```

This command will build the code and the transpile it into JavaScript. The JavaScript file is also saved in the same location where we had TypeScript. If there is any build issue, `tsc` will show these messages on the command line only.

As you can imagine, running the `tsc` command manually for medium- to large-scale projects is not a productive approach. Hence, we prefer to use an editor that has TypeScript integrated.

The following table shows the most commonly used TypeScript compiler configurations. We will be discussing these in detail in upcoming chapters:

Compiler option	Type	Description
allowUnusedLabels	boolean	By default, this flag is `false`. This option tells the compiler to flag unused labels.
alwaysStrict	boolean	By default, this flag is `false`. When turned on, this will cause the compiler to compile in strict mode and emit use strict in the source file.
module	string	Specify module code generation: None, CommonJS, AMD, System, UMD, ES6, or ES2015.
moduleResolution	string	Determines how the module is resolved.
noImplicitAny	boolean	This property allows an error to be raised if there is any code which implies data type as any. This flag is recommended to be turned off if you are migrating a JavaScript project to TypeScript in an incremental manner.
noImplicitReturn	boolean	Default value is false; raises an error if not all code paths return a value.
noUnusedLocals	boolean	Reports an error if there are any unused locals in the code.

`noUnusedParameter`	boolean	Reports an error if there are any unused parameters in the code.
`outDir`	string	Redirects output structure to the directory.
`outFile`	string	Concatenates and emits output to a single file. The order of concatenation is determined by the list of files passed to the compiler on the command line along with triple-slash references and imports. See the output file order documentation for more details.
`removeComments`	boolean	Remove all comments except copyright header comments beginning with `/*!`.
`sourcemap`	boolean	Generates corresponding `.map` file.
`Target`	string	Specifies ECMAScript target version: ES3(default), ES5, ES6/ES2015, ES2016, ES2017, or ESNext.
`Watch`		Runs the compiler in watch mode. Watches input files and triggers recompilation on changes.

TypeScript to-do list application

It's time to create our to-do list application. In this application, we will have the following features:

- Add a new item with its description to the to-do list
- View all the items in the list

The application is very simple, as our focus is on looking at how TypeScript helps build better web applications. With this application, we intend to show you how to create an application with TypeScript, showcase the basic features of TypeScript, show you how to debug TypeScript code in the browser, and give you an overview of the JavaScript code that's generated by TypeScript.

You can find the source code on GitHub at `https://github.com/sachinohri/TypeScriptTodo.git`.

The following screenshot shows what the application looks like:

The application has no dependencies on any JavaScript library and is purely written in TypeScript. In this application, we have written all our code in a single file (todo.ts) just to keep it concise, although in real-world applications, we would want to create separate files to reduce code complexity and have separation of concerns.

Starting a new project in VS Code is fairly simple: just select **Open Folder** and browse to the folder where you would want to create a new project. If you are opening an existing project, then browse to that folder and VS Code will open the project for you. Our *Todo* application has a very basic code structure with the following folders/files:

- The .vscode folder which was created by VS Code when we configured our build task. You can refer to the *Installation and setup* section of this chapter for more details on how this folder is created.
- The app folder where we have our todo.ts file. When we build our project, the TypeScript compiler generates todo.js and todo.js.map files for our TypeScript file in the same folder.
- We also have a site.css file to provide some basic styling to our project, in addition to bootstrap.
- The tsconfig.json file is used by the TypeScript compiler to configure its build task.
- The index.html file is our user interface and has reference to the todo.js file. This file just has basic features such as an input group to add a new item and a list group to show the existing items.

Our main code lies inside the todo.ts file and we will focus on that.

todo.ts

The `todo.ts` file contains a couple of classes—`todo` and `todolist`—and has an interface `ITodo`.

We have a `Todo` class, which has three properties: name, description, and completed. The `Todo` class implements an interface `ITodo`:

```
interface ITodo{
    name:string;
    description: string;
    completed: boolean;
}
```

Implementing an interface helps maintain code consistency; in large applications, if any class implements an interface, that would act as a contract between the class which implements the interface and the class/module which creates an object of this class. An interface provides code abstraction and helps us create more manageable code. As we discussed earlier, an interface is just a TypeScript concept and, upon compilation, no JavaScript code is generated.

TypeScript provides a couple of ways to declare and assign values to member variables of a class:

- We can create three variables and then assign values to them inside the constructor function as follows:

```
class Todo implements ITodo{
    public name:string;
    public description: string;
    public completed: boolean;
    constructor(name:string, description:string,
completed:boolean){
        this.name = name;
        this.description = description;
        this.completed = completed;
    }
}
```

Here we have three public variables in a class which is initialized inside the constructor.

- Another way, which is more concise, is seen in the following code snippet. Here, in the constructor itself, we declare the variables and TypeScript makes sure that they get initialized as well when the object of the class is created:

```
class Todo implements ITodo{
    constructor(public name: string,
                public description: string,
                public completed: boolean){}
}
```

We have another class, `TodoList`, which contains all the logic for our application. We have a static property of the type `Todo Array` which will persist all the `Todo` elements. It has two functions, `createTodoItem` and `allTodoItems`, which are responsible for creating a new `todo` task and returning all the `todo` tasks respectively:

```
class TodoList{
    public static allTodos: Todo[]= new Array;
    createTodoItem(name:string,description:string):number {
        let newItem = new Todo(name,description, false);
        let totalCount: number = TodoList.allTodos.push(newItem);
        return totalCount;
    }

    allTodoItems():Todo[]{
        return TodoList.allTodos;
    }
}
```

We will go deeper into classes of TypeScript in later chapters; here, we will just look at the basic syntax and how functions are defined inside the class.

Classes in TypeScript

Declaring a function is straightforward, with the function name, set of parameters, and then, inside curly braces, the implementation. After the set of parameters is declared, we can also annotate the function with the data type of the return value from the function. By default, all properties and functions inside the class are *public*.

Before we look at the remaining functions in our class, let's look at the JavaScript generated so far for our code. If you are following along then, to generate the JavaScript file, use *Ctrl + Shift + B* on Windows and *Cmd + Shift + B* on macOS. This command will build the code and generate a corresponding JavaScript file. If we have the sourcemap flag turned on in our taskconfig.json then the build will generate another file with the name filename.js.map, which in our case is todo.js.map.

As we discussed earlier, for an interface, no code is generated, hence we just see the code for our two classes in the JavaScript file:

```
var Todo = (function () {
    function Todo(name, description, completed) {
        this.name = name;
        this.description = description;
        this.completed = completed;
    }
    return Todo;
}());
var TodoList = (function () {
    function TodoList() {
    }
    TodoList.prototype.createTodoItem = function (
                                    name, description) {
        var newItem = new Todo(name, description, false);
        var totalCount = TodoList.allTodos.push(newItem);
        return totalCount;
    };
    TodoList.prototype.allTodoItems = function () {
        return TodoList.allTodos;
    };
    return TodoList;
}());
TodoList.allTodos = new Array;
```

You will see that for both of our classes, the TypeScript compiler generated an **immediately invoked function expression** (**IIFE**) and assigned it to the variables Todo and TodoList respectively. An IIFE is a JavaScript function which is auto-executed when the JavaScript file is parsed. To identify the IIFE, look at the parentheses at the end of the function. The methods createTodoItem and allTodoItems are converted to prototype functions in JavaScript. The prototype is a JavaScript function which allows us to add behavior to our objects. In this case, the createTodoItem and allTodoItems functions introduce new behavior to the TodoList object. We had an allTodos static array in our TodoList class, which in JavaScript is just an array.

Functions in TypeScript

The next function in our file is a `window.onload` function which is called when the browser is loaded. The `window.onload` function is a standard JavaScript function and here is a good example of TypeScript being a superset of JavaScript. All JavaScript functions can be used directly in TypeScript. In the `window.onload` function, we just attach the event listener to the add button:

```
window.onload = function(){
    let name= <HTMLInputElement>document.getElementById("todoName");
    let description = <HTMLInputElement>document.getElementById(
                     "todoDescription");
    document.getElementById("add").addEventListener(
        'click',()=>toAlltask(name.value, description.value));
}
```

TypeScript allows us to type cast one type of value to another using `<>` or the `as` keyword. We will discuss this in more detail in later chapters; here, we should just know that `document.getElementById` returns a type of `HTMLElement` and, because we know that this element is a input element, we type cast that into `HTMLInputElement`. The last function, `todoAllTask`, is called every time we click and add a function, which takes a name and description entered by the user as input, calls the `createTodoItem` function of the `TodoList` class and then fetches the updated list of all `Todo` items and assigns that to a `div` using an ordered list. These two functions, when looked at in a JavaScript file, will be almost the same as what we wrote in TypeScript.

Debugging TypeScript code

Browsers don't understand TypeScript; they can only execute JavaScript code. That's why in our `index.html` file, we have a reference to `todo.js` and not to `todo.ts`. Our application is very small in size and it would not be difficult to debug the JavaScript code in the browser, but real-world applications are often large-scale with many files, each with hundreds of lines of code, and it would not be easy to debug the JavaScript generated by the TypeScript compiler. TypeScript provides a workaround to help developers debug their TypeScript code directly in the browser by using a special file with a `.map` extension. These are called source map files and we need to enable a flag in our `tsconfig.json` to allow the compiler to generate this file. The source map allows a relationship to be created between a JavaScript file and its corresponding TypeScript file. Once we generate the source map file, we can see the TypeScript file in our browser's source tab along with the JavaScript file.

In our code, we have already set the source map flag to `true` and you will see that the map file is generated when the compiler creates the JavaScript file. In the browser, press *F12* on Windows or *Cmd + Opt + I* on macOS to open the developer tools. Then navigate to *sources* and you should see `index.html`, `site.css`, and an `app` folder. Inside the `app` folder, you should have both `todo.js` and `todo.ts` files. The following screenshot shows a snapshot of the developer tools in Chrome. On the left side is the list of files that were downloaded to the browser:

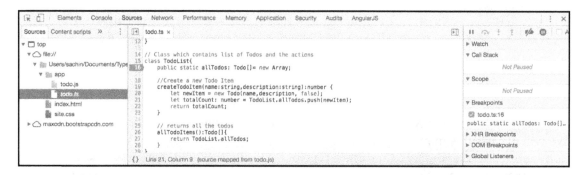

We can open the `todo.ts` file and add breakpoints; when the code is executed by the browser, our breakpoints will be hit and we will be able to debug the code therein. This makes it very easy for developers to debug the code that they have written rather than the code generated by the compiler.

Playground

The official TypeScript website provides a playground where you can write a TypeScript code and it will convert that to JavaScript code. You can also run the code and see the output in a new window. TypeScript has added samples as well, showcasing some of the features, such as Classes, Types, Inheritance, and Generics:

```typescript
1  class Greeter {
2      greeting: string;
3      constructor(message: string) {
4          this.greeting = message;
5      }
6      greet() {
7          return "Hello, " + this.greeting;
8      }
9  }
10
11 let greeter = new Greeter("world");
12
13 let button = document.createElement('button');
14 button.textContent = "Say Hello";
15 button.onclick = function() {
16     alert(greeter.greet());
17 }
18
19 document.body.appendChild(button);
```

```javascript
1  var Greeter = (function () {
2      function Greeter(message) {
3          this.greeting = message;
4      }
5      Greeter.prototype.greet = function () {
6          return "Hello, " + this.greeting;
7      };
8      return Greeter;
9  }());
10 var greeter = new Greeter("world");
11 var button = document.createElement('button');
12 button.textContent = "Say Hello";
13 button.onclick = function () {
14     alert(greeter.greet());
15 };
16 document.body.appendChild(button);
17
```

This is a very handy tool if you just want to try out TypeScript without getting into the details of creating a whole web application.

Summary

In this chapter, we gained an overview of TypeScript, and learned why TypeScript is such a popular language and what features make it so popular. We discussed what the problems of JavaScript are, and how TypeScript solves them.

We also did a step-by-step configuration of VS Code, which will be our IDE of choice.

In the next chapter, we will start digging deeper into some of the concepts of TypeScript by creating some real-life projects.

2
Our First Application – Sports News Combinator

In the last chapter, we got a glimpse into the world of TypeScript. We looked at the features of TypeScript, which allow us to write more manageable, robust, and error-free code. TypeScript is a powerful language that provides the right balance between the flexibility of JavaScript and features, such as types and interfaces, which provide checks at design and compile time.

In this chapter, we will start by digging deeper into the feature set of TypeScript, and will also introduce the Angular framework. As with the subject of this book, we will use real-world examples to gain a better understanding of the features.

This chapter will focus on the following topics:

- **Sports News Combinator (SNC)**: We will start by introducing our first application and its feature set, which we will build.
- **Types in TypeScript**: Types play an important role in TypeScript, and we will delve deeper into the various types available in TypeScript, type inference, and type declaration.
- **Classes in TypeScript**: To be able to build robust web applications, we have classes. TypeScript implements classes to provide the object-oriented feature.
- **Introduction to Angular**: The SNC application is built with TypeScript and Angular, so it is important to introduce Angular and its basic concepts, such as components and data binding.
- **Project setup, configuration, and code setup**: In this section, we will start building our application by first looking at various ways to create **single-page applications (SPAs)** with Angular, and then using the Angular CLI to create our application's skeleton.

- **The architecture of SNC:** We will look at the high-level architecture of SNC and discuss the various components that will be created.
- **Building our first component:** We will be creating our first component, which will be used to display the news content on the page.

By the end of this chapter, we will have a simple working app with hardcoded data, as well as an understanding of types in TypeScript, and the basic fundamentals of Angular.

Sports News Combinator (SNC)

SNC is a single-page web application that provides a unified interface to view the latest sports news from various news outlets. We will be fetching news from NFL, Fox Sports, ESPN, and BBC Sport. We will have four tabs in SNC, each providing the top 10 articles from the respective news outlet. When the user clicks on any of the article links, SNC will redirect the user to the respective website.

This application will be large enough to showcase application features, and small enough not to distract us with the intricacies of applications, and will help us learn the fundamental concepts of TypeScript and Angular.

The following screenshot shows the final version of our application:

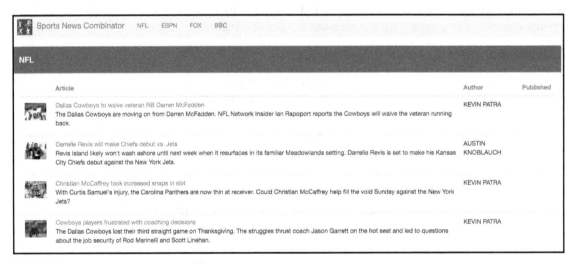

Downloading the code

The code for SNC can be downloaded from GitHub at `https://github.com/sachinohri/SportsNewsCombinator.git`. We will build our application incrementally, with each chapter adding features while discussing the concepts of TypeScript and Angular. So, it makes sense that we provide code for each chapter as well, apart from the final application. To achieve this goal, we have created multiple folders under the main master branch, with each folder providing the final code, which we will create at the end of each chapter. The naming convention for each folder is based on the chapter number.

For this chapter, you can find the code in the `Chapter 02` folder, as shown in the following screenshot:

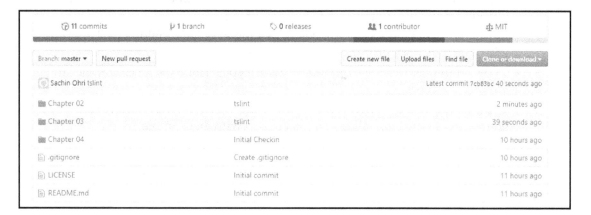

The feature set of SNC

In this chapter, we will be focusing on creating the bare minimum of our application to showcase the features of TypeScript and Angular. SNC will have the following functionalities by the end of this chapter:

- The application will have just one tab to show the news from the NFL network.
- Data in this tab will be hardcoded just to show how data binding works. We will be making a live web service call in `Chapter 4`, *Sports New Combinator - the Final Version*.
- We will design a single component for our application, which will host the main content.

Type System

If there is one feature in TypeScript that stands out from its competitor, it is Type System, and how TypeScript uses types to help write better code. Types in TypeScript are one of the easiest features to understand and use, thus providing the maximum productivity boost for a new developer to TypeScript.

To develop any application with TypeScript, understanding types and their features is very important. Hence, we will look at the following topics in this section, which will then help us when we start working on our application:

- **Variables**: We will start by looking at how to declare variables and constants in TypeScript. We will also look at the `let` and `const` keywords, which were introduced in ES 2015 to provide better scoping.
- **Types**: We will then shift our focus to looking at types provided by TypeScript, which include both primitive and custom types.
- **Type inference**: Then we will look at how TypeScript uses type inference to help identify the types.
- **Type compatibility**: TypeScript has a feature wherein we can relate types based on members only; we will take a look at this with an example.

 Types are a TypeScript concept and are not emitted in the transpiled JavaScript. They are only used at design and compile time.

Variables

If you have done any JavaScript programming, you will be aware of the `var` keyword for declaring variables. In ES 2015, a couple of new keywords were introduced to allow declaring variables, namely `let` and `const`. The `var` keyword allowed us to declare a variable, but it had its quirks with regard to how scoping and access to the variables worked; `let` tries to solve this problem.

The var keyword

Variables declared with the `var` keyword have a global scope in which they are declared; this means that they can be accessed by any function sharing the same scope. The following example shows the scope of the variable `value` in `innerFunction`:

```
1    function outerFunction(){
2        var value=10;
3        function innerFunction(){
4            console.log(value);
5        }
6        return innerFunction;
7    }
8    var func = outerFunction();
9    func();
```

Also, variables declared with the var keyword are subject to hoisting. This means that if we declare a variable at the end of a function, the runtime will hoist it to the top and we will not have any error if we would have used that variable before being declared. In the following example, we see an example of hoisting. Although the value variable was declared at line 9, we were able to access it at lines 3 and 6. When this function is executed, the JavaScript runtime hoists the variable declaration to the top of the function, and hence, is available at lines 3 and 6. The output of the following code will be **1** and **0** respectively:

```
1    function scopingExample(hasValue){
2        if(hasValue){
3            value=1;
4        }
5        else{
6            value=0;
7        }
8        console.log(value);
9        var value;
10   }
11
12   scopingExample(true);
13   scopingExample(false);
```

Let and const keywords

The `let` and `const` keywords solve these problems by providing block scoping for the variables, and do not support hoisting. Block scoping means that the scope of a variable is restricted to the scope in which it is declared, which is normally defined by curly braces. So, if a variable is defined inside a loop or an `if` condition, that variable is not available outside this block, as seen in the following example. Line 6 throws an exception of **x is not defined**, but we do get the correct response of `10` on line 4:

```
1    function letExample(hasValue){
2        if(hasValue){
3            let x= 10;
4            console.log(x);
5        }
6        console.log(x);
7    }
8    letExample(true);
```

This helps reduce errors in code because we make sure we are using the variables in the correct scope. Also, the `let` keyword does not support hoisting, which means that variables are not moved to the top at runtime. They are accessible only after they are declared.

The `const` keyword is another way to declare variables and follows the same scoping principles as the `let` keyword. The only difference between `const` and `let` is that the values declared with `const` cannot change once they are bound. So, if you know that the variable you are declaring cannot and should not be allowed to reassign, then declare it with `const`, else use the `let` keyword.

Types in TypeScript

The JavaScript language does not have a concept of explicitly defining types of variables which end up being one of the main reasons for errors at runtime. We can assign one type to a variable and then later assign a different type to the same variable. TypeScript, with its type annotation, allows us to assign types to each variable, function, object, or class. Types act as a contract, which that variable has to follow, and the TypeScript compiler makes sure that there are no deviations from this contract. TypeScript does this with static and dynamic type checking. Types provide a set of rules which the compiler needs to follow for that variable; these rules also allow an autosuggest feature in IDEs by providing the most relevant options available. For example, by having types, we can make sure that while calling a function, we are passing the right set of variables.

TypeScript is an *optional statically typed* language, which means that it is not mandatory to assign types to each variable or function. This is why every JavaScript code is a valid TypeScript code. TypeScript provides a way to infer types for the variable based on the value assigned to the variable or the code flow. TypeScript will try to infer the best possible type, and then have checks in place to make sure that all the further operations do not contradict with the type. TypeScript also provides an option to explicitly opt out of the type for a variable by assigning the any keyword. For a variable with type any, TypeScript does not perform any type checking. This feature allows us to have existing JavaScript migrated to TypeScript without any issues.

 TypeScript emits JavaScript even if there are type errors at compile time, allowing us to progressively update the JavaScript code.

Type annotation

To specify a type to a variable or a function, TypeScript provides a syntax for defining a type preceded by a colon. Type annotation comes after the variable identifier. Types can be primitive types, or arrays, or complex types using classes and interfaces. The following example shows the basic syntax of defining types of variables and functions:

```
let num: number=42;
function example(name: string, age:number): number{
  return 42;
}
```

In the first line, when defining a `num` variable, it's optional to assign a value as well. In the `function` example, we see that we can define the type of the input parameter, and also for the `return` value. This helps us in making sure that all function calls are maintaining the correct signature contract.

Primitive types

TypeScript primitive types relate very closely to the types in JavaScript and follow the same principles. The primitive types available in TypeScript are as follows.

Number

A `number` data type can contain a double precision 64-bit floating point value. In TypeScript, the number has the same meaning as in JavaScript and represents all numbers, including decimals and hexadecimal. The following is an example of a number variable:

```
let num:number = 42;
let decimal = 42.0;
```

String

The `string` data type represents textual data in UTF-16 format. To assign a string value to a variable, we use single (') or double (") quotes. We can also create a string that spans multiple lines, and is called a template string. The following is an example of declaring strings:

```
let firstName: string = 'John';
let templateHTML: string = `
<h1>Title</h1>`
```

In the preceding code, `templateHTML` is an example of using a template string. This is one of the features that is very frequently used in Angular to define inline templates for its components. We will see these when we start working on our application.

The strings also have an ability to add dynamic expression in its definition, as shown in the following example. The result variable will be **Top 10 news feed from ESPN**:

```
let news: string = "ESPN";
let count: number = 10;
let result: string = `Top ${count} news feed from ${news}.`
console.log(result);
```

The preceding code, when transpiled to JavaScript, produces the following output:

```
var news = "ESPN";
var count = 10;
var result = "Top " + count + " news feed from " + news + ".";
console.log(result);
```

Boolean

The `boolean` data type can be assigned a `true` or `false` value as shown in the following example:

```
let hasvalues: boolean = false;
```

Arrays

Like JavaScript, TypeScript has an array type to allow assignment of multiple values. The array is specified by adding a square bracket after the type. Every time a new value is added to an array, the compiler checks for type compatibility and alerts if there is a type mismatch. The following is an example of defining an array:

```
let scores:number[] = [10,20,30,40];
```

Arrays are accessed based on zero index, which means that the first element is at zeroth index, as shown here:

```
let scores:number[] = [10,20,30,40];
console.log(scores[0]);
```

The output of the console statement will be the value **10**.

Tuples

Tuples can be seen as an advanced type of an array wherein we can have an array with elements not of the same type. For example, we can have any tuple that will have the first element of type string and the second element as a number, as shown here:

```
let details:[string, number];
details= ['John', 42];
```

The preceding code allows us to manage different data types in a single structure, which provides flexibility.

Any

The any keyword is a special type in TypeScript that allows us to opt out of type checking for that variable. This type is very useful when we are migrating the old JavaScript code to TypeScript. We can have the variables defined as any, and TypeScript will not perform any type checking on those. The following example shows the use of the any type:

```
let item: any;
item = 10;
item = 'John';
item = [10,20,30];
```

In the preceding code, the compiler does not complain when we assign a number, string, or array to the same variable.

> It is recommended to not use any type in TypeScript code until and unless we are in the process of migrating the code from JavaScript. Having the any type takes away all the benefits of compile-time type checking from our code, which can result in unintended behavior.

Void

The void keyword is used to represent a scenario where there is no type. This is useful in the case of functions that do not return any value. These functions are annotated with void as a return type. In the following example, the doSomething function does not return any value, and hence has a void as return type:

```
function doSomething(num: number):void{
  console.log(num);
}
```

Null and undefined

The null and undefined types are special types that can be assigned to any variable. They are not very useful on their own, as seen in the following example:

```
let value = null;
value = 42;
```

Here, the value variable is of the any type, because null is a subtype of all the types and the compiler assigns *any* to the variable.

Union types

Most of the time, we are aware of what type of data a specific variable can hold, and we can annotate the said variable with that type. This helps in type checking at compile time, and makes sure we don't misuse the variable. But there are times when a variable may not be confined to one specific type, but can have multiple types of values. This is common in scenarios where we are migrating JavaScript code, or using reference of JavaScript libraries.

TypeScript has the **union type** to solve this problem. A union type allows us to define a variable with multiple types; for example, a variable can have number and string types. This is achieved by using the *pipe (|)* symbol between the types, as shown here:

```
let data : string | number;
data = 10;
data = 'John';
```

Here, the data variable can hold both number and string, which allows us to have the flexibility to use both data types. The TypeScript compiler makes sure that it alerts us if we try to assign a type of value that was not defined.

Like union types, we have intersection types, which allow us to combine multiple types into one type. This is mostly used when we are using classes and interfaces for type declaration, hence we will look into this type when we discuss interfaces in the subsequent chapter.

Type inference

As we discussed in the *Types in TypeScript* section, TypeScript is an optional statically typed language, which means that TypeScript does provide types, but explicitly assigning types to variables is optional. TypeScript has an ability to infer types if not declared. Let's look at an example:

```
let firstName = "John";
firstName = 10;
```

In the line firstName = 10, the compiler alerts us with the error that the variable firstName is a string, and a number cannot be assigned to a string. How does TypeScript identity this mismatch? TypeScript uses type inference to identify the type for the firstName variable.

In this case, TypeScript identified based on the assignment of the value at the time of variable declaration. If we had not assigned `"John"` to the `firstName` variable, the type inferred by TypeScript would have been `any`, as in the example shown here:

```
let lastName;
lastName = 10;
lastName = 'jj';
```

This is called **type inference through declaration**. Another place where you can see type inference in action is the return type of a function. TypeScript looks at the code and, based on the code flow path, decides the best suitable type. The following is one such example:

```
function doSomething(num:number){
   return "name";
}
```

In this case, TypeScript infers the return type as the `string`. Type inference is very useful in cases when we are working on legacy code of JavaScript; TypeScript will make sure to infer types for variables and functions based on the code flow.

Type checking

Once TypeScript has identified the types, it uses these for type checking in the program. TypeScript checks if we try to assign a type of value to a variable that contradicts the type defined for that variable, or when a function is called, TypeScript checks if we are passing correct types for the parameters and the return value is being assigned to the correct type of variable. The only exception to this type checking is the `any` keyword. If a variable or property is defined with the `any` keyword, the TypeScript compiler does not perform type checking for that variable.

Take a look at the following example of type checking:

```
let age:number;
age=10;
age="42"; //Compile Error: string can not be assigned to a number
```

In the preceding example, the TypeScript compiler alerts us on the last line with the message that *42 can not be assigned to a number*, because although we are passing a *number*, we are passing it as the string. TypeScript, unlike JavaScript, does not coerce the types. TypeScript not only does type checking for primitive types, but also for arrays and custom types such as classes. We will look at an example of classes in the next chapter.

Apart from the types we have discussed in the preceding sections, there are other types in TypeScript as well, such as enum, generics, intersection types, and optional types. We will be looking into these types as and when we use them in our example application.

Classes in TypeScript

If we are developing any application using TypeScript, be it a small-scale or a large-scale application, we will use classes to manage our properties and methods. Prior to ES 2015, JavaScript did not have the concept of classes, and we used functions to create class-like behavior. TypeScript introduced classes as part of its initial release, and now we have classes in ES6 as well. The behavior of classes in TypeScript and JavaScript ES6 closely relates to the behavior of any object-oriented language that you might have worked on, such as Java or C#.

Object-oriented programming in TypeScript

Object-oriented programming allows us to represent our code in the form of objects, which themselves are instances of classes holding properties and methods. Classes form the container of related properties and their behavior. Modeling our code in the form of classes allows us to achieve various features of object-oriented programming, which helps us write more intuitive, reusable, and robust code. Features such as encapsulation, polymorphism, and inheritance are the result of implementing classes.

TypeScript, with its implementation of classes and interfaces, allows us to write code in an object-oriented fashion. This allows developers coming from traditional languages, such as Java and C#, feel right at home when learning TypeScript.

Understanding classes

Prior to ES 2015, JavaScript developers did not have any concept of classes; the best way they could replicate the behavior of classes was with functions. The function provides a mechanism to group together related properties and methods. The methods can be either added internally to the function, or using the `prototype` keyword. The following is an example of such a function:

```
function Name (firstName, lastName) {
   this.firstName = firstName;
   this.lastName = lastName;
   this.fullName = function() {
```

```
      return this.firstName + ' ' + this.lastName ;
   };
}
```

In this preceding example, we have the `fullName` method encapsulated inside the `Name` function. Another way of adding methods to functions is shown in the following code snippet with the `prototype` keyword:

```
function Name (firstName, lastName) {
   this.firstName = firstName;
   this.lastName = lastName;
}
Name.prototype.fullName = function() {
   return this.firstName + ' ' + this.lastName ;
};
```

These features of functions did solve most of the issues of not having classes, but most of the dev community has not been comfortable with these approaches.

Classes make this process easier. Classes provide an abstraction on top of common behavior, thus making code reusable. The following is the syntax for defining a class in TypeScript:

```
1   class News{
2       public channelNumber : number;
3       public newsTitle: string;
4       private author: string = "ESPN";
5
6       format():string{
7           return `${this.channelNumber} : ${this.newsTitle} was written by ${this.author}`;
8       }
9   }
10  let espn = new News();
11  espn.channelNumber = 1;
12  espn.newsTitle = 'NFL Today';
13  console.log(espn.format());
```

The syntax of the class should look very similar to readers who come from an object-oriented background. To define a class, we use a `class` keyword followed by the name of the class. The `News` class has three member properties and one method. Each member has a type assigned to it, and has an access modifier to define the scope. On line 10, we create an object of a class with the `new` keyword. Classes in TypeScript also have the concept of a constructor, where we can initialize some properties at the time of object creation. We will look at constructors and other concepts of classes in `Chapter 3`, *Sports News Combinator – Adding Features*.

Access modifiers

Once the object is created, we can access the public members of the class with the dot operator. Note that we cannot access the `author` property with the `espn` object because this property is defined as private. TypeScript provides three types of access modifiers.

Public

Any property defined with the `public` keyword will be freely accessible outside the class. As we saw in the previous example, all the variables marked with the `public` keyword were available outside the class in an object. Note that TypeScript assigns `public` as a default access modifier if we do not assign any explicitly. This is because the default JavaScript behavior is to have everything public.

Private

When a property is marked as private, it cannot be accessed outside of the class. The scope of a private variable is only inside the class when using TypeScript. In JavaScript, as we do not have access modifiers, private members are treated similarly to public members.

Protected

The `protected` keyword behaves similarly to private, with the exception that protected variables can be accessed in the derived classes. The following is one such example:

```
class base{
  protected id: number;
}
class child extends base{
  name: string;
  details():string{
  return `${name} has id: ${this.id}`
```

```
        }
    }
```

In the preceding code, we extend the `child` class with the `base` class, and have access to the `id` property inside the `child` class. If we create an object of the `child` class, we will still not have access to the `id` property outside.

Readonly

As the name suggests, a property with a `readonly` access modifier cannot be modified after the value has been assigned to it. The value assigned to a `readonly` property can only happen at the time of variable declaration or in the constructor. We will look at constructors in Chapter 3, *Sports News Combinator – Adding Features*; here, we will see an example of a `readonly` property when initialized at the time of declaration:

```
1    class HelloWorld{
2        readonly name:string = 'John';
3
4        changeName(){
5            name = 'Jane';
6        }
7    }
```

In the above code, line 5 gives an error stating that property name is `readonly`, and cannot be an assigned value.

Transpiled JavaScript from classes

While learning TypeScript, it is important to remember that TypeScript is a superset of JavaScript, and not a new language on its own. Browsers can only understand JavaScript, so it is important for us to understand the JavaScript that is transpiled by TypeScript. TypeScript provides an option to generate JavaScript based on the ECMA standards. You can configure TypeScript to transpile into ES5 or ES6 (ES 2015) and even ES3 JavaScript by using the flag `target` in the `tsconfig.json` file. We discussed this setting in Chapter 1, *Getting Started with TypeScript*. The biggest difference between ES5 and ES6 is with regard to the `classes`, `let`, and `const` keywords which were introduced in ES6.

Even though ES6 has been around for more than a year, most browsers still do not have full support for ES6. So, if you are creating an application that would target older browsers as well, consider having the target as ES5.

So, the JavaScript that's generated will be different based on the target setting. Here, we will take an example of class in TypeScript and generate JavaScript for both ES5 and ES6. The following is the class definition in TypeScript:

```
1    class News{
2        public channelNumber : number;
3        public newsTitle: string;
4        private author: string = "ESPN";
5
6        format():string{
7            return `${this.channelNumber} : ${this.newsTitle} was written by ${this.author}`;
8        }
9    }
10   let espn = new News();
11   espn.channelNumber = 1;
12   espn.newsTitle = 'NFL Today';
13   console.log(espn.format());
```

This is the same code that we saw when we introduced classes in the *Understanding Classes* section. Here, we have a class named News that has three members, two of which are public and one private. The News class also has a `format` method, which returns a string concatenated from the member variables.

Then, we create an object of the News class in line 10 and assign values to public properties. In the last line, we call the format method to print the result.

Now let's look at the JavaScript transpiled by TypeScript compiler for this class.

ES6 JavaScript

ES6, also known as ES 2015, is the latest version of JavaScript, which provides many new features on top of ES5. Classes are one such feature; JavaScript did not have classes prior to ES6. The following is the code generated from the TypeScript class, which we saw previously:

```
1    class News {
2        constructor() {
3            this.author = "ESPN";
4        }
5        format() {
6            return `${this.channelNumber} : ${this.newsTitle} was written by ${this.author}`;
7        }
8    }
9    let espn = new News();
10   espn.channelNumber = 1;
11   espn.newsTitle = 'NFL Today';
12   console.log(espn.format());
13
```

If you compare the preceding code with TypeScript code, you will notice minor differences. This is because classes in TypeScript and JavaScript are similar, with just types and access modifiers additional in TypeScript. In JavaScript, we do not have the concept of declaring public members. The `author` variable, which was defined as private and was initialized at its declaration, is converted to a constructor initialization in JavaScript. If we had not have initialized `author`, then the produced JavaScript would not have added `author` in the constructor.

ES5 JavaScript

ES5 is the most popular JavaScript version supported in browsers, and if you are developing an application that has to support the majority of browser versions, then you need to transpile your code to the ES5 version. This version of JavaScript does not have `classes`, and hence the transpiled code converts classes to functions, and methods inside the *classes* are converted to prototypically defined methods on the functions.

The following is the code transpiled when we have the *target* set as ES5 in the TypeScript compiler options:

```
1    var News = (function () {
2        function News() {
3            this.author = "ESPN";
4        }
5        News.prototype.format = function () {
6            return this.channelNumber + " : " + this.newsTitle + " was written by " + this.author;
7        };
8        return News;
9    }());
10   var espn = new News();
11   espn.channelNumber = 1;
12   espn.newsTitle = 'NFL Today';
13   console.log(espn.format());
14
```

As discussed earlier, the basic difference is that the class is converted to a function. The interesting aspect of this conversion is that the News class is converted to an **immediately invoked function expression (IIFE)**. An IIFE can be identified by the parenthesis at the end of the function declaration, as we see in line 9 in the preceding code snippet. IIFEs cause the function to be executed immediately, and help to maintain the correct scope of a function rather than declaring the function in a global scope. Another difference was how we defined the method format in the ES5 JavaScript. The prototype keyword is used to add the additional behavior to the function, which we see here.

A couple of other differences you may have noticed include the change of the let keyword to var, as let is not supported in ES5. All variables in ES5 are defined with the var keyword. Also, the format method now does not use a template string, but standard string concatenation to print the output.

TypeScript does a good job of transpiling the code to JavaScript while following recommended practices. This helps in making sure we have a robust and reusable code with minimum error cases.

SNC – 101

It's time to jump in over our heads by building our first application. At the start of the chapter, we briefly discussed what the application is all about and how the finished product will look. We will be building this application gradually, starting in this chapter and then adding features to the application in `Chapter 3`, *Sports News Combinator - Adding Features*, and `Chapter 4`, *Sports News Combinator - the Final Version*. With each new feature, we will first discuss the feature and then implement it.

SNC is an SPA built with Angular and TypeScript. We will be using Angular 4 as our frontend framework, and all the code written in Angular will be in TypeScript. This book does not assume that the reader is proficient in Angular, and hence we will be explaining Angular concepts as we go along.

In the second-half of this chapter, we will focus on the following items of our SNC application:

- **Introduction to Angular**: As our application is built on top of the Angular framework, it makes sense for us to first understand the basics of Angular.
- **First step**: To start building the application, the first step is to set up the code structure. We will briefly discuss the multiple ways to set up Angular code; more details will be in `Chapter 8`, *Trello – Using Angular CLI*.
- **Building our first component**: Once the basic code is set up, we will start developing our application by building our first component.

By the end of this chapter, we will have one simple component to display a list of data with images. We are intentionally not adding many features to our application in this chapter because we would like to have more focus on the concepts of Angular and TypeScript. Once we have our basics clear, it will be very easy to look at other features and implement them in our application.

Angular – the superhero framework

In this book, we will be creating three applications, and all the applications will be built with the Angular and TypeScript framework. So, it makes sense for us to spend some time understanding what Angular is, and its basic concepts.

In this section, we will learn just enough concepts to help us start with our first application. In subsequent chapters, as we add features to our applications, we will look at other features of Angular along with TypeScript in detail.

SPAs

In the last couple of decades, web applications have come a long way, from static web applications to web applications with some JavaScript, to jQuery, where we were building dynamic web applications. As the need for web applications increased, technology also evolved to handle the ever-changing needs. Earlier, it was fine to go to the server for each user request, for each page navigation. But, as the need changed, we were looking for ways to make our web applications more fluid, have shorter load time, and reduce the number of requests to the server.

In came SPAs, which provided just the right concepts to improve application performance. The basic premise of an SPA is to have a single HTML page, and just keep swapping the inner content of HTML as the user interacts with the application rather than always loading a whole new page. This approach lets us reduce the request count, reduce the size of the application, and in turn, increases application responsiveness.

Angular is not the only SPA framework on the market at the moment; there are other frameworks such as React, Aurelia, and Vue, which also try to provide a mechanism to create SPAs, though Angular is the most popular one.

Angular – the concepts

Angular is an open source JavaScript/TypeScript framework for building rich client-side applications. Angular uses HTML, CSS, and TypeScript or JavaScript as its building blocks. If you have used jQuery before and are wondering how Angular differentiates itself from jQuery, then you can look at the features it provides. Angular is a full-fledged web application development, unlike jQuery, which is more of a wrapper for JavaScript functions helping in providing a common API for handling different browsers.

Angular provides features to create HTML pages and embed CSS into them, routing to help navigate between pages, services to provide an interface to interact with the backend, and components to stitch all these together. Angular is an opinionated framework, in the sense that it provides guidance on how we should create web applications.

We can easily build our web applications without using Angular as our framework in just plain JavaScript but, in doing so, we would end up defining all the underlying features that can help develop the application. Angular provides many standout features over creating custom frameworks for web applications, as shown in the following diagram:

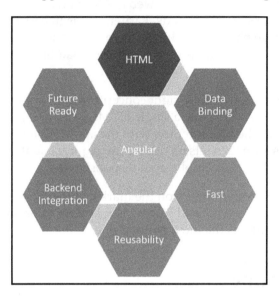

- **Adds power to the HTML**: Angular provides structural directives, which help add flexibility to HTML. With the help of Angular, we can make our HTML more expressive.
- **Better data binding with models**: Angular provides a mechanism to bind data models with UI, and help track changes. It has features such as one-way binding and two-way binding, which allows applications to set up a channel between the models and their respective UI elements.
- **Faster load time**: Angular has one of the fastest load times, which allows for better rendering and more fluid applications.
- **Reusability**: One of the guiding principles of Angular design is its ability to help create a modular design. Angular is designed in a modular way, wherein each feature of Angular is available as a separate module to help manage the dependencies. Modularity allows building components and features that are reusable.
- **Integrates well with backend systems**: Angular has specific functionalities that provide interfaces to help communicate with backend servers.

- **Futureproof**: Angular follows all the modern practices. It takes advantage of the latest features in JavaScript and TypeScript such as classes, interfaces, and decorators.
- **Better productivity**: With all the features of Angular, you will see the productivity improving exponentially when developing any web application. Angular provides a framework that makes it easy to start and implement features and functionalities.

Angular – the architecture

Angular is a modular framework that provides separation of concerns with regard to features and technology. All Angular features are also managed in separate modules; you have a core module, which is responsible for basic features such as components and NgModule, then there are modules for services, pipes, and internationalization, among others. This provides us with the opportunity to create our applications with Angular in more modular fashion to provide us with reusability and ease of use.

Angular application on a high level is comprised of components and services that help us create features and bind them together to make an application. Multiple components can be clubbed together in a module to provide a functionality. For example, we can have a component for report filter and a component for report result. Both these components can be bound together inside a module. The following figure shows a high-level view of how an Angular application is composed:

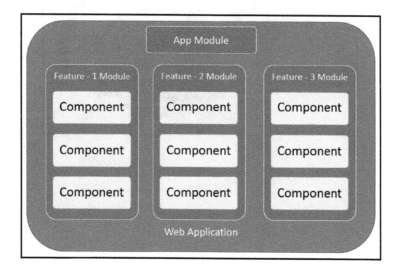

Components are further divided into three main parts:

- HTML, which forms the UI of the component called *template*. These UI templates form the view of the application. Templates have a 1:1 relationship with the component, and can be defined either inline or in a separate HTML file.
- A class that is written in TypeScript and contains all the properties and methods that are required by the view. Properties are the data members that are bound to the view and used to display the data. Methods are action events that are performed from the view, such as a button click.
- Angular needs a way to identify a class defined above as a component so that it can process it to display on the screen. This information is provided to Angular by the form of metadata.

The following is a graphical representation of a component:

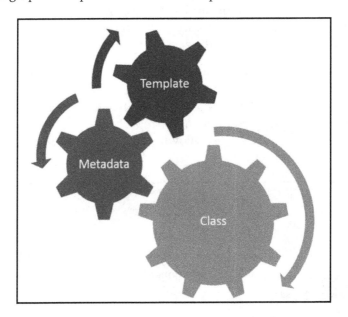

This approach of having multiple components to form a module and multiple modules to form an application allows us to have separation of concerns and create multiple reusable components that can be used in different applications.

When we navigate to the URL of an Angular application, the first component that is loaded is always a root application component, and then the Angular router uses the routing configuration defined to match the component with the URL, and loads that component. The components template is then displayed in the browser, with data fetched from the server. A component can be made up of multiple smaller components, which are then loaded subsequently.

SNC – the architecture

Before we start developing our application, it is a good idea to look at the high-level architecture of what we will be building. The architecture provides us with the blueprint for designing our application, which in this case, will define the components that we will be building and their hierarchy. The following is an architecture diagram of SNC:

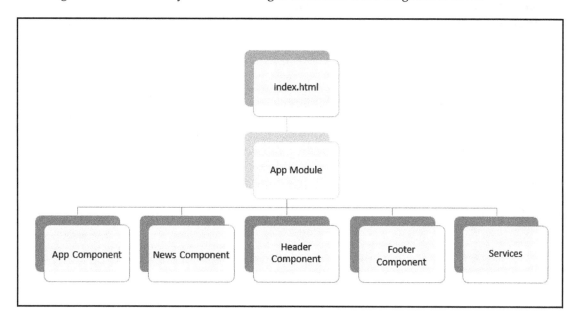

This application is comprised of the set of components and modules with `index.html` as our starting point. From `index.html`, we have an `app` component, which is the parent component. Then we have two components, namely header and footer, to provide with common content. Our main application is made of one component, `news`, which provides the primary user interface. We also have a service layer, which is used to make a backend call to fetch the top 10 news stories for a specific channel. The `news` component will show all the stories in a list format. This is achievable because of the hierarchical setup of components, with *news* as a parent component and `story` as a child component. In this chapter, we will keep it simple and develop only one component, which will have the list of stories; we will be adding components and their interaction in `Chapter 3`, *Sports News Combinator - Adding Features*, and `Chapter 4`, *Sports News Combinator - the Final Version*.

SNC – code setup

Angular provides multiple ways to set up the initial code structure, with options ranging from quick seed project, found at `https://github.com/angular/quickstart`, to **Angular Command Line Interface (Angular CLI)**, which is an npm package and allows you to create applications that can run immediately. There are also multiple startup projects provided by various Angular enthusiasts, each with something different. Angular is a frontend framework that needs to be hosted on a server to run. It supports various servers such as node, IIS, and even Tomcat.

As we saw earlier, Angular is built with modules, with each module loading different components. Angular supports module loaders such as SystemJS and Webpack. You will find startup projects with either of the module loaders. For our application, we will use Angular CLI to create our initial project structure. We will look at Angular CLI and other startup projects in detail in `Chapter 8`, *Trello – Using Angular CLI*; here, just follow the steps we discuss and we should have our application running in no time.

If we had to manually set up a project from scratch, we would have to perform the following steps:

1. First, we would need to create an application folder, a traditional `app` folder.
2. Add package details and other configuration files.
3. Install these packages using npm.
4. Then we need to create an Angular root module. As we discussed in the *SNC - architecture* section, each application has one root module, which is required to load the application.

5. Create a file called `main.ts`, which will load the module.
6. Create an `index.html` file that will be our one and only fully HTML file.
7. Develop your first component, which will be called from the `app` component.
8. Define Angular routes to help Angular identify which component to load based on the URL request.

As you will notice, there are quite a few steps that need to be performed, and doing these manually is time-consuming and error-prone. This is where Angular CLI comes in. It creates all these files and also some boilerplate code for our first component. Angular CLI also provides commands to create new components/services/pipes/directives, among others. Angular CLI code comes with a built-in server from the Node that helps run the application in the development mode.

 The Angular CLI package helps create an initial web application for Angular with Webpack and node server built in. It follows best practices as defined by the official Angular team, and helps to provide us with the correct folder structure to manage the code.

Angular CLI setup

To start using Angular CLI, you will need to install the Angular CLI package from npm. **npm**, or **Node Package Manager**, is a package manager for all the client-side repositories. If you don't have npm and node on your machine, you can install it by downloading the executable from Node's website at `https://nodejs.org/en/download/`. If you think you already have node and npm, you can check which version you have with the following command executed in the Terminal window:

```
node -v
npm -v
```

These commands will give you the version you already have installed on your machine. Before Angular CLI can help you build web applications, you need to install Angular CLI itself from npm with the following command on a Terminal window:

```
npm install -g angular-cli
```

This command will install the `angular-cli` package in your global npm scope.

Application setup

Once we have CLI installed, then we can start creating our application. Creating an application with CLI is as simple as running the following command in your Terminal window:

```
ng new <<projectname>>
```

The project name will be the name you would like to give to your project, which in our case, will be SportsNewsCombinator. The following screenshot shows the executed command and the result:

```
Sachins-MacBook-Pro:Git sachin$ ng new SportsNewsCombinator
installing ng
  create .editorconfig
  create README.md
  create src/app/app.component.css
  create src/app/app.component.html
  create src/app/app.component.spec.ts
  create src/app/app.component.ts
  create src/app/app.module.ts
  create src/assets/.gitkeep
  create src/environments/environment.prod.ts
  create src/environments/environment.ts
  create src/favicon.ico
  create src/index.html
  create src/main.ts
  create src/polyfills.ts
  create src/styles.css
  create src/test.ts
  create src/tsconfig.app.json
  create src/tsconfig.spec.json
  create src/typings.d.ts
  create .angular-cli.json
  create e2e/app.e2e-spec.ts
  create e2e/app.po.ts
  create e2e/tsconfig.e2e.json
  create .gitignore
  create karma.conf.js
  create package.json
  create protractor.conf.js
  create tsconfig.json
  create tslint.json
Installing packages for tooling via npm.
Installed packages for tooling via npm.
Project 'SportsNewsCombinator' successfully created.
```

As you can see in the preceding screenshot, the CLI created a load of files and folders for our project. If you compare the files that we discussed in the previous section when listing down the manual steps to configure a new project, you will find all those here. In addition, there are files for e2e test cases, which we will not focus on at this time. As we discussed earlier, the CLI provides the built-in node server for us to run our application; the following command does that exactly:

```
ng serve
```

This command builds the projects and starts the web server. Once this command is executed, we can just navigate to our browser and open the URL `http://localhost:4200`.

You should see a page similar to the following:

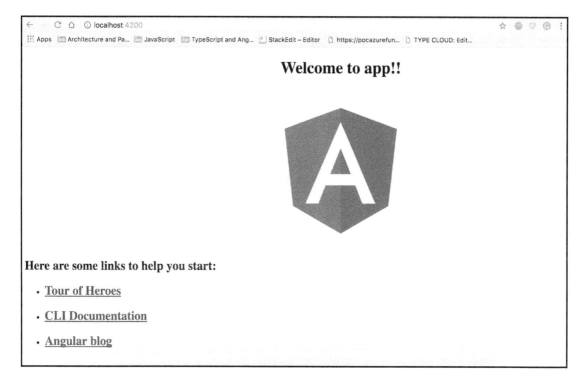

And we are up and running. Though this is nowhere close to how our application will look, this step helps us to start our application.

SNC – folder structure

Angular CLI creates the folder structure, which is one of the recommended ones from the Angular team. Although you can create your own custom folder structure and follow the practices as per your organization, Angular CLI helps to get you started with minimal effort. The following screenshot shows the folder structure that was created for our project:

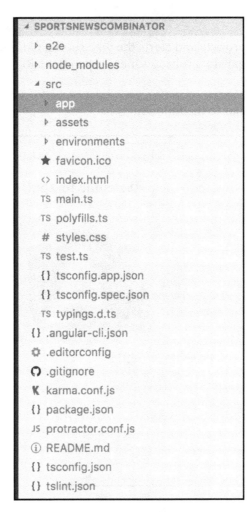

The following are the folders created by Angular CLI:

- e2e: This folder is used for creating and managing end-to-end test cases for the application. In this example, we will not focus on writing test cases. We will cover how to write test cases later in the book.
- node_modules: All the packages that we define in package.json are downloaded by npm under this folder. We never check-in this folder with our code base and always expect users to run npm install to download the packages. If you are downloading this code from GitHub, do remember to run the npm install command.
- src: All our application code resides in this folder. We have an app folder inside the src, which will have all the application-related files and an assets folder, which will have all external assets such as icons and images.
- environments: The purpose of this folder is to provide environmental configurations when you are building your application. You may have different configurations for different environments, and this folder helps you manage that.
- Other files: We have other files in our src folder which are used at startup, such as main.ts, index.html, and tsconfig.app.json. We will look at these files when developing our application.

Now it's time to get our hands dirty.

Creating our model

Before we start building our first component, let's first create our model. A model is an entity that represents some logical data. Here, in our case, we will have two primary models, namely news and articles. The article model represents the articles that are fetched from the specific website, and the news model is the enclosing model of articles that will contain the array of articles.

In this chapter, we are not making a live web service call to fetch the articles, but will just hardcode the data to show the initial binding aspect of the application. But it is useful to understand the data format from the web service response so that we can identify the model structure that needs to be created. The following is one such response from NFL news:

```
{
"status": "ok",
"source": "nfl-news",
"sortBy": "top",
```

```
"articles": [
    {
     "author": "Lakisha Jackson",
     "title": "Mike Williams denies report on season-
    ending surgery",
     "description": "Los Angeles Chargers first-round pick
    Mike Williams is denying reports that he might need
    season-ending back surgery. The rookie wideout
    addressed the rumors during Alshon Jeffery's camp
    on Saturday.",
     "url": "http://www.nfl.com/news/story/
    0ap3000000821316/article/mike-williams-denies-
    report-on-seasonending-surgery",
     "urlToImage": "http://static.nfl.com/static/content/
    public/photo/2017/07/22/
    0ap3000000821315_thumbnail_200_150.jpg",
     "publishedAt": "2017-07-22T23:21:00Z"
    },
    {
     "author": "Jeremy Bergman",
     "title": "Tamba Hali, upset with snaps, launches
    tweetstorm",
     "description": "We've got ourselves a Saturday
    afternoon tweetstorm in late July, courtesy of
    Chiefs pass rusher Tamba Hali. The veteran bemoaned
    his lack of snaps in the Chiefs' playoff loss to
    Pittsburgh.",
     "url": "http://www.nfl.com/news/story/
    0ap3000000821309/article/
    tamba-hali-upset-with-snaps-launches-tweetstorm",
     "urlToImage": "http://static.nfl.com/static/content/
    public/photo/2017/07/22/
    0ap3000000821310_thumbnail_200_150.jpg",
     "publishedAt": "2017-07-22T20:30:00Z"
    }
]
}
```

As we can see, the JSON has two parts to it. The first part provides us with basic information about the web service call, such as status, source, and criterion with which we called the web service. The second part is the array of articles that are returned by the new website. The article array consists of article objects that have the following properties:

- author
- title
- description

- url
- urlToImage
- publishedAt

Under the `src` folder, add a new folder named `models`. This folder will contain all our models that will be required to manage data for our application. Once the folder is created, let's create our first file, `article.ts`.

The `Article` model looks like the following:

```
export class Article{
  author:string;
  title:string;
  description: string;
  url:string;
  urlToImage:string;
  publishedAt:Date;
}
```

Here, we created all the properties in the `Article` class we had identified in our web service response. All the properties are public in their scope as that is the default access modifier in TypeScript.

Next up is the `news.ts` file, which will be our parent model and will have an array of articles and status details. The following is the model that we created:

```
export class News {
  status:string;
  source:string;
  sortBy:string;
  articles: Article[];
}
```

Here, as we are referencing another file (article), we need to import that in our news class by writing the following code at the top of the news.ts file:

```
import {Article} from './Article';
```

This takes care of our models. Now let's create our first component.

First component – NewsComponent

Components are the building blocks of the Angular application. Each component represents some functionality of the application which, when combined with other components, provides a rich user experience. Angular components consist of four parts:

- Template
- Class, which is written in TypeScript
- Metadata, which tells Angular about the class
- Import statements, which provide reference to other components and services of the application

The following is a graphical representation of the composition of a component:

```typescript
1   import { Component, OnInit } from '@angular/core';
2   import {News} from '../../../models/news';
3   import {Article} from '../../../models/article';
4
5
6   @Component({
7     selector: 'snc-news',
8     templateUrl: './news.component.html',
9     styleUrls: ['./news.component.css']
10  })
11  export class NewsComponent implements OnInit {
12    latest_news: News = new News();
13
14    constructor() {
15    }
16
17    ngOnInit() {
18    }
19
20  }
```

Import

Metadata

Class

Template

The template provides the user interface of the component. It's created in HTML and details the elements that are represented in that component. The template for the component can be defined either inline, or in a separate file. We can create an inline template in two ways:

- We can use a `template` property in the `@Component` decorator and define the HTML in single or double quotes. We will read about the `@Component` decorator in the next chapter. The following is a code example of an inline template:

  ```
  template: "<h1>{{article.title}}</h1>"
  ```

- If the HTML is more than a couple of lines long, then we can use ES2015 backticks to define the HTML in multiline. There is no difference between either of these ways, apart from readability. Defining inline templates with backticks allows us to create multiline strings, which are more readable:

  ```
  template: `
  <li>
    <div>
      {{article.description}}
    </div>
  </li>`
  ```

With our view and logic in one file, in one place, it helps to keep track of our bindings with the HTML properties. But, if our HTML is longer than a few lines, then the inline template may not provide many advantages. The inline template is a string, and hence we do not get any IntelliSense support for the HTML tags and syntax checking. The bigger our HTML, the more challenging it becomes to define inline templates.

In these cases, it's better to define the HTML in the separate HTML file and have it linked to the component using the `templateUrl` property. In the `templateUrl` property, we define the path of our HTML file, which is relative to `index.html`. The following is an example of the `templateUrl` property:

```
templateUrl: './news.component.html'
```

Component class

The component class is where the brain of the component resides. This class is written in TypeScript, and has properties and methods. The properties define the data members of the component, and are bound to the template using Angular binding syntax. The methods provide interface for the events that are triggered on the user interface.

As we have learned, each class is defined by the `class` keyword followed by the class name. One of the best practices defined for the component class is to name the class followed by the component keyword, such as `newsComponent`. The `export` keyword in front of the class allows the class to be available to the other components of the application. The following is an example of one such class:

```
export class itemComponent{
  item: string;
  itemCount: number;
  constructor(){
  console.log('Constructor called');
  }
  printItemDetail(){
  console.log('${this.item} has total ${this.itemCount}
  copies');
  }
}
```

Metadata of the component

The definition of metadata is information about the data, which means when we provide details of the data we use, those details are called metadata. For Angular to understand that the class defined is a component, we need to provide metadata, which in this case would be the information to Angular informing it what the class is about. The metadata also provides Angular with details such as the template for that component, CSS styles for the HTML, and the selector that would be used to represent the component.

The metadata is defined using a decorator on top of the class. The decorator is a JavaScript concept that is proposed for ES7 and is implemented in TypeScript. You can identify the decorator by looking for the @ sign. The component decorator is defined by Angular and has options that allow providing details about the component. Some of the frequently used options are the following:

- **Template/templateUrl**: As we discussed in the previous section, this property allows us to define the template for the component.

- **Selector**: This defines the component's directive name; using this name, Angular identifies the HTML to be loaded.
- **StyleUrl**: This property helps us to define the path of the CSS file for that component. As is the case with the template, we can define CSS either inline or in a separate file.

The following is a code sample for the metadata:

```
@Component({
  selector: 'snc-news',
  templateUrl: './news.component.html',
  styleUrls: ['./news.component.css']
})
```

To refer to this component in any other HTML file, we will use the selector property as an HTML tag.

Import

In most cases, the components you are going to create will refer to some external function, or a class. This class can be another component, a model that defines the custom data type, or even a third-party library. To be able to access these functions, we need to import them in our component. Angular allows such imports by using the `import` keyword.

The `import` keyword is similar to the `using` statement we have in C# language. This helps us to access the external methods and properties. One `import` statement that you will have in your component class would be from Angular. We import the `component` keyword from the Angular core module, which is used as a decorator in our class. The following is the syntax of the `import` keyword:

```
import { Component, OnInit } from '@angular/core'
```

The import syntax requires that the members we need should be defined in curly braces, followed by the path of the module that contains that member. In the above case, we are importing `component` and `OnInit` members from Angular core module.

newsComponent

For our SNC application, we will be creating our first component named `newsComponent`. The purpose of this component will be to display the latest news from the news source. When we launch our application, this will be the main component that will be loaded. For this chapter, as we decided, we will just have a basic component with some hardcoded data, hence we will just add a few lines of news articles and display them on the user interface.

Angular CLI provides us with the command to generate components for our application. It not only generates the barebone class for the component, but also the external template, and adds the reference to the component in the `app` module. The syntax of generating a new component is as follows:

```
ng generate  component <<componentname>>
```

The following screenshot shows the command we execute for our `newsComponent`, which generates the required files. We will be creating our component in a `dashboard` folder under the `app` folder:

```
Sachins-MacBook-Pro:SportsNewsCombinator sachin$ ng generate component dashboard/news --spec false
installing component
  create src/app/dashboard/news/news.component.css
  create src/app/dashboard/news/news.component.html
  create src/app/dashboard/news/news.component.ts
  update src/app/app.module.ts
Sachins-MacBook-Pro:SportsNewsCombinator sachin$
```

Here, we mentioned that our component is a `news` component under the `dashboard` folder, and Angular CLI created three files. Angular CLI creates a folder for the component with the component name, `news` in our case, to make sure we have separation of concern.

The flag `spec false` informs Angular CLI not to create the spec files for test cases. By default, Angular CLI, when generating the component or service or pipes, will create an additional file for writing test cases. We will be looking at how to write test cases in an Angular application in `Chapter 8`, *Trello – Using Angular CLI*.

You will have noticed here that there is an update to the `app.module` file as well. This file defines all the components that are under the `app` module. We will discuss modules in more detail in the following chapter; here, we just want to understand that each component that is created needs to be a reference in the module file. Angular uses this module file to identify which components are associated, and load them appropriately.

Now let's add some code in our newly created component.

newsComponent business logic

Our news component will be very simple and will have the following logic in it:

1. We will first import the reference to our models, namely `News` and `Article`:

```
import {News} from '../../../models/news';
import {Article} from '../../../models/article';
```

2. Then we will create an object of our `News` model inside the `newComponent` class:

```
latest_news: News = new News();
```

We will have a private method in our class, which will seed our `news` object. This method will just create some hardcoded objects, which we will display on the screen:

```
private seedNewsData(): News{
    let news:News= new News();
    news.status = "ok";
    news.source="nfl";
    news.sortBy="top";
    news.articles = this.seedArcticles();
    return news;
}
private seedArcticles():Article[]{
    let articles:Article[] = new Array();
    articles.push({
    ......
    return articles;
}
```

This private method will be called from the `ngOnInit` method.
The `ngOnInit` method is one of the life cycle hooks provided by Angular. The life cycle hooks are the methods that are exposed by the Angular for us to add logic to the component load and unload event. The `ngOnInit` method is exposed from the Angular core module, and in the following code snippet we see how to use this:

```
ngOnInit() {
    this.latest_news = this.seedNewsData();
}
```

3. Once we have assigned the news data to the new object, we can then bind this news property to the HTML template for the new component.

newsComponent template logic

You will have noticed that when we created the component from Angular CLI, it created a separate file for the template. We will be using this file to define our HTML for news details and bind the news property which we defined in the component to display the data.

As our news articles are a list, we will be using one of the built-in Angular structural directives, `*ngFor`. Angular has predefined directives called **structural directives**, which enable us to change the structure of the HTML at runtime based on the input provided. These directives add power and flexibility to our HTML by providing features such as `for` loops and `if` logic. Here, we are using `ngFor` to loop through our list of news articles and print each article as a separate element. The following is the code where we use `ngFor` on the news article:

```
<li *ngFor="let article of latest_news.articles">
```

The preceding statement tells Angular to loop through all the articles in the news object and assign each article to the variable article defined after the `let` statement. This allows us to access the article properties by using the dot syntax.

Angular provides interpolation for binding the values of properties from the class to the HTML, by using the syntax of double curly braces `{{}}`. When Angular finds these double curly braces, it evaluates the expression inside these and displays the result as the value in an HTML element. For example, we have the following HTML in our `newComponent` file:

```
<div class="para">
{{article.description}}
</div>
```

Angular here evaluates the expression `article.description` and prints the result on the screen. You can find the whole HTML on the GitHub page.

Now, once we have defined our component and its respective HTML, it's time to run our application and see the output.

SNC – running the code

As we discussed before, Angular CLI provides a built-in server that builds the application and hosts it on the local node server. We can now run our application using the same command of `npm serve`. Once you run this command, navigate to `http://localhost:4200` in your browser and it should present you with our first cut of the SNC website, as shown in the following screenshot:

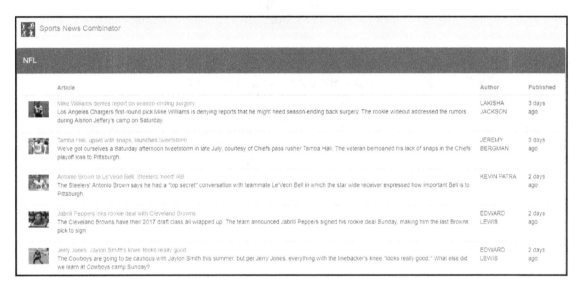

Summary

In this chapter, our focus was to start with our first application and, in doing so, go through some of the features of TypeScript and Angular. We learned about data types in TypeScript, and the type inference feature of TypeScript, which allows TypeScript to identify the types implicitly for the variable defined. Then we looked at the classes provided in TypeScript and how TypeScript provides us with the object-oriented feature to help produce better code.

Our application is built with Angular and TypeScript, so it was necessary to have an understanding of Angular concepts, which was the next topic that we discussed. We looked at Angular architecture, and discovered what components are and how are they composed. We are building our application with Angular CLI, a command-line interface that provides the ability to create a barebone project with all the required configuration in place.

Then we started building our project by defining its high-level architecture and code setup. We looked at some concepts such as creating components and templates, and basic data binding, and used these components to create our first application component, *newsComponent*.

In this chapter, the focus was to build our basics, hence our `newsComponent` did not have much functionality. We just created static data and used that to display on the main page.

In the next chapter, we will continue our journey by adding features such as adding basic routing and data format to the SNC application. In doing so, we will focus on writing more object-oriented code using features such as interfaces in TypeScript. We will discuss classes in detail, with constructors, functions, and optional parameters. From the Angular perspective, we will delve deep into components, templates, and binding.

3
Sports News Combinator – Adding Features

In the previous chapter, we started on our first application, **Sports News Combinator** (**SNC**). We created a simple component to display a set of news articles on a page. We hardcoded our data and focused more on the basics of Angular and TypeScript. We covered types, type constructs, and type inference in TypeScript, and had a brief look at classes, Angular framework, and components.

The focus of the previous chapter was to get us off the ground and to look at some of the primary concepts. In this chapter, we are going to build on top of our application and look at some other features of TypeScript and Angular.

This chapter will focus on the following topics:

- **Functions in TypeScript**: With types, the functions in TypeScript provide flexibility to set up rules.
- **Deep dive into classes and interfaces**: We will look at the features of classes, such as constructors, scoping, and member declarations. Interfaces allow us to create a more object-oriented style of code.
- **Features in SNC**: We will enhance our existing application by adding a couple of other components for headers and footers.
- **Angular templates and modules:** With our application, we will look at how templates and data binding work in Angular. We will look at modules in Angular and how we defined a module in our application.

By the end of this chapter, we will have added new features to our application and, along the way, understood some more features of TypeScript and Angular.

Functions

Functions are the building blocks of the JavaScript programming language, which allow us to write readable, maintainable, and reusable code. Functions define the action to be performed. If you have done any JavaScript development you would have written functions. TypeScript functions are not very different from JavaScript functions, with the addition of some new features that allow us to write code that is more understandable and error-free.

Here is an example of how a TypeScript function is defined:

```
function printFullName(firstName:string,lastName:string):string{
  return firstName + " " + lastName;
}
```

This example shows how a function is defined in TypeScript. We have a `function` keyword, which is prefixed to the function name, followed by a list of parameters. In TypeScript, we mostly use functions inside classes as methods, with one difference that the `function` keyword is not required.

In the following section, we will cover the features of TypeScript functions, which help us write better code, and provide flexibility and error checking.

Types in functions

Functions in TypeScript use types to define parameters and return values. This allows us to have a concrete signature of a function that needs to be followed by anyone who is calling the function. Since JavaScript, natively, does not support types, we can't do a similar thing in JavaScript. If you take a look at the preceding example, where we had a function called `printFullName`, you can see that we have two parameters—`firstName` and `lastName`—whose type is defined as a string.

When we call this function, the type of value passed is checked by the compiler to confirm whether it matches the types defined in the function declaration. These types are also available inside the function body, which allows us to use features such as auto-completion and type checking. In addition to the types defined for parameters, TypeScript also allows us to define the type of the return value. Each `return` statement is then checked to confirm whether it has the same type, as defined by the function signature.

Types make writing and using functions more intuitive and provide checks, which were missing in JavaScript.

Arrow functions

Also known as fat arrow or lambda function, Arrow functions have been newly introduced in ES6. Arrow functions allow us to write concise code for anonymous functions. With an arrow function, we don't need to write the `function` keyword; we can directly just define the function.

Check out the following example of a function written in a traditional way:

```
function printFullName(firstName:string,lastName:string):string{
    return firstName + " " + lastName;
}
```

This same function can be written in a concise format using arrow notation, as shown here:

```
(firstName: string, lastName: string) => firstName + " " + lastName;
```

An arrow function is an equals symbol (=) followed by the greater than symbol (>). To the left of the arrow are the parameters for the function; in this case, we have two parameters. To the right of the arrow is the body of the function, which, in this case, just returns the concatenation of `firstName` and `lastName`. We don't have to use the function keyword, wrap the function in curly braces, or type the `return` keyword.

There are some subtle differences in how we can manage the parameters in an arrow function, as described here:

- **Empty parameters**: In the following example, we do not have any input parameter; hence, we need to have an empty set of parentheses to the left of the arrow:

    ```
    () => console.log("Hello World!!");
    ```

- **Single parameter**: If we have a single parameter to pass in an arrow function, then we don't need to wrap the parameter in parentheses, as shown here:

    ```
    id => console.log(id);
    ```

- **Multiple parameters**: In case we have multiple parameters, as we saw in the first example of arrow functions, we need to wrap the parameters in parentheses, as follows:

    ```
    (firstName: string, lastName: string) => firstName + " " +
    lastName;
    ```

- **Multiline function body**: All the preceding examples have a single line of code in the function body. If we have a function that spans across multiple lines, we can very well wrap them in curly braces, as shown here:

```
(firstName, lastName, age): number => {
console.log(firstName + ' ' + lastName);
return age + 1;
// do more stuff here
};
```

The this keyword in arrow functions

The `this` keyword in JavaScript has always been a cause of confusion for developers. In traditional JavaScript, the lexical scope of the *this* keyword is based on the time when a function is executed.

Take a look at the following example to understand how the significance of `this` changes:

```
function Book(title) {
  this.title = title;
  this.printTitle = function () {
  this.title = this.title + " by Sachin Ohri";
  console.log(this.title);
  }
}
var typeScript = new Book("TypeScript By Example");
setTimeout(typeScript.printTitle, 1000);
setTimeout(function() { typeScript.printTitle(); },2000)
```

When the preceding function is executed, we get the following output:

```
undefined by Sachin Ohri
  TypeScript By Example by Sachin Ohri
```

In the first `setTimeout` function, when the `printTitle` method is called after 1 second, the scope of `this` inside the `printTitle` method is windows and, hence, `this.title` is `undefined`. But, in the second `setTimeout` function, the scope of `this` is the `Book` class, which results in printing the `title` value.

Arrow functions solve the problem of lexical scoping by assigning `this` at the time of function declaration, and not execution, which would then be based on the outer function. The following is the updated example of using arrow functions, which will return the output as `TypeScript By Example by Sachin Ohri` for both the `setTimeout` functions:

```
function Book(title) {
  this.title = title;
  this.printTitle = () => console.log(this.title + " by Sachin Ohri");
}
var typeScript = new Book("TypeScript By Exmaple");
setTimeout(typeScript.printTitle, 1000);
setTimeout(function () { typeScript.printTitle(); }, 2000);
```

 If you specifically need to use the *this* keyword in the context of execution, then you should avoid using arrow functions.

Optional and default parameters

JavaScript is a very flexible language and one of the flexibilities it provides is that every parameter in a function is optional. You can call a function that accepts a parameter and not pass any parameter to it, and JavaScript will still not complain. On the other hand, in TypeScript, all the parameters are required until explicitly defined as optional.

In the following example we have a parameter, length, which is optional:

```
function Book(title: string, length?:number){
}
```

As you can see in the preceding code snippet, the only syntax change required to make a parameter from mandatory to optional is to add a question mark (?) after the parameter name. One thing to note is that optional parameters are only allowed after all the required parameters have been defined.

Default parameters let us specify a default value to be used for optional parameters or for required parameters (when the caller passes undefined values). In the following example, we assign a default value to the length parameter:

```
function Book(title: string, length:number=300){
}
```

So, if anyone calling this function does not pass the length parameter, the function will assume the value of 300. If the default parameters are at the end of all the required parameters, then TypeScript assumes it as an optional parameter.

Rest parameters

Rest parameters allow us to pass a variable number of parameters to a function and accept them as an array. A rest parameter is defined by prefixing the parameter name with ellipses (three dots). When the function is called, we can pass multiple parameters to that function, and the function will accept them in an array format. Check out the following example, where we define a function with rest parameters:

```
function School (name: string, ...id:number[]){}
let harvard = new School("Harvard", 1,2,3,4,5);
```

Here, all the parameters passed to the second parameter are combined together and added to the number array.

Function overloads

Function overloads allow us to define multiple functions with the same name but different implementations. This concept is very prevalent in traditional object-oriented languages but not so much in JavaScript. TypeScript does allow function overloads but the syntax and implementation are a bit clunky.

In TypeScript, function overload is accomplished by providing multiple function definitions, but only one implementation. The implemented function, then, has to make sure that it handles all the different function definitions and perform an action based on the definitions. In the following example, we will define two function overloads and one implementation, which will also handle the overloaded functions:

```
function getCustomer(name:string):string;
function getCustomer(id:number):string;
function getCustomer(property:any):string{
  if(typeof property == 'string'){
    //return customer info based on customer name
  }
  else if(typeof property == "number"){
    //return customer info based on customer id
  }
  return "customer";
};
```

In the preceding example, we have two overloads of the getCustomer function: one takes a string as the input parameter and the other takes a *number* as the input parameter. The third function is an implemented function, which takes any as the type of input parameter. In this function, we provide the implementation of getCustomer based on the typeOf input variable passed. This type of behavior in TypeScript for function overload is because there are no types in JavaScript. The following is the transpiled code for the preceding example into JavaScript:

```
function getCustomer(property) {
  if (typeof property == 'string') {
  //return customer info based on customer name
  }
  else if (typeof property == "number") {
  //return customer info based on customer nidame
  }
  return "customer";
};
```

Note that there is no transpiled version of the overloaded functions.

Classes in TypeScript

Classes have been some of the most sought-after features of TypeScript. Classes and interfaces are the cornerstones of writing object-oriented code. Object-oriented programming provides the following features:

- Inheritance
- Polymorphism
- Encapsulation
- Abstraction

In this section, we will look at classes in TypeScript and see how we can write code in an object-oriented fashion. We will start by looking at what classes are and how they are defined in TypeScript. Then, we will look at a special keyword called constructor, which is used to initialize the properties of a class. From there, we will look at how we can write and access the properties and methods of a class. To cement our understanding of classes, we will create an example of a class and see all the features in it.

Classes in TypeScript have additional features, such as declaring static properties, abstract class, and inheritance. We will look at these topics as well in this section.

Class definition

If you have a background in programming languages such as C# and Java, then you will be familiar with the concept of classes. Even if you have used JavaScript version ES6, you will have an understanding of what classes are. But JavaScript developers who have worked in ES5 would not have used classes before.

Class is like a logical container composed of *related* properties and method. The *related* word here is of special significance. So, if we define a class named Book, then this class will contain things related to books, such as author, title, publisher, and so on. If we define a class named TVShow, then this class will contain things related to TV shows, such as cast, description, duration, and so on. The class helps us to organize our code in a logical format with every entity having an independent structure.

Class forms a template containing properties and methods used for creating objects. Each object will have same properties and methods. The most important feature of the class is to provide encapsulation to reusable code, which can be used throughout the application.

TypeScript supports classes out of the box and makes it easy for us to encapsulate our code in a logical form. As we saw in the previous chapter, TypeScript can be transpiled into ES5 or ES6 format, which provides us the flexibility of using these features and not worrying about the browser support for native JavaScript.

TypeScript classes also have constructors and access modifiers, along with support for inheritance and abstract classes. All of the functional programming goodness of JavaScript is retained, but TypeScript adds to that the object-oriented constructs familiar to many developers. The following is a simple example of a class definition:

```
class Book{
  public author:string;
  public title: string;
  public length: number;
  getFullTitle():string{
    return `${this.title} by ${this.author}`;
  }
}
let typeScript = new Book();
typeScript.title = "TypeScript by Example";
typeScript.author = "Sachin Ohri";
typeScript.length = 300;
```

A class is defined by the class keyword followed by the name of the class. Then, inside the curly braces, we have properties and methods associated with the class. As in the preceding example, we have a class named Book with three properties and a method.

To create an object of a class, we use the `new` keyword and define an object name.

> All the public properties and methods can be accessed by the object using the *dot* operator (.), as seen in the preceding code with the `typeScript` object.

Constructors

A constructor is used to initialize a new instance of a class. If we need to pass some starter values to the properties of a class at the time of object creation, we use the constructor. A constructor looks like any other function in a class with the exception of its name—it is always named as `constructor`. In the following example, we have a constructor of the `Book` class, which initializes its properties:

```
class Book {
   public author: string;
   public title: string;
   public length: number;
   constructor(author:string, title:string, length: number){
   this.author = author;
   this.title = title;
   this.length = length;
}
   getFullTitle(): string {
      return `${this.title} by ${this.author}`;
   }
}
let typeScript = new Book("Sachin Ohri","TypeScript by Example",300);
```

When you create a new instance of a class, you pass the parameters expected by the constructor. Note that you don't execute the constructor by calling it by name; you use the class name and the `new` keyword; however, this will execute the `constructor` function and return a new instance of the class.

In TypeScript, there can only be one constructor function per class, unlike traditional languages where we can have multiple constructors with different parameters. In TypeScript, we can achieve similar goals through the use of optional parameters. In the following example, we have a constructor that takes three parameters; however, the last parameter is optional because of the use of the question mark (?).

This allows the single constructor to behave as if it has multiple forms:

```
constructor(author:string, title:string, length?: number){
}
```

Constructor parameters

In the preceding example, we saw how we can initialize properties at the time of object creation using the constructor. We pass the parameter to the class, and, then, inside the constructor, we assign these parameters to the properties of the class. Parameter properties allow a short form to define these properties in a class.

In the following example, we have a class with three properties, namely, title, author, and length. The constructor takes three parameters which are then assigned to the property:

```
class Book {
  public author: string;
  public title: string;
  public length: number;
  constructor(author:string, title:string, length: number){
    this.author = author;
    this.title = title;
    this.length = length;
  }
}
```

We can accomplish the same thing with the following code, which is much shorter. Here we don't explicitly declare a new property, instead, we place the `public` keyword in front of the constructor's parameter name. This tells the TypeScript compiler that we want a property with the same name as the parameter, and that it should be set equal to the value passed to the constructor.

```
class Book {
  constructor(public author:string,
    public title:string, public length: number){
  }
}
```

Properties and methods

Classes can contain properties and methods which provide data and behavior. We will look at interfaces in next section, but one important difference between *classes* and *interfaces* is that classes contain the actual implementation of the methods.

Properties

There are two ways to define the properties in a class. One we have used and seen in the preceding examples, where we defined properties such as author, title, and length. We can set and get the values of these properties using the dot syntax, as we have already seen.

The second way is it define properties using custom *accessors*.

Accessors

Accessors are getter and setter functions that give us more control over how property values can be accessed. They have their own special syntax. In the following example, we have accessors for a the `title` property. You define them by using the `get` and `set` keywords. On a high level, accessors are just functions, but they both have the same name:

```
class Book {
  private _title:string;
  get title():string{
    return this._title;
  }
  set title(value:string){
    if(value != ""){
    this._title = value;
    }
  }
}
let typeScript = new Book();
typeScript.title = "TypeScript By Example";
```

The *getter* will always contain an empty set of parentheses after the name. The *setter* must be passed exactly one parameter, and you are not allowed to specify a return type for it. Inside the bodies of the accessors, you can perform any special logic you need for the property. The object of the class will access the property with the dot syntax.

Methods

Methods are pretty straightforward. They're just functions defined inside the class. The following is the example of a method that we'd defined in our `Book` class earlier:

```
getFullTitle(): string {
  return `${this.title} by ${this.author}`;
}
```

Here, the `getFullTitle` method can be accessed by the class using the same dot syntax.

Static properties

Static properties are properties of the class itself and not of the class instances, like we saw in the preceding example of the `Book` class. The advantage of static properties is that they allow us to store data specific to the class and do not change with different instances of the class. In the following example, we have a `Book` class with a static property named `publisher`:

```
class Book {
   public author: string;
   public title: string;
   public length: number;
   static publisher: string = "Packt Pub";
   constructor(author:string, title:string, length: number){
   this.author = author;
   this.title = title;
   this.length = length;
}
   getFullTitle(): string {
      return `${this.title} by ${this.author}`;
   }
}
let typeScript = new Book("Sachin Ohri","TypeScript by Example",300);
let publisher = Book.publisher; //Publisher property is available on the
class
```

The properties `title`, `author`, and `length` are parameter properties available in all the instances of the class. Each instance can set the property equal to whatever value is appropriate for that instance.

The `publisher` property is a static property, which is defined by having the name prefixed with the `static` keyword. It is, therefore, only available in the class and not on instances of the class. If we want to reference the `publisher` property, we must reference it through the `Book` class itself.

Inheritance

Inheritance is one of the features of object-oriented programming, and TypeScript allows us to use this feature in writing code for JavaScript. Inheritance is a behavior of extending an existing class with additional features to create subclasses. The advantage of inheritance is code reuse; we can have common properties and methods defined in the parent class and have child classes inherit those properties and methods. We can then add specific functionalities to them.

To create a child class, TypeScript defines a keyword, extends, which is added to the child class followed by the name of the parent class.

The following is the example of implementing inheritance:

```
1  class Book {
2      constructor(public author:string, public title:string, public length: number){
3      }
4      getFullTitle(): string {
5          return `${this.title} by ${this.author}`;
6      };
7  }
8
9  class TypeScript extends Book{
10     public releaseDate:string;
11 }
12
13 let typeScript = new TypeScript("Sachin Ohri","TypeScript by Example",300);
14 typeScript.
15             author              (property) Book.author: string
16             getFullTitle
17             length
18             releaseDate
19             title
20
```

As we can see on line number 9, we created a new class, TypeScript, which extends the parent class, Book. The TypeScript class has only one property, which is, releaseDate, but as you can see in line number 14, when we create an object of the TypeScript class, we have access to the properties of the parent class as well.

If we extend this example, we can create multiple child classes that inherit from the parent class, and we will have access to all the properties and methods of the parent class in addition to the properties and methods defined in the child class.

Super

Super is a TypeScript keyword that refers to the parent class. If we define a constructor to the child class, it's mandatory to call the constructor of the parent class explicitly, using the `super` keyword. In the following example, we have a constructor for our child class, `TypeScript`:

```
class Book {
  constructor(public author:string,
    public title:string, public length: number){
  }
  getFullTitle(): string {
    return `${this.title} by ${this.author}`;
  };
}
class TypeScript extends Book{
  constructor(author:string,title:string,
    length: number, public releaseDate:string){
    super(author,title,length);
  }
}
```

In this case, we need to call `super` so as to pass the required parameters to the constructor function of the parent class.

 If the parent's constructor expected some parameters and the child class didn't define a constructor, the parameters expected by the parent must be passed when creating new instances of the child class.

Abstract class

An abstract class is a special type of class, which does not need to have an implementation of all the methods it defines. The primary use of an abstract class is to have a base class that defines all the common behaviors and lets the child classes manage the differences. This concept is very useful in writing large-scale object-oriented applications, where we want to define the behavior of a parent entity.

The following example shows how to define an abstract class and abstract methods:

```
abstract class Book {
  constructor(public author:string, public title:string,
    public length: number){
  }
```

```
    abstract getFullTitle(): string ;
}
```

To define a class as abstract, we just need to prefix the class name with
the `abstract` keyword; the same goes for the methods of the class, as seen earlier. Here, we
have an abstract `Book` class with three properties and one abstract method. Now, we can
create a child class that can extend the parent class and provide the implementation of the
`getFullTitle` method, as shown in the following code snippet. This child class,
`TypeScript`, can be used to create an object and access the properties and methods:

```
class TypeScript extends Book{
  getFullTitle(): string {
    return `${this.title} by ${this.author}`;
  }
}
```

 An abstract class can have fully implemented properties, constructors,
methods, and accessors.

Another important difference in abstract classes is that we cannot instantiate the class
directly but can only create the object of a child class.

Interfaces

Interface is a TypeScript concept and there is no alternate version in JavaScript; hence, when
we write an interface, it does not get transpiled into JavaScript. Interfaces play an important
role in TypeScript of providing us with a contract that can be enforced in a class. In
TypeScript, interfaces allow us to create our own custom types and provide compile-time
checks to make sure the types are used correctly.

An interface is a collection of properties and methods but with no implementation. Its basic
purpose is to provide the shape of an object. This means that we can have an interface that
defines a couple of properties and a method that accepts one parameter. This interface will
not specify how this method is implemented, just the method signature. The
implementation will be the responsibility of the class implementing this interface.

Definition

The following is the example of how an interface is defined in TypeScript:

```
interface IArticle{
  // properties
  author:string;
  title:string;
  description: string;
  // optional properties
  url?: string;
  //methods
  getFormattedDate():string;
}
```

An interface is defined by the `interface` keyword followed by the name. The definition of the interface is placed inside the curly braces. As we can see in the preceding example, we have three properties defined in the interface, with each property having its own data type.

Similar to optional parameters in functions, we can define optional properties in an interface by using the question mark (?), as you can see with the `URL` property in the preceding example.

The interface also provides a definition of the methods but no implementation, as in the preceding example, where we have a `getFormattedDate` method that does not take any parameters but returns a string.

Duck typing

Duck typing in computer science means that if an object has the same properties and methods as defined in any known type, then the object can be treated as that type and it does not need to be explicitly marked as that type. The interfaces in TypeScript are a form of duck typing, as we will see in the following example:

```
 1    interface IArticle{
 2        // properties
 3        author:string;
 4        title:string;
 5        //methods
 6        formatdDate():void;
 7    }
 8    class Article{
 9        author:string;
10        title:string;
11        //methods
12        formatdDate():void {
13            // implementation detail
14        }
15    }
16    function news (article:IArticle){
17        // implementation
18    }
19    let espn = new Article;
20    news(espn);
```

Here, we define an interface with two properties and one method. We also have an `Article` class, which has the same signature as that of the interface. Then, we have a function named `news`, which takes one parameter of the `IArcticle` type. As you can see in line number 20, we can pass the object of the `Article` class to this function, which expects the `IArticle` type even when we have not explicitly defined that the class `Article` is of the `IArcticle` type. This is called duck typing and it forms a very useful part of developing applications in TypeScript by providing flexibility of types.

Extending interfaces

As we saw in classes, interfaces can also be extended from other interfaces. This allows us to create new custom types from existing types and make our code more reusable. When we extend an interface, the child interface automatically inherits all the properties and methods of the parent interface, much like classes. The following example shows how we can extend interfaces:

```
interface IArticle{
  author:string;
  title:string;
}
interface IEspn extends IArticle{
  description: string;
}
let news: IEspn = {
  author:"ESPN",
```

```
    title: "Latest news",
    description:"Latest ESPN news"
}
```

To extend an interface, TypeScript provides the `extends` keyword followed by the interface name. As you can see in the preceding example, the `IEspn` interface extends the `IArticle` interface and, thus, has all the properties of `IArticle` in it. Extending interfaces provides us with the flexibility of defining multiple custom types derived from other custom types.

Implementing interfaces

Once we have custom types defined using interfaces, the next step is to implement these interfaces using classes. TypeScript allows classes to implement interfaces using the `implements` keyword. When a class implements an interface, the TypeScript compiler checks to see whether all the properties and methods have been implemented in the class. This check helps in making sure that the class follows the contract defined by the interface.

The following example shows how we can implement an interface in a class:

```
interface IArticle{
  author:string;
  title:string;
  formatdDate():void;
}
class Article implements IArticle{
  author:string;
  title:string;
  formatdDate():void {
    // implementation detail
  }
}
let espn:IArticle = new Article();
```

The `Article` class in the preceding example implements the `IArticle` interface, which tells the TypeScript compiler that `Article` should have at least all the properties and methods defined in `IArticle`. The `Article` class can have other properties and methods as well, but it must have the properties and methods defined `IArticle`.

Adding features to SNC

In the previous chapter, we started with our *Sports News Combinator* application, created one component, and populated the data in it. We are using Angular and TypeScript for our application built with Angular **CLI** (**command-line interface**). The following is the *Sports News Combinator* architecture, which we defined in the previous chapter:

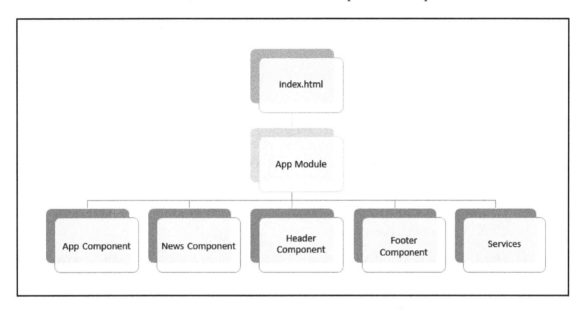

In the previous chapter, we developed **News Component** and **App Component**. In this section, we will refactor our existing code to add features that you learned in this chapter, such as interfaces and functions to make the app more robust. We will also add a couple of components for header and footer to provide a better look and feel to our application. From Angular perspective, we will also look at binding and interpolation techniques.

Restructuring the models

In the previous chapter, we defined two models: articles and news. The news model contained three properties and a reference to the article model. Now, we will use our knowledge of interfaces to define an interface for an article and have the Article class implement that interface.

Adding interface to the Article class

We start by creating a new file called `IArticle` in our model's folder and add the following code to the `IArticle` interface:

```
export interface IArticle{
  author:string;
  title:string;
  description: string;
  url:string;
  urlToImage:string;
  publishedAt:string;
  getFormattedDate():string;
}
```

The `IArticle` interface contains all the properties required by the `Article` class and a `getFormattedDate` function, which is responsible for converting the date from ISO format to yyyy-mm-dd format. In the first line, before the `interface` keyword, you can see that there is another keyword, `export`. We will discuss `export` in the next chapter but, for now, let's look at the basic definition of the `export` keyword and why it is used. As we know that an interface only provides the definition and not the implementation, we need to implement this interface in a class.

For us to refer to a specific class/interface in another class/interface, we need a way to notify TypeScript that we want to import that entity. This is achieved by prefixing the class/interface with the `export` keyword, which needs to be imported. In our case, we want to refer to `IArticle` in the `Article` class; hence, we need to export the `IArticle` interface and then import the interface in the `Article` class.

As we know that the interface only provides the definition and not the implementation, we need to implement this interface in a class.

We already have a class that we created in the previous chapter, called `Article.ts`. Now, let's implement the `IArticle` interface on the `Article` class. This just requires us to add the `implements` keyword after the class name followed by the interface name:

```
export class Article implements IArticle{
  .....
}
```

As we discussed earlier, we need to import the `IArticle` interface in the `Article` class; hence, we need to add the following line of code on top of the `Article.ts` file:

```
import {IArticle} from './IArticle';
```

These changes have helped us to write a class that follows a predefined contract by the IArticle interface. The advantage of defining an interface is that, if required, we can use the same interface to provide shape to a different class, or we can extend the IArticle interface with other properties to make the code reusable.

Modifying the news model

The purpose of the news model class is to encapsulate the set of articles for each news channel. Let's refactor this class to now use the IArticle interface and a constructor. The following is the code of the original news.ts file:

```
import {Article} from './article';
export class News {
  status:string;
  source:string;
  sortBy:string;
  articles: Article[];
}
```

We have four properties, out of which, one is for an array of articles. The first change will be to use the constructor function that we learned in this chapter to accept the values of the three properties:

```
constructor(public status:string, public source:string, public
sortBy:string ){}
```

As we know, in TypeScript, we can define a property and initialize its values in constructor parameters, which provides us a concise way to code. The preceding code tells the TypeScript compiler that we need to define three public properties and assign values to them, which are passed by the caller at the time of object creation.

The other change we will do is modify the Article array property to define it as an accessor. This allows us to define the get and set properties for the Article arrays and have a special logic to make sure we only assign the expected value. We first define a private property of the IArticle type and then have setters and getters, which will assign and return the values, respectively.

Here's the code for the modified `News` class:

```
1    import {IArticle} from './IArticle';
2
3    export class News {
4
5        private _articles: IArticle[];
6        constructor(public status:string, public source:string, public sortBy:string ){}
7
8        get Articles():IArticle[] {
9            return this._articles;
10       }
11
12       set Articles(value: IArticle[]){
13           if(value.length > 0 ){
14               this._articles = value;
15           }
16       }
17   }
18
```

As you can see in line number 1, we import the `IArticle` interface so that we can refer and assign the `IArticle` type. On line number 8 and 12, we define getters and setters for the private variable, `_articles`.

Features such as interfaces, properties, constructors, accessors, and types help us to write better, more robust, easily understandable, and error-free code.

Core components

In the previous section, we refactored our code to make it more object-oriented and reusable using the features of TypeScript. These changes did not have any impact on the user interface of our application but did make our code more robust and easy to maintain. In this section, we will focus on adding a couple of new components to our application: a header and footer.

In the previous chapter, we had a header to our application but it was part of the news component itself. This approach is not very extensible because, whenever we need to add a new component/feature to our application, we would need to make sure that we have a header HTML also included in the same component. Angular solves these problems by allowing us to compose the page with multiple components stitched together.

The header component

Our header component will have our application image with application name and navigation for our four news outlets. When the user navigates to our application, we will have NFL news as our default selection. As we saw in the last chapter, the Angular CLI provides us with the `ng generate` command which generates the component along with its template and style sheet. The Angular CLI also adds reference to the component in the app module. This time, we will not use the CLI but, rather, manually add these files and references just to show the steps executed by the CLI to generate a component for us:

- The first step is to create the header component. Our header and footer components will reside under the core folder, so let's create the core folder. Inside the core folder, we will create a new folder called `header`.
- A component consists of three parts, and for each part we will create a separate file:
    - **Component file**: We will create a new file, named `header.component.ts`. This file will consist of our component code, including the header component class, and the reference to the component HTML and style sheet.
    - **HTML file**: The next file is our HTML file, which will contain the navigation and related HTML. We'll name this file as `header.component.html`.
    - **StyleSheet file**: Similar to the HTML file, we will have one file for style sheet, with the name, `header.component.css`.

 We could have added HTML and CSS inline in our component file, but because our HTML and CSS are more than a few lines long, it's always better to have these in a separate file and reference them in the component decorator.

Now, let's look at each of these files and the `app` module changes to make a working header.

The component file

We don't have much logic in our header file as of now, apart from the HTML and some routing link. Hence, in our component file, we just define the component decorator and bind the HTML and CSS to the component. Check out the code for our component file:

```
import { Component, OnInit } from '@angular/core';
@Component({
```

```
    selector: 'snc-header',
    templateUrl: './header.component.html',
    styleUrls: ['./header.component.css']
})
export class HeaderComponent implements OnInit {
  constructor() { }
  ngOnInit() {
  }
}
```

The interesting thing to note here is that, had we generated our header component with the Angular CLI, it would have autogenerated the preceding code. In the preceding code, we just have a component decorator, which defines the component selector, its HTML template file, and its style sheet file.

The selector is used as a directive for referring to the header component in other component files. We will be referring to the header component in the app component file later in this chapter.

The HTML file

For the header component, this is the meat of the code. We define our navigation bar with the application logo and the links to our news outlets. Check out the code for our `header.component.html` file:

```html
<nav class="navbar navbar-light" style="background-color:whitesmoke">
  <a class="navbar-brand" href="#" style="padding: 10px">
    <img src="assets/Logo.png" width="35" height="35" alt="">
  </a>
  <div class="container-fluid">
    <div class="navbar-header">
      <a class="navbar-brand" href="#">Sports News Combinator</a>
    </div>
    <ul class="nav navbar-nav">
      <li><a routerLink="/nfl" routerLinkActive="active" >NFL</a></li>
      <li><a routerLink="/espn" routerLinkActive="active" >ESPN</a></li>
      <li><a routerLink="/fox" routerLinkActive="active" >FOX</a></li>
      <li><a routerLink="/bbc" routerLinkActive="active" >BBC</a></li>
    </ul>
  </div>
</nav>
```

We use a twitter bootstrap for our styling; hence, to show the header in the form of a navigation bar, we use the `nav` tag. The rest of the HTML is pretty straightforward, apart from the two properties that we see in our anchor tags. The `routerLink` and `routerLinkActive` properties are used by Angular to provide routing.

Routing is a way of defining the rules of navigation. In Angular, we use routing techniques to map the URL with the component that needs to be loaded on `index.html`. The `routerLink` defines the URL that would be initiated when the user clicks on the link. Angular achieves routing using `routingLink` and routes modules defined under `@angular/route`. We will cover routing in the next chapter.

The footer component

The footer component is very similar to the header component, with only one difference in the HTML. We will create our footer component in the core folder, as we did for the header component. You can refer to the code on GitHub for the HTML and CSS of the footer.

The app component

In Angular, we have `app.module`, which is the startup module and is responsible for declaring all of the dependencies of this module, including the startup component. If you look at our `app.module.ts` file, you will see a `bootstrap` property in `NgModule`, which defines the component that Angular should use as a startup component. The following is the code snippet from our `app` module file:

```
10  @NgModule({
11    declarations: [
12      AppComponent,
13      NewsComponent,                          Declarations: Components
14      HeaderComponent,                        that are part of this module
15      FooterComponent,
16      PublishedComponent
17    ],
18    imports: [
19      BrowserModule                           Imports: External modules
20    ],                                        which are imported
21
22
23    providers: [],                           Providers: Contains reference
24                                              to services
25
26    bootstrap: [AppComponent]
27  })
```

Bootstrap: Define the startup component

This screenshot shows the various components of NgModule and their purpose. When Angular loads the app.module file, it checks for the bootstrap component and, then, renders this component. In our case, this component is AppComponent. Hence, in our case, we will declare our header and footer components along with the news component in the appcomponent.html file, which would make Angular load all the three components to form a single web page.

Templates and interpolation

In Angular, there are two basic topics which make for a majority of the implementation: components and templates. We saw components in some detail in the previous chapter and we will deep-dive into components and its features in the upcoming chapters as well. Here, we will discuss templates, data binding, and interpolation.

To create our user interface in Angular, we define HTML, but just having a basic HTML does not really provide us with the flexibility of creating rich and powerful user interfaces. Angular provides us with data binding and directives to really power up our user interface. Angular data binding provides functionalities to help display information and respond to user actions, and with Angular directives, we can add logic to our HTML, such as if statements and for loops.

Templates

As we discussed templates in the previous chapter, we will just have an overview of the templates here. Our focus here will be on data binding and directives.

We have seen, when we created our components, that we had a separate file for our HTML components. The reference to this file was defined in the templateUrl property of the component metadata in the component class. When Angular loads the component, it checks the component metadata for various properties such as where the template resides and where the CSS resides. On identifying the template, Angular then processes and renders the component's HTML on the page.

Angular provides a couple of ways of defining templates for a component:

- **Inline templates**: These are the HTML components defined right inside the component file, and we do not create a separate file for the user interface. This is useful if we have a couple of lines of HTML, which can be easily managed inside the component decorator.

- **Linked template**: If our HTML is bigger than a few lines of code, then it's better to define our template in a separate file. The link to this file is then defined in the `templateURL` property of the component metadata. Having the HTML in a separate file helps in managing the code and providing proper IntelliSense to the HTML.

Directives

Directives have been part of Angular since its inception. Angular 1 (AngularJS) had loads of directives, but in Angular 2/4 only a select few remain. Directives are custom HTML tags that allow us to extend our HTML. Angular directives allow us to create small HTML components, which can be infused together to create an entire web page. This approach allows us to create multiple reusable templates, which can be shared in an application. You can think of directives as custom controls, which can be used as plug-and-play templates.

We have been using Angular directives in our current application. Let's look at our implementation and understand how directives work.

When a component has a selector defined in its component metadata, as we have in `NewsComponent`, `HeaderComponent`, and `FooterComponent`, we can use the said component as a directive. What this means is that we can insert this component into any other component by referencing the selector as an HTML tag. The following code snippet shows how we can define the components selector:

```
7    @Component({
8        selector: 'snc-news',
9        templateUrl: './news.component.html',
10       styleUrls: ['./news.component.css']
11   })
12   export class NewsComponent implements OnInit {
```

This code is from our `NewsComponent`, where we define our component selector in line number **8**. The selector, `snc-news`, represents the HTML associated with the news component. When we reference this selector in any other component, this selector can be referred to as a directive.

The following is the code snippet from the `AppComponent` HTML file where we have used `snc-news` as a directive; check out line number **3** for the news component directive:

```
1  <div>
2    <snc-header></snc-header>
3    <snc-news></snc-news>
4    <snc-footer></snc-footer>
5  </div>
6
```

Similarly, we have the header and footer directives referenced here.

So, the initial step to use a directive is to use the selector name of a component as an HTML tag in another component. When the template of this component is displayed, Angular looks for a component that has a selector with this name. In this case, when Angular displays the `AppComponent` template, it will then check the component for the header, news, and footer components. This way, we can define hundreds of small and specific templates, which can then be used as directives to provide us with reusable, easily maintainable, and loosely-coupled code base.

So, how does Angular know where to find this directive and how it ends up loading the HTML represented by the said directive?

The Angular loading process for directives

As we saw earlier, we had used the `snc-news` directive in our app component HTML page, but how does Angular know what `snc-news` is, where to reference this directive, and what needs to be replaced as an HTML for this directive? The answer to these questions is how Angular looks at the modules.

As we discussed earlier, an Angular application is made up of multiple modules, with each module working as a container of multiple components and directives. This module works as a boundary in which the component resolves its directives and dependencies. So, when Angular has to load a directive, it checks the module of the component to determine which directives are visible to that component.

Every Angular application should have at least one module: the `root` module, called `AppModule`. In our application, `AppModule` defines our `root` component, that is, `AppComponent`. This means that `AppComponent` now belongs to `AppModule`.

An Angular component can belong to one and only one Angular module.

If we look at our `AppModule` file, we will find that this module not only contains `AppComponent` but also `NewComponent`, `HeaderComponent`, and `FooterComponent`. Hence, when Angular loads `AppComponent` and finds that there are directives referenced in the `AppComponent` template, it first identifies the module in which `AppComponent` resides, which, in this case, is `AppModule`, and then checks to find if the directive is referenced in this module:

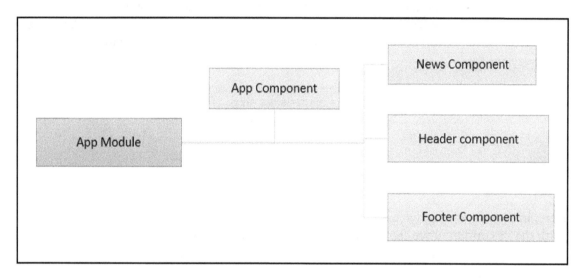

There are two ways of exposing a directive in an Angular module. We can declare the component in the Angular module, as we did for `NewComponent`, `HeaderComponent`, and `FooterComponent`. Alternatively, if the component is already declared in another Angular module, we can import that module, similar to how we import `BrowserModule` in the `NgModule` metadata.

Angular built-in directives

Similar to the directives that we created in our application, Angular also provides some built-in directives. Here, we will look at two of those built-in directives: `*ngIf` and `*ngFor`.

These directives are called structural directives because they modify the structure of the existing template by adding, removing, and modifying the existing elements. These directives are available in `BrowserModule` and, hence, can be referenced and used in any module that imports `BrowserModule`, as we did in our `AppModule` code.

The asterisk sign prefixing the directive is a terminology used by Angular to identify structural directives.

The *ngIf directive

As the name suggests, `*ngIf` provides us with an `if` condition, which can be used to remove or add an element to HTML based on whether the `if` expression is `true` or `false`. If the expression evaluates to `true`, then we end up adding an element into `dom`; else if the expression evaluates to `false`, then we remove the element. The following example shows the usage `*ngIf`:

```
<div class='table-responsive'>
  <table class='table' *ngIf='articles && articles.length'>
    <thead> ...
    </thead>
    <tbody> ...
    </tbody>
  </table>
</div>
```

Here, in the second line, we used `*ngIf` to evaluate an expression for the `article` array. With the `if` condition, we check if the `article` array is not null and has some length (size); if so, we show the HTML elements inside the condition, else we bypass them.

The *ngFor directive

The `*ngFor` directive is used to repeat a set of elements in `dom`. We define an HTML block for a single row and wrap it with `*ngFor`. When Angular encounters the `*ngFor` directive, it knows to repeat this HTML block a number of times, based on the expression evaluated in it. Let's look at the following example of using `*ngFor`:

```
<tbody>
  <tr *ngFor='let article of latest_news.Articles'>
    <td></td>
    <td>{{ article.urlToImage }}</td>
    <td>{{ article.title }}</td>
    <td>{{ article.description }}</td>
    <td>{{ article.author }}</td>
```

```
        <td>{{ article.publishedAt }}</td>
    </tr>
</tbody>
```

In the preceding example, we want to display each article in the row of a table. We define one table row and its child elements. This table row element and its children are then repeated for each article in the list of articles. We define each object with the `let` keyword, which can be referenced anywhere on this element, on any sibling element, or on any child element.

Bindings

To be able to build highly interactive applications, we need a mechanism to be able to bind the data from our components to the template. We also need to make sure that, if there is any change in data value on the template, or if any event is triggered, the application should be able to identify the responsible property or method in the component and call it. All this is achieved in Angular using data binding techniques.

Angular provides several types of binding, and we'll look at each of them.

Interpolation

Interpolation provides one-way binding between a component and a template. One-way binding means that the data flow happens only from the `component` property to the `template` tag it is associated with. These values do not get updated on the component side if there is any change in the template. Here are some examples of how we can use interpolation in our template:

```
1    <h4>{{source}}</h4>
2    <h4>{{'News Outlet: ' + source}}</h4>
3    <h4 innerText={{source}}>/h4>
4    <h4>{{getSource()}}</h4>
```

Its corresponding component code is shown here:

```
12   export class NewsComponent implements OnInit {
13
14       source:string = "nfl";
15
16       getSource():string {
17           return this.source;
18       };
```

As you can see, in the preceding example, there are multiple ways of implementing interpolation. All the four examples will result in the same output of `nfl` being shown on the user interface. Line number **1** shows the simplest form of interpolation, where a property from the component (as seen in line number **14**) is directly mapped to the HTML element.

Interpolation is defined by properties or expressions enclosed in curly braces.

We can even perform operations such as concatenation, like on line number **2**, or call a method in the component class, as shown in line number **4**. In line number **3**, we show that we can use interpolation to populate the values of the HTML element attributes.

When Angular finds the interpolation syntax, it looks inside and evaluates the expression mentioned based on the component to which this template is associated. After evaluating the expression, Angular assigns the value to the HTML element.

Property binding

Property binding is another form of interpolation. It allows us to bind the existing properties of the HTML elements with the properties or methods defined in the component. Here is the syntax of property binding:

```
<img [src] ='article.url'></img>
```

In the preceding example, we have bound the source property of `img` tag to the URL property of the `article` object. The following is the example of how we can write the same binding in interpolation:

```
<img src ={{article.url}}></img>
```

Here in interpolation, the attribute is not enclosed in the square brackets, but the binding is enclosed in curly braces. As with interpolation, property binding is also one-way binding.

Two-way binding

Using interpolation allows us to have one-way binding between the HTML template and component properties. There is an instance where one-way binding does not satisfy our requirements. We would want to make sure whether the user modified any value on the user interface that gets reflected in the component as well. This is called two-way binding.

In Angular, two-way binding is achieved by using the ngModel directive. The following is a sample syntax of ngModel:

```
<input [(ngModel)]="name">
```

The ngModel directive is enclosed in square brackets, which enclose parentheses and the model name. The square bracket indicates property binding from the component to the HTML input elements, and the parentheses indicate event binding to manage notifications of user actions.

In this case, whenever the value inside the input box is modified, an event is generated, which informs the component of the event fired. If any change happens on the component property, then it gets propagated to the user interface.

With all the preceding changes, we now have our intermediate application with header and footer components. The following screenshot shows how our application looks now:

You can see that there is not much change in our application layout or the data presented. We will make our final changes in the next chapter.

Summary

In this chapter, the focus was on learning some new concepts of TypeScript and Angular. We looked at functions, classes, and interfaces in TypeScript, and templates and interpolation in Angular. We enhanced the user interface of our application by adding headers and footers, and made our code more object-oriented by using interfaces and modifying the code structure in our class. At this time, you have enough knowledge to create web applications with TypeScript and Angular, apart from features such as making web service calls and routing.

In the next chapter, we will add more features to our *Sports News Combinator* application, including making a web service call to fetch the sports news. You will be reading about decorator patterns and how they are used in Angular; then, we will also learn about the HTTP module and routing in Angular.

4
Sports News Combinator – the Final Version

In this chapter, we will add the finishing touches to our application, **Sports News Combinator (SNC)**. So far, we have a running application, but the data is all hardcoded and we do not have routing for our different news sources.

In the last chapter, we learned about TypeScript functions, classes, interface, and how to write more object-oriented code. We also focused on Angular templates and binding, which form the backbone of how our application is able to present the data from the components.

In this chapter, we will focus on the following topics:

- **Decorators in TypeScript**: We have used decorators in our application by the names of `@Component` and `@NgModule`. Here, we will understand what decorators are and how we can create our own.
- **Adding features in SNC**: We will add the final pieces to our application by adding services, making web service calls to fetch the live data, and routing to provide navigation between different tabs.
- **Angular services**: While adding features to our application, we will also introduce the concept of services in Angular.
- **Angular routing**: To achieve routing, we will be using the built-in Angular concept of routing based on the URL. We will take a brief look at routing concepts here.

By the end of this chapter, we will have our application production-ready with all the features stitched in.

Decorators

Decorators are not a new programming concept, but are one of the structural design patterns, along with the facade and flyweight patterns. In JavaScript, we do not have any implementation of the decorator pattern as of now, though currently they are in a stage two proposal. In TypeScript also, decorators are an experimental feature that may end up changing in implementation depending on how ECMA finalizes the implementation in JavaScript.

Let's first look at what the decorator design pattern states and where is it applicable. Following that, we will look at the TypeScript implementation of the decorator pattern. In Angular, we have decorators such as `@Component`, `@NgModel`, and `@Injectable`, which we will take a brief look at.

Decorator design pattern

The decorator design pattern is one of the structural patterns that allows us to extend the functionality of a class without modifying the class. This is achieved by creating a separate class and wrapping the `main` class with this new class, which allows us to add new functionality. This pattern allows us to make sure we are able to follow the single responsibility principle with our classes. Our classes can continue to focus on their primary responsibility, and any new functionality that needs to be added can be added using a decorator that would be triggered when the class is initialized. Because the logic of the decorator class gets executed at the time of creation of the object, the decorator pattern allows us to focus on specific instances rather than all of them. If you have worked in languages such as Java or C#, you will have used decorators in the form of annotations and attributes respectively. These annotations and attributes provides extended functionality to the class or method that is decorated.

In TypeScript, we have a wrapping decorator pattern, which basically allows us to add functionality by adding an annotation to the affected class. The advantage of a wrapping pattern is that it's unobtrusive to the existing code and can be used as a plug and play on specific classes. Aspect-oriented programming is based on the decorator pattern only where we add annotations to our classes and functions, and provide external functionalities such as logging and exception handling.

You can refer to `http://www.dofactory.com/net/decorator-design-pattern` to gain an in-depth understanding of the decorator design pattern. We will focus on understanding how the decorator pattern is used in TypeScript.

Decorators in TypeScript

Decorators are a proposed feature in JavaScript, currently in stage two, and will most likely take another year or so to be finalized. In this time, there are chances that the current feature set of decorators may change.

In TypeScript, decorators were introduced in version 1.5. TypeScript transpiles decorators in functions that are exactly what they are. So, we can use decorators today with TypeScript and not worry about compatibility with the browsers.

 Decorators are an example of how TypeScript is future driven and allows us to dabble with features of JavaScript that are not yet available in browsers.

In TypeScript, decorators are defined as functions, which can then be attached to classes, properties, and methods to add functionalities. There are different forms of decorators in TypeScript, each focusing on a specific target, such as decorators for classes and decorators for methods. The main difference between all these decorators in TypeScript lies in the decorator signature. As the decorator is just an experimental feature, we need to explicitly enable them in our TypeScript projects. In the tsConfig.json file under the compilerOptions property, we need to add the following flag that informs TypeScript that we will use decorators in our project:

```
"compilerOptions": {
"experimentalDecorators": true,
.....
}
```

In our SNC application, you will find that this flag is already turned on. This is because Angular uses decorators extensively to differentiate classes with component classes, and when we create our project with the Angular CLI, it adds this flag by default.

Definition of decorators in TypeScript

Decorators in TypeScript are just the function definition, so ideally we can just write a TypeScript function and use it as a decorator. The only difference is the type of parameters the decorator accepts. The following is the simplest possible example of a decorator function and how it is used in a class:

```
1    //Decorator Definition
2    function logger (target:Function) {
3        // Implement decorator logic
4    }
5
6    // Decorator used on class
7    @logger
8    class Book {
9        constructor(private title: string){}
10   }
11
```

On line number two, we define a standard TypeScript function that takes one parameter. The parameter is of type `Function` in this case. Then we use this decorator on line number seven by just referencing it with its name and prefixed with an @ sign. The @ (at) sign tells TypeScript that this is a decorator and TypeScript will plug in its execution in the class execution cycle.

This type of decorator is called a **class decorator**. Class decorators just take one parameter, which is the constructor of the class. As we know, constructors are just functions and that is why the `target` property is of type `function`. We can even ignore the type and TypeScript will assign *any* type it the parameter by default. When TypeScript executes the class, it passes the constructor of the class as a parameter to the decorator, and hence we don't need to explicitly pass any parameter when we use the decorator, as in line number seven.

Decorator factory

In the previous example, we saw how we can create a simple decorator and annotate that on a class. But if this was the only thing decorators did in TypeScript then they would be very restrictive. In real-world applications, you would want to have the flexibility to pass some custom values to the decorator from the class or a function. This is where the decorator factory comes in.

The decorator factory allows us to define additional parameters that can then be used to pass values from the class to the decorator. Let's refactor the logger decorator we defined earlier to pass a parameter to it. The first step is to create a function similar to what we created earlier for the `logger`, but now have the parameters of the function that we want the decorator to accept from the class. The second step is to return the function from this function, which would have the signature of the class type decorator. The following is the refactored code for `logger`:

```
1    //Decorator Definition
2    function logger (name:string) {
3        return function(target:Function){
4            console.log ('Class is:  ${name}');
5        }
6    }
7
8    // Decorator used on class
9    @logger("Book")
10   class Book {
11       constructor(private title: string){}
12   }
```

In the preceding code, we see that our decorator is now a function that accepts a string as a parameter rather than function. So, here we can have as many parameters defined for the `logger` function that the class would need to pass to the decorator. This function is called a **factory function** because this function returns another function that would have the signature required for defining the class decorator. As we know, class decorators accept one parameter of type `function`, which is passed the constructor of the class by TypeScript, so our inner function has a signature accepting a single parameter, as seen in line number three.

Because of a feature called closure in JavaScript and TypeScript, we have the ability to accept the parameters that we defined on the decorator function, inside the factory function. Hence, on line number four, we see that we have access to the `name` property.

These parameters are passed as an argument to the decorator when it's annotated on the class, as seen in line number nine.

So, the decorator factory allows us to define decorators that can accept parameters from the class, function, or property where they are annotated, and this is achieved by creating a factory function that returns the decorator function.

Class decorator

From all the possible type of decorators we can define, class decorators are the most common ones. Class decorators allow us to enhance the functionality of the class, as TypeScript injects the logic implemented in the class decorator to the constructor of the said class. In our SNC application, as well as the applications that we will build in our remaining chapters, we use decorators, which are defined by Angular as `@Component`. These are class decorators and allow Angular to identify a specific class as a component and add behavior to it at runtime.

The class decorator can be defined in two ways, namely, a decorator that does not replace the constructor function and a decorator that does. This distinction happens based on the return type we define in the class decorator function.

The class decorator takes one argument only, which is of the type of constructor of the class, as shown in the following snippet:

```
function logger (target: Function): void{
  console.log("Logging implemented");
}
```

In the preceding code, we have defined a `function logger` that takes one argument of type `Function` and prints a string. When we use this decorator on a class, TypeScript passes the class constructor to the decorator as a parameter. This type of decorator does not return anything and just executes the code inside and returns the flow back to the constructor of the class, hence the return type as `void`.

Having `void` as a return type for the class constructor tells us that we will not be replacing the behavior of the constructor, but will be adding additional behavior on top of it. Whereas, if the decorator had a return type of the function, then we would have replaced the behavior defined in the constructor of the class with the implementation of the decorator.

In this decorator, we are just logging a statement notifying that the decorator function was called successfully. Now, let's use this decorator on a class, as shown in the following code:

```
// Decorator used on class
@logger
class Book {
  constructor(private title: string){}
}
```

Using a decorator is as simple as annotating the required entity (class/function/property) with the decorator name prefixed by the @ the sign. This tells TypeScript to call the decorator function and pass the constructor of the `Book` class as the parameter, execute the function, and the come back to the constructor. In this case, we would have a `Logging Implemented` message printed in the console.

As we have not implemented our decorator as a decorator factory, we cannot pass any custom values to the decorator. Let's look at how we can do this in the next section.

Passing parameters to the decorator

Our previous example was good enough to show how to create decorators in TypeScript; now let's add some flexibility to our decorator. TypeScript defines a concept of the decorator factory that we saw earlier that allows us to pass custom values to our decorator and use them in processing. This feature is extremely necessary because we would want our decorators to be able to execute based on various criterions defined by the class.

The following is the refactored code for our logger decorator, which takes one parameter as a name:

```
//Decorator Definition
function logger (name:string) {
  return function(target:Function){
  console.log ('Class is: ${name}');
  }
}
```

In this case, we wrap our decorator function inside the main function which takes the `name` as an input parameter. Now, when we use the decorator on the `Book` class, TypeScript will inform us that we need to pass a string value to a `name` parameter, as seen in the following screenshot:

```
13
14     // Decor  logger(name: string): (target: Function) => void
15     @logger()
16     class Book {
17         constructor(private title: string){}
18     }
```

TypeScript passes this parameter value to the decorator along with the constructor function of the class. The following is the updated code of the `Book` class:

```
// Decorator used on class
@logger("TypeScript")
class Book {
 constructor(private title: string){}
}
```

Overriding constructors in decorators

By default, the class decorators in TypeScript do not override the constructors, but add logic on top of the constructor implementation. But, there are instances where we would like to have a decorator that overrides the existing constructor and returns a new constructor implementation. This is where TypeScript excels. The syntax of the decorator that overrides the current implementation of the constructor is very similar to the syntax we have been looking at in the earlier sections, with the main difference in the type that is returned from the decorator.

The following is the syntax of a class decorator that replaces the constructor of the class with a new constructor:

```
1    function logger (name:string){
2    return function <newFunction extends Function> (target: newFunction): newFunction{
3        let newConstructor : Function
4        // Implement the new constructor
5        return <newFunction> newConstructor;
6    }
7    }
8
```

The preceding code is for the scenario where we are overriding the constructor and our decorator takes a `string` parameter. Line number one is exactly the same as what we have for decorators that do not override the constructor, where we have one input parameter that would be used when we annotate the class with our decorator. The magic starts at line number two.

In the earlier case, we used to have a function that had a single input parameter of type `Function` that accepts the constructor of our class, and the return type of this function was void. The following code snippet shows such an example:

```
10    //Decorator Definition
11    function logger (name:string) {
12        return function(target:Function){
13            console.log ('Class is:  ${name}');
14        }
15    }
```

In our case where we want to override the constructor, we would have to return some value, and this value has to be of the same type as that of the constructor that was passed to our decorator. So, we extend the function type into another generic type named `newFunction`. This `newFunction` will represent the type of our constructor that is returned.

We know that the type that is returned should be same as the type that we received as an input parameter for the constructor, and hence our `target` property is also of type `newFunction`. In the end, we make sure that we return a new constructor from the decorator and assign relevant values to it. Using this decorator is exactly the same as how we used the logger decorator when we were not overriding the constructor.

Method decorator

As with the class decorator, the method decorator is used to annotate methods and provide additional functionality. The following is the syntax of a method decorator:

```
function writable(target: Object,
  propertyKey: string,
  descriptor: PropertyDescriptor) {
  console.log(`Setting ${propertyKey}.`);
  descriptor.writable = true;
  }
```

A method decorator takes three parameters, unlike the class decorator which takes only one. The first parameter in a method decorator is the same as that of the class decorator, a reference to the constructor function if the method is static or a class prototype for the instance member. The second parameter is the name of the method that would be decorated. The third parameter is the property descriptor that can be used to control the properties of the method decorated.

The property descriptor is an interface in TypeScript and was introduced in JavaScript in ES5. The property descriptor has multiple properties that can be used to control the behavior of the method. Some of those properties are are follows:

```
interfacePropertyDescriptor{
configurable?: boolean;
enumerable?: boolean;
value?: any;
writable?: boolean;
get? ():any;
set? (v:any): void;
}
```

Using the method decorator is straightforward, where a method is annotated with the decorator name, similar to the glass decoration technique:

```
class Book {
 constructor(private title: string){}
 @writable
 getDetails(name:string){}
}
```

We can even pass values to the method decorator much the same way as we did in the class decorator, by creating a wrapper function that returns this function and the parameter. The following is the modified version of the `writable` function that accepts one parameter:

```
function writable (name:string){
return function (target: Object,
 propertyKey: string,
 descriptor: PropertyDescriptor) {
 console.log(`Setting ${propertyKey}.`);
 descriptor.writable = true;
 }
}
```

Property decorator

The property decorator is very similar to the class decorator, with the only change in the syntax is an additional parameter signifying the name of the decorated property. The following is a code snippet showing a property decorator:

```
function propertyDecorator(target: Object, propertyKey: string) {
  // add decorator logic
}
```

As you can see, there are two parameters to a property decorator. The first parameter is the constructor of the class if the object is a static, else it will be the prototype of the class containing the property. The second parameter is a string, which defines the name of the property decorated in the class.

The use of the property decorator is similar to the class and method decorators; we just annotate the required property with the property decorator name, prefixed with an @ sign.

Parameter decorator

The only difference between the parameter decorator and the property decorator is an additional third parameter. The parameter decorator is applied to the specific parameter in a function. To identify which parameter in a function is decorated, we use this third parameter. The following is the syntax of a parameter decorator in TypeScript:

```
function parameterDecorator(target: Object, propertyKey: string,
index:number) {
  // add decorator logic
}
```

The first two parameters are exactly the same as the property decorator, with the first parameter signifying the constructor of the class, and the second parameter being the name of the function to which the parameter belongs.

The third parameter, `index`, specifies the location of the parameter in a function that is decorated. This index is a zero-based index; hence, the first parameter's index would be zero.

Decorators in SNC

The best use case of decorators is available in Angular implementation. We have been using decorators since Chapter 2, *Our First Application – Sport News Combinator*, when we created our first component, NewsComponent. In Angular, we have used the class decorators to help identify the component and its metadata. The following is the decorator used in NewsComponent:

```
@Component({
  selector: 'snc-news',
  templateUrl: './news.component.html',
  styleUrls: ['./news.component.css']
})
export class NewsComponent
```

As we can see in the preceding code, we have a decorator named Component, which is of the type class Component and has multiple parameters associated with it. Some of the parameters that we use often are selector, templateUrl, and styleURLs.

Additional features in SNC

Now it's time to start working on the final phase of our application, *Sports News Combinator*. So far, we have created one main component, NewsComponent, which shows the latest sports news, and a couple of core components, namely, HeaderComponent and FooterComponent, which provide us with the standard header and footer for our application.

NewsComponent currently fetches the data that is hardcoded in the application and binds that data to the user interface. The following diagram shows the application architecture that we have been developing so far:

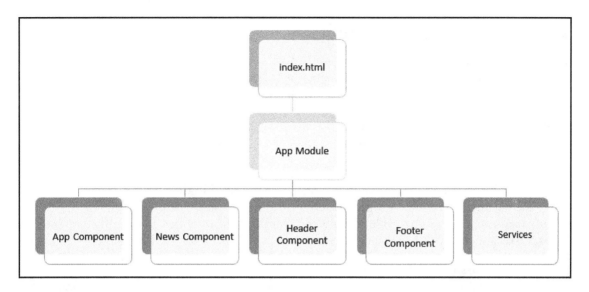

We have created our `index.html` file that has a reference to our only module, the `App`
module. All our components are part of this `App` module. The primary component we have
is **App Component**, which is basically made of a combination of other components such as
`NewsComponent`, `HeaderComponent`, and `FooterComponent`. To add the final touches to
our application, we need to implement the following functionalities:

- **Services**: We need to add services to our application that will host the logic for
  web service calls
- **HTTP call**: In the services layer, we will use Angular's HTTP interfaces to make
  the required `GET` call to fetch the latest sports news
- **Routing**: We need to allow users to navigate between different news sources, and
  that will be achieved using Angular routing

In the next three sections, we will explore these topics and add code to our application.

Adding services in SNC

The components are essential feature of any application built with Angular, but components can only take us so far. The purpose of components is to provide us with a placeholder for the user interface and its respective logic. The component is a combination of a UI template, its style, and the UI logic to display the data. For any meaningful application, we would also have associated business logic which is not directly related to a specific view, or a need to share data between multiple components, and this is where services come in.

Application logic can be broadly divided into two forms: **UI logic**, which resides in components, and the **business logic**, which resides in services. The business logic encapsulates commonly shared logic between components, data persistence that can be shared across them, and HTTP service calls.

A service is a class with a very specific purpose, used to implement functionality independent of the components. This approach allows us to follow the single responsibility principle effectively with clear responsibilities for components and services. This allows us to build code that is robust and easier to test and reuse.

Creating a service

Creating a service in Angular is a three-step process, as illustrated in the following diagram. You will notice that these steps are very similar to the steps of creating a component. We will discuss these steps now:

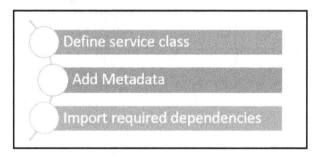

The first step to implement a service is to create a service class. So, let's create a new folder called `service` under the `app` folder. This folder will contain our new service file named `Newsapi.service.ts`. In this file, let's just define a standard TypeScript class named `NewsapiService`, as shown in the following snippet:

```
export class NewsapiService {
}
```

The `export` keyword is used so that this service can be accessed from any other part of our application. The `NewsapiService` will have one method to fetch the latest sports news from a web server based on the news source selected.

Next, we need to identify this class as a service for Angular, and for this we have a decorator defined by Angular. The decorator is `@Injectable()`, which allows a simple class to be used a service.

The third and final step is to import the required dependencies to our class. One dependency that is required for a service is for the Angular core module to refer the `@Injectable()` decorator.

Now, we have a service class ready, but it does not have any methods. For our SNC application, we will have one main method in this class which will be responsible for fetching the data. Let's add the skeleton of this method in our class for now and we will work on making a web service request and fetching the data in the next section.

Now our service class looks like the following:

```
import {Injectable} from '@angular/core';
@Injectable()
export class NewsapiService{
  constructor(){}
  //This method will be responsible for fetching the data from web server
  public fecthNewsFeed(){}
}
```

As we can see from the preceding code, we are using a service to encapsulate the data access layers, which allows us to keep separate responsibilities for data and its display logic.

Now that we have our service, next up will be registering the service with Angular, and after that injecting the service in our component.

Registering our service

Angular provides a neat way to register our services in an application using the built-in injector. The Angular injector creates an instance of our service and holds on to that single instance, providing us with a singleton behavior. It acts as a container for all the services registered with Angular. The following diagram shows an example of the injector managing multiple services, with each service having a single instance:

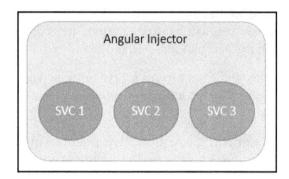

The advantage of the injector maintaining the service instance is two-fold. First, it takes away our responsibility of managing instances, which Angular will now do. Secondly, having a single instance of the service allows us to use the service as a mechanism to share data between components.

So, to register our service with the Angular injector we use providers. The provider is the code that is responsible for creating and returning the service instance. We can define the provider either in the component or in the module. Based on where we register the provider, the service will be accessed in that respective hierarchy. So, if we register a provider in our `NewsComponent`, then we will have access to our service in `NewsComponent` and any child component. If we register a provider in an `app` module, then the service is available throughout our application and acts as a global service. So, it's very important to decide where we should register our service.

If we register our provider with multiple components, then Angular will maintain multiple instances of that service and it will not act as a singleton. So, we should try to make sure that the provider is registered at the correct level in the application.

For our application, we will register our provider in the app module so that it is available everywhere. The following code snippet shows our app module, where we have a providers property in the NgModule decorator, which takes an array:

```
@NgModule({
  declarations: [
  AppComponent,
  NewsComponent,
  HeaderComponent,
  FooterComponent
  ],
  imports: [
  BrowserModule,
  routing,
  HttpModule
  ],
  providers: [NewsapiService],
  bootstrap: [AppComponent]
})
```

We have added a reference to our NewsapiService in this provider array. To be able to add a reference we also need to import the NewsapiService in the app module, as follows:

```
import {NewsapiService} from './service/newsapi.service';
```

Now we have our service registered with Angular, and it can be injected anywhere in our application.

Injecting the service

The last step for our service is to inject it into the component that needs it. When a component needs a service instance, it defines the dependency for the said service, and Angular is responsible for resolving the dependency. This process is called **dependency injection**, wherein the class just defines the dependency it needs and it receives the dependencies from the external source rather than creating it itself.

As Angular creates a single instance of the service and is responsible for injecting it into components, we can use the service to share data between the components. Angular injects the dependencies into the component at the time of object creation of the component. Hence, it makes sense to have dependency injection in the constructor of the class.

We need to use our service in the `NewsComponent` class, hence we will be adding a constructor in the class that would have `NewsapiService` defined as the dependency, as shown in the following line of code:

```
constructor(private _service:NewsapiService){}
```

We don't need to add the service provider in our `NewComponent` class because we have already added that in our `app` module, and Angular can now inject this service in any component that is part of the `app` module.

In the previous code, we created a local `_service` variable of type `NewsapiService`, which would be assigned the value when the object of the `NewsComponent` class is created. The last thing that needs to be done is to add an `import` statement for `NewsapiService` in the `NewsComponent` class.

Now when the new instance of `NewsComponent` is created, Angular injects the `NewsapiService` instance into the `_service` property, which can then be used to call the functions defined in the `service` class.

The next step is to make the web service call using HTTP, and we will do that in our `service` class.

Implementing HTTP calls in SNC

Most web applications use HTTP to retrieve the data from the web server, and that is what our application, SNC, will do. We will be fetching data from the `newsapi` web server, which provides feeds for more than 30 news outlets. `Newsapi` provides a convenient API interface that can be used to fetch the latest news stories.

In HTTP flow, the application (SNC in our case) issues a web request to the web server (`newsapi`). This web request can be a `GET`, `POST`, `PUT`, or `DELETE` depending on the type of operation to be performed. Then the web server retrieves the data type from a data store and sends the response back to the web application in an HTTP response. The web application then uses this data to display the required content on the web page.

Angular uses observables to fetch the data from HTTP. There are other ways as well as promises that can be used to fetch the data asynchronously. We will focus on observables, as that is the way recommended by Angular. We will start by introducing observables and then look at how we can send web requests using observables. Once the web request is sent, we need to subscribe to the observables to be able to listen to the HTTP response. We will also look at how we can handle exceptions when making a web service call.

Observables in HTTP

The observables represent the stream of data coming from the backend server asynchronously. The data stream could be of any kind, such as notifications or a set of events to be processed. Angular uses a third-party library called **Reactive Extensions (Rx)** to implement observables. We can think of observables as an asynchronous array whose elements are populated from the backend. So, we can get the first element in response, and then after a while the second element may come in, as represented in the following diagram:

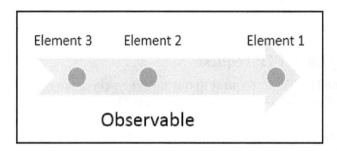

This type of behavior allows us to handle a web response that is sent in chunks, rather than the whole response being sent at once. And, having observables as a form of the array allows us to use operators such as map, catch, and do to handle the response effectively. Using Reactive Extensions, we can subscribe to the observable that would allow us to get notified when a new stream of data arrives from HTTP. Once the data arrives, we can then modify the data as needed for our application using operators provided by the Reactive Extensions library.

If you have experience of using promises for handling asynchronous HTTP calls, you will notice some differences here. For one, the promises are used to handle the single response from the web service call, whereas in observables we have multiple values (stream of data) coming in over a period of time. Secondly, the promises are not cancellable, whereas observables are, which is very useful when you are developing a feature wherein you make multiple web service calls based on continuous user input—for example, an auto-complete feature where we would want to provide IntelliSense support whenever a user types in a character. So, using observables we will have the option to cancel the previous request and only handle the response to the most current request.

HTTP request flow with observables

Let's now start implementing the HTTP request for our web service to fetch the latest sports news. There are two parts to this implementation:

- Implementing the HTTP request to make the GET call
- Subscribing to the HTTP response and using the data to populate the UI

These two steps are performed in two different files, with the HTTP call implemented in newapi.service.ts, and the subscription to the HTTP response being done in NewsComponent.ts.

Implementing the HTTP request

To implement the HTTP GET request in our service class, we need Angular's HTTP module. To use this module we need to define HTTP as a dependency in our NewsapiService class. As we know, to define a dependency in TypeScript we use a constructor function of the class. Angular then makes sure to pass the instance of that module to the class when we create an instance of the class. The following is the updated code of our NewsapiService class:

```
import {Injectable} from '@angular/core';
import {Http} from '@angular/http';
@Injectable()
export class NewsapiService{
 constructor(private _http:Http){}
}
```

We are using the HTTP client module in our service call, so we need to import the HTTP module class from the Angular HTTP module, which will be done in our AppModule under the import section of the NgModule decorator.

We can see there are two main changes in our code, one adding a dependency of HTTP in our constructor, and the other adding the import statement to import the given module. The HTTP client provides us an interface to make the web service call. This interface has methods such as GET, PUT, POST and DELETE. We will be using the GET method to fetch the latest news. The GET method of the HTTP client returns an observable which would then be typecasted into our news model. To achieve the web service call we add a new method to our class, fetchNewsFeed, which would take a single parameter, source. This parameter will tell us for which news outlet we are fetching the sports news. As the HTTP GET returns an observable, our method will also return the observable of type News model. The following shows the updated code:

```
import { Injectable } from '@angular/core';
import { Observable } from 'rxjs/Observable';
import { Http, Response } from '@angular/http';
import 'rxjs/add/operator/map';
import 'rxjs/add/operator/catch';
import 'rxjs/add/operator/do';
import { News } from '../../models/news';
@Injectable()
export class NewsapiService {
  baseUrl: string;
  static apiKey: string = "b07f98f6575d47d99fd6057668f21cb2";
  constructor(private _http: Http) {
    this.baseUrl = 'https://newsapi.org/v1/articles';
  }
  public fetchNewsFeed(source: string): Observable<News> {
    return this._http.get(`${this.baseUrl}/?source=
      ${source}&sortBy=top&apiKey=${NewsapiService.apiKey}`)
    .map((response: Response) => <News>response.json())
    .do(data => console.log('All: ' + JSON.stringify(data)))
    .catch(this.handleError);
  }
  private handleError(error: Response) {
    console.error(error);
    return Observable.throw(error.json().error || 'Server error');
  }
}
```

Let's go through all the changes we made to our code:

1. The first thing is the `apiKey` and `baseUrl`. To fetch the news articles from the `newsapi` web server, we need to register them and generate a unique key, which is required when we make a service call.

2. Next up is the `fetchNewsFeed` method. Here, we are calling a `GET` method of HTTP client and passing the URL. The URL consists of the `baseUrl`, `source`, `sortBy`, and `apiKey`. As we are looking for the top 10 news items, our `sortBy` value will always be `top`.

3. We know that the `GET` method returns an observable, hence we use the `map` operator in the `fetchNewFeed` method to typecast the response we received into our news model.

4. In the `do` function, we are just logging the response data into our console for debugging purposes.

5. It is always recommended to handle exceptions when making a web service call, and this is what we are doing on the last line of HTTP `GET`. The Reactive Extensions (rxJs) library provides us with the `catch` operator that takes a function as a parameter. If the web service call fails, the control goes to the `catch` block and the function is executed.

6. We wrote a `handleError` function that logs the error and then throws the error message returned from the web server.

With these code changes, we are now ready to make a live web service call to fetch the news stories. But before that, we need to subscribe to the observable which would be returned from the `fetchNewsFeed` method.

Subscribing to HTTP response

In the previous section, we added the dependency of the `NewsapiService` to our `NewsComponent` class. Now it's time to use that dependency to call the `fetchNewsFeed` method and subscribe to the observable response. As we want to make sure that the new articles are loaded when we load the page, we would need to make the call to our web service in the `ngOnInit` method of the `NewsComponent` class.

The `ngOnInit` method is one of the life cycle hooks that are provided by Angular to help us intercept the page load cycle. The `subscribe` method from the rxJs observable library has two overloaded implementations:

```
this._service(successFunc, errorFunc);
this._service(successFunc, errorFunc, completeFunc);
```

The `successFunc` is called when the observable returns the response without any error. If there is an error returned from the web server, the `errorFunc` is called. The `completeFunc` is used to unsubscribe from an observable. If we know that we don't need to listen to the response anymore, we can use the `completeFunc` to unsubscribe from the observable.

The following is the code that would be implemented to call the `newapi` service class method:

```
this._service.fetchNewsFeed(this.feedType)
.subscribe(
items => this.latest_news = items,
error => {this.errorMessage = 'Could not load ' + this.feedType + '
stories.'; console.log(this.errorMessage)}
);
```

Here, we subscribe to the `fetchNewsfeed` response, and on success assign the response returned to the local `latest_news` variable. In case there is any error returned, we set the `errorMessage` property with the text string and log the error in the console. In the method call, we are passing a `feedType` property, which represents the news source for which we want to fetch the data. We will be covering the `feedType` property and how we can fetch data for all four of our news outlets in the following section on routing.

We use the `errorMessage` property in our template file of `NewsComponent` to check if there are no error, and only then show the table which would be populated with the web service response. Otherwise, we show the error message to the user.

Routing in SNC

Thus far, our application is in a half-baked state. We have implemented components with `NewsComponent` as our primary component, which shows the latest news from a news source. We have header and footer components that provide us with the layout of the screen. We have also implemented the services and HTTP call to `newsapi` to fetch the latest sports news. But, our application currently does not handle any sort of navigation, no hyperlinks that we created in `HeaderComponent` work, and the web service call needs the name of the news source to fetch the data. This will all be achieved by routing.

Routing is a concept that allows navigation between multiple views in an application. An application achieves routing by defining unique routes for each view to be displayed. When a user selects an option on a screen, be it a menu, a button, or a link in a navigation bar, its respective route is activated, which results in loading the selected component and its template.

In our application, we have four routes defined for each news outlet, and when the user clicks on any one of the links we use routing to identify the link clicked and display the information accordingly. We will start by defining the routes, then we will stitch these routes to the links in our header, and lastly, in our `NewsComponent`, we will fetch the clicked route and use that to retrieve the news and display it on the screen.

Defining routes

In our application, we need to configure routes for all four links. Angular provides us with a router module that allows us to register the routes, provides an interface for router directives which provides the use of `RouterLink` and `RouterOutlet`, and provides a mechanism to expose the configured routes. So, the first step would be to import the `RouterModule`. The following is the code for doing so:

```
import { Routes, RouterModule } from '@angular/router';
```

To provide better separation of concerns, we will be creating a new module called `newsroutingmodule`, which will host all our routes. So, let's first create a new file, `app.route.ts`, which will have reference to the `RouteModule` from Angular. In the preceding code, we are also importing `Routes`. `Routes` provides us with an array of all the defined routes. These `Routes` are then attached to the `Router` module. Also, to be able to create a new module, we need to refer to the `ModuleWithProvider` module from Angular, so let's import that as well:

```
import { ModuleWithProviders } from '@angular/core';
```

Application routes

The router must be configured with the list of route definitions, with each definition specifying the route. We imported the route module from Angular in preceding section. This `route` module provides us with the `Route` property, which takes an array of objects with each object defining a specific route. Let's look at our `Route` array as defined in our `app.route.ts` file:

```
import { ModuleWithProviders } from '@angular/core';
import { Routes, RouterModule } from '@angular/router';
import { NewsComponent } from './dashboard/news/news.component';
const routes: Routes = [
 {path: '', redirectTo: 'nfl', pathMatch: 'full'},
 {
 path: 'nfl',
 component: NewsComponent,
```

```
data: {feedType: 'nfl-news',source:'nfl'}
},
{
path: 'espn',
component: NewsComponent,
data: {feedType: 'espn',source:'espn'}
},
{
path: 'fox',
component: NewsComponent,
data: {feedType: 'fox-sports',source:'Fox Sports'}
},
{
path: 'bbc',
component: NewsComponent,
data: {feedType: 'bbc-sport',source:'BBC Sports'}
},
{
path:'**',
redirectTo: 'nfl', pathMatch: 'full'
}
];
```

As we can see on the first line after the `import` statements, we define a constant variable route of type `Routes`, which contains an array of objects.

Each route object has a `path` property that defines the URL's path segment. When the specific route is activated, this path property is appended to the application URL. So, for example, when the NFL route is activated, our application URL would be `http://localhost:4200/nfl`, and when the FOX route is activated, our application URL would change to `http://localhost:4200/fox`. This allows us to maintain the unique URLs for each route, which can then be bookmarked by the user to directly jump to that page.

Each route object also has a `component` property that signifies the component where the application should be routed when the selected route is activated. In our code, because we just have one component, the `NewsComponent`, all our routes have the same component value in their object.

After the route declaration, we have defined all our possible route definitions. Apart from first and last one, other routes should be fairly obvious, with definitions for NFL, ESPN, FOX, and BBC.

The first route defined is called a default route. The default route is activated when a user comes to our application by hitting the URL `http://localhost:4200`. The `redirectTo` property defines the route that we would want the user to be redirected to when they come to our default page, which in our case is NFL. The `pathMatch` property tells us that we should only do the redirect if the path exactly matches to the path we have defined, which in this case is an empty string, meaning the URL of our application without any URL segment.

The last route is called a wildcard route, and is denoted by `**`. The wildcard route defines any route that does not match any of the previously defined routes. So, for example, if the user tries to redirect to the URL `http://localhost:4200/wrongPath`, the application will redirect the user back to `http://localhost:4200/nfl page`. Normally, the wildcard route redirects the user to a custom page that would display some form of **404** error message.

 In routing, the order of the routes is important. We should always place specific routes before the generic routes because Angular uses a first-match policy when resolving the routes.

We have one more property defined in our route object; `data`. The Angular route allows us to define custom properties that can be useful in passing data to our components, which can then be used for processing. In our case, we are passing two properties, namely `feedType` and `source`. We will be using these properties in our `NewsComponent` to identify the link and display in the header.

Adding to the router module

The next step for us is to bind the routes we defined previously to the `router` module we created. The Angular router module provides a `forRoot` method that creates the `router` module with all the `route` providers and directives. We will pass our `route` property to this function, which returns a module that would be assigned to our newly created `newsroutingmodule` module. The following is the code we use to create our module:

```
export const newsroutingmodule: ModuleWithProviders =
RouterModule.forRoot(routes);
```

This now creates our route module with specific routes defined for each news outlet and its respective component.

Importing in the app module

The last thing to do here with regards to defining routes is to import our newly created `newsroutingmodule` module into our main module, which is the `app` module. The modules are imported into the `imports` property of the `NgModule`, as seen in the following code. This tells Angular to load the `newsroutingmodule`, which can then be accessed from any part of the application:

```
imports: [
BrowserModule,
newsroutingmodule,
HttpModule
],
```

Implementing a router link

Now that we have defined our routes, we need to tie these routes with our user actions. Angular's routing module provides us with the directive that helps us define the URL segment, which in turn is used by the routing engine to map the respective route. Let's look at our `HeaderComponent` template where we have defined our user options and attached the routing directive:

In large-scale applications, we may have sub-menus and sub-options, but for our application we will just have these four menu options, each displaying the news articles for their respective website. The menu options are tied to the route using the following code:

```
<ul class="nav navbar-nav">
<li><a routerLink="/nfl">NFL</a></li>
<li><a routerLink="/espn">ESPN</a></li>
<li><a routerLink="/fox">FOX</a></li>
<li><a routerLink="/bbc">BBC</a></li>
</ul>
```

To tie each menu option with the route we use the `routerLink` directive. The `routerLink` directive allows us to define the URL path segment for each menu option, and the router uses this to locate the associated route in our `route` module.

The `routerLink` directive is an attribute directive, which means that it's used as an attribute on an HTML tag, in this case on the anchor tag. For each anchor tag, we have a unique `routeLink` defined. When the user selects any link, the associated route is activated, which displays the component view for that route. But, where would Angular display the view?

The routing module from Angular also has one more directive, `router-outlet`. This tells Angular where it should display the component of a selected route. We add this directive to the component where we want all other components to be embedded, which in our case would be the `app` component. We add the following code to our `app` component template file:

```
<div>
<snc-header></snc-header>
<router-outlet></router-outlet>
<snc-footer></snc-footer>
</div>
```

When Angular finds the `router-outlet` directive, it understands that any template to be displayed will be displayed here. This allows us to compose multiple components together to make a full screen.

Accessing routes in NewsComponent

So, now we have routes defined and they have been stitched together using `routerLink` with the menu options. When we click on any of these menu options, Angular changes the URL of the browser and loads the respective component, which would be `NewsComponent` in our case.

The last step is to be able to access the menu option selected, and make the web service call with that selected news outlet so as to fetch the news articles. The following is the code we have in our `ngOnInit` in the `NewsComponent.ts` file:

```
ngOnInit() {
  this.route.data.subscribe(data => {
  this.feedType = (data as any).feedType;
  this.source = (data as any).source;
});

this._service.fetchNewsFeed(this.feedType)
  .subscribe(
    items => this.latest_news = items,
    error => {this.errorMessage = 'Could not load ' +
```

```
        this.feedType + ' stories.';
        console.log(this.errorMessage) }
    );
}
```

Here, we see that in the first line of the `ngOnInit` method we subscribe to our route and fetch the data object for the selected route. In our routes, we used the data custom object to pass the values of `feedType` and `source`. The `feedType` property is used by the API service call as the news outlet source, and we use the `source` property to find the table header on our `NewsComponent` page.

Final product

With all the changes to our application we made in this chapter, our application is now up and running. We have live data coming from the `newsapi` service for all four news outlets, and we have routing working so that we can navigate to each tab. We used many concepts of TypeScript to make our application robust, reusable, and maintainable. We employed concepts such as strong typing, classes, interface, inheritance, and decorators, which help us write object-oriented code for client-side applications.

If you face any issues while following along, or just want to take a look at the final code version, you can access the code at `https://github.com/sachinohri/SportsNewsCombinator`.

We have created three folders here, one for each chapter, which hold the final version of the code that we have created in each respective chapter. The `Chapter 04` code is the final code for our application, *Sports News Combinator*. You can just clone the repository and run the following commands on the `Chapter` folder to run the application:

```
npm install // this will install all the npm dependencies for our project
ng serve // this will build the application and deploy on localhost:4200.
```

Then we can just navigate to the URL to access the application, which should look something like the following:

Summary

In this chapter, we added the final touches to our application. We modified our code from hardcoded data to live data from a web server. We then added routing to manage navigation. We learned about decorators in TypeScript and how we can create our own decorators. We also looked at how decorators are used by Angular.

In the next chapter, we will start with our second application of the book. We will focus on some advanced topics of TypeScript and Angular while developing our application. In this application, we will also write test cases for our code to showcase the testing capabilities of Angular.

5
Application 2 – Trello

It's time for us to shift gear and move on to more complex topics. In the previous chapter, we finished our first application and, in doing so, learned quite a few concepts of TypeScript and Angular. We will continue this practice in this chapter as well. We will start with our second application, **Sample Trello board**, and during the course of building this application, we'll learn more concepts of TypeScript and Angular.

We will cover the following topics in this chapter:

- **An introduction to the sample Trello application**: First off, we will take a brief look at the application we will be building and the feature set it will have.
- **TypeScript namespace and modules**: We'll look at how TypeScript provides an opportunity to write modular code with namespaces and modules.
- **TypeScript generics**: One of the most powerful features of TypeScript is generics, which allows us to write better object-oriented code.
- **Angular advanced components**: While building our application, we will look at how Angular provides us with mechanisms to allow communication between multiple components.
- **Angular life cycle hooks**: Another feature of Angular that we'll use very frequently is life cycle hooks. We will look at its implementation in our *Trello* application.

By the end of this chapter, we will have a working model of our application and a detailed understanding of many of the advanced concepts of TypeScript and Angular.

An introduction to the sample Trello application

Our *Trello* application will be a smaller, trimmed down version of real *Trello*. Our primary purpose is to learn the new features of TypeScript and Angular while creating the application; hence, our focus will be on the features of the language rather than on the features of the application. *Trello*, in the real world, is a task management application, wherein we can group our tasks on different boards, and each high-level task will have multiple subtasks. These subtasks can then be moved to different stages, such as pending, in-progress, and completed. In our sample *Trello* application, we will not have the latter part, but we will have a dashboard page with multiple boards, so we can drill down into each board to see the tasks and their respective subtasks.

Application overview

With this scope, we will make sure that our application is meaningful and, at the same time, not overly complex, in order to ease your learning process. The following are the screenshots of our final *Trello* dashboard and the task screen.

This screenshot shows our homepage where we will display all our **Boards** and the total number of tasks in each board. We also have an option to create a new board on the **Homepage**:

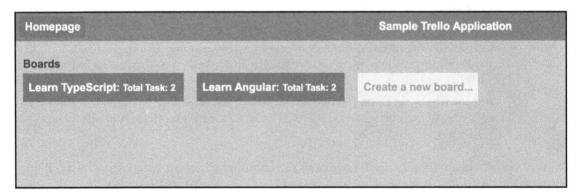

In the following screenshot, you can see how the **Board** screen looks when one of the boards is selected from **Homepage**. Each board will show the tasks and subtasks associated with the selected board.

In addition, here we can add new tasks and subtasks to the board:

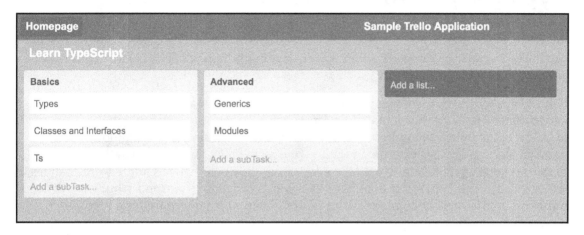

As our book is primarily focused on TypeScript and Angular, we will not be looking at persisting this information on the server. However, if you are interested in learning how we can manage the server and save the details, you can dig into Node.Js or even look at in-memory browser storage techniques, such as `localStorage`.

Technical overview

In our previous application, *Sports News Combinator*, we had one component that will display the result of all four news outlets. In our sample *Trello* application, we will add another component and showcase how we can provide options for data sharing between components. We will also see how we can use singleton services to persist and use the data between components.

In our application, we will use most of the TypeScript and Angular features that you have already learned. We will also delve deeper into additional features, such as namespace, modules, and generics for TypeScript, and advanced components and life cycle hooks for Angular. In the next chapter, we will add functionality to our application and learn more about observables, async programming, and more. Then, to finish our application, we will look at how we can write test cases, and we will learn that by adding a few test cases for our sample *Trello* application.

So let's get started.

TypeScript namespace and modules

A well-organized code is one of the few important aspects of any application development, which normally does not affect your ability to churn out features but affects how fast you can make changes to your code without breaking anything. TypeScript allows us to write organized code by using features such as namespace and modules.

Before TypeScript 1.5, there was no concept of namespace; in fact, we had internal and external modules. TypeScript team in effort to align the naming convention with ECAMScript standards modified internal and external modules. Internal modules were named `namespaces` and external modules were named just `modules`, as in the case of ECMAScript 2015 (ES6). Now, with the naming conventions changed, there were changes in the syntax as well. TypeScript does have backward compatibility support, but we will keep our focus on the latest and greatest features and, hence, on namespaces and modules.

The universal namespace

JavaScript, by default, adds all our classes and functions under a `window` namespace. The `window` namespace is like a universal namespace that contains all the functions, classes, and events that are associated with the current window. These functions, classes, and events are accessible everywhere in the web application. Now, having our functions and classes under the window namespace may not sound bad considering we can access them from everywhere, but if we are building a fairly large application, this quickly turns into a problem.

Having all our functions and classes in a universal namespace has one major problem: name conflict. So, for example, if we create a `getData` function and, then, someone else in our team also writes a new function with the same name but for a different purpose, we will have a name conflict. The universal namespace can only have one function with one name; hence, it will overwrite the previous function with the new one, which may not behave in the way we expected it to.

If you go to your developer tools in your browser and type in the following code, you will see the behavior of our universal namespace:

```
function getData() {
  return "true";
};

function getData() {
  return "false";
};
```

```
window.getData();
"false"
```

The preceding example is of pure JavaScript code; TypeScript, with its built-in features, will show a red squiggly line if we try to declare two classes or functions with the same name in the same scope, as we can see in the following code snippet:

```
1   class getData{
2       getJsonData(){
3           return "No result available";
4       }
5   }
6
7   class getData{
8       getFileData(){
9           return "No result available";
10      }
11  }
12
```

Just for illustration purposes, we had defined two same classes in one file; this issue will still persist if we have these in two different files.

To solve this problem, we have containers (namespaces and modules). Having containers allows us to reduce the chances of naming conflicts, with each class or function encapsulated inside these containers and only the container name being exposed to the universal namespace. So, for the preceding example, we have one container with the name `JsonData` and other containers with the name `FileData`; both have a `getData` function.

The TypeScript namespace

TypeScript provides a keyword, `namespace`, which allows us to encapsulate the related functions, classes, and interfaces under one umbrella. The syntax of defining `namespace` is very straightforward, as follows:

```
namespace WebServiceResponse{
}
```

All the functions, classes, and interfaces will go inside the curly braces of the namespace. Anyone outside the namespace can access these by using the dot notation–that is, `<<namespace name>>.<<function/class name>>`.

Now, by default, all the functions and classes that will be defined under the namespace will not be visible to anyone outside the namespace, as shown in the following code snippet:

```
1    namespace WebServiceResponse{
2        class WebResponse{
3            getResponse(){
4                return "Success";
5            }
6
7            sendResponse(){
8                return "200 Ok";
9            }
10       }
11
12       let localResponse = new WebResponse();
13       localResponse.getResponse();
14       localResponse.sendResponse();
15
16   }
17
18   let response = new WebServiceResponse.WebResponse();
19
```

In line number **18**, we have a warning from the TypeScript compiler, mentioning that the `WebResponse` property does not exist on the type of `WebServiceResponse`. And we can see in line number **12** that we are able to access our class inside the namespace.

This allows us to have a nice encapsulation of our logic without worrying that someone else may modify the behavior of our classes or functions from outside the namespace, which was very much possible in the case of the universal namespace.

The export keyword

TypeScript provides us with the `export` keyword, which allows us to expose the selected members of our namespace to the outside world. We can just prefix the `export` keyword on a class, function, interface, or even on a variable inside the namespace and, then, we can access them outside immediately. The `export` keyword works like a `public` keyword, which we saw in the preceding chapter.

So, if we modify our preceding example by adding the `export` keyword to our `WebResponse`class, we will then be able to access the class outside, as you can see in the following code snippet:

```
namespace WebServiceResponse{
```

```
export class WebResponse{
getResponse(){
return "Success";
}
sendResponse(){
return "200 OK";
}
}
let localResponse = new WebResponse();
localResponse.getResponse();
localResponse.sendResponse();
}
let response = new WebServiceResponse.WebResponse();
response.getResponse();
response.sendResponse();
```

Nested namespace

TypeScript also allows us to create nested encapsulation by adding a namespace inside another namespace. The nested namespace to be exposed outside should also be prefixed with the export keyword. The following is an example of how we can use nested namespaces:

```
namespace WebServiceResponse{
   let url: string;
   export namespace ServiceResponse{
     export class WebResponse{
       getResponse(){
         return "Success";
       }
       sendResponse(){
         return "200 OK";
       }
     }
   }

   let localResponse = new ServiceResponse.WebResponse();
   localResponse.getResponse();
   localResponse.sendResponse();
}
let response = new WebServiceResponse.ServiceResponse.WebResponse();
response.getResponse();
response.sendResponse();
```

As you can see in the example, we have introduced a nested namespace, `ServiceResponse`, and a class inside it. So, to access the `WebResponse` class, we need to reference it using the outer namespace, followed by the inner namespace, and, then, the class name. This provides us an opportunity to test the functionalities based on the features and sub feature set.

Namespaces transpired to JavaScript

Now, let's look at the JavaScript generated for our namespace by the TypeScript compiler. As we had mentioned earlier as well, looking at the generated JavaScript provides us an opportunity to understand the features of the TypeScript in more detail.

We will look at the JavaScript of the previous example, where we had one namespace and one class, as follows:

```
1
2   namespace WebServiceResponse {
3       let url: string;
4       export class WebResponse {
5           getResponse() {
6               return "Success";
7           }
8
9           sendResponse() {
10              return "200 Ok";
11          }
12      }
13
14      let localResponse = new WebResponse();
15      localResponse.getResponse();
16      localResponse.sendResponse();
17
18  }
19
20  let response = new WebServiceResponse.WebResponse();
21  response.getResponse();
22  response.sendResponse();
23
24
```

```
1
2   var WebServiceResponse;
3   (function (WebServiceResponse) {
4       var url;
5       var WebResponse = (function () {
6           function WebResponse() {
7           }
8           WebResponse.prototype.getResponse = function () {
9               return "Success";
10          };
11          WebResponse.prototype.sendResponse = function () {
12              return "200 Ok";
13          };
14          return WebResponse;
15      }());
16
17      WebServiceResponse.WebResponse = WebResponse;
18      var localResponse = new WebResponse();
19      localResponse.getResponse();
20      localResponse.sendResponse();
21
22  })(WebServiceResponse || (WebServiceResponse = {}));
23
24  var response = new WebServiceResponse.WebResponse();
25  response.getResponse();
26  response.sendResponse();
27
```

The right-hand side shows the generated JavaScript. We can see that the `WebServiceResponse` namespace is just a function in JavaScript, which has an inner function, `WebResponse`. Line number **22** makes sure that we have the `WebServiceResponse` variable only in our global scope and not the inner functions. This helps keep our code more organized.

TypeScript modules

TypeScript modules are an extension of the ES5 modules that we have in JavaScript. They serve the same purpose as namespaces, that is, to provide an opportunity to manage the code in a more modular fashion and prevent naming conflicts. We have been using modules since our first application. One of the biggest advantages of using modules instead of namespaces is that they allow us to use modular loaders to provide asynchronous behavior for loading the JavaScript file and hence speed up the application flow. There are multiple module loaders available and they differ from each other mainly in terms of syntax and how they manage the modules.

Definition

TypeScript modules are defined by the filesystem, meaning that every file is a separate module and the filename becomes the module name. There's no special keyword to define a module. So, we can create a new file, which becomes a module; all the content inside the module is encapsulated and cannot be accessed from outside, unless explicitly defined.

For example, as shown in the following code snippet, we create a file named `service.ts`, which has a class and a function. This would create a module named `service`, which can then be referenced in another module:

```
interface iBoardService{
 url: string;
 getBoardInformation();
}
class BoardService{
 url: string;
getBoardInformation(){
 return "No boards available";
 }

}
```

Exporting a module

Our code in the current shape does not expose the class or interface to outside the module. We can continue to reference them inside the `service.ts` file, as follows:

```
interface iBoardService{
    url:string;
    getBoardInformation();
}
class BoardService{
    url:string;
    getBoardInformation(){
        return "No boards available";
    }
}
let boardService = new BoardService();
boardService.getBoardInformation();
```

We are able to create an instance of the `BoardService` class and call its methods. However, if we try to do the same in another file, we will get an error.

To be able to expose the members of the module, we should use the `export` keyword. The `export` keyword behaves similarly as in the case of `namespace`. It allows us to explicitly define which members of our module can be exposed outside the module and which ones cannot be.

 Only the members that are exported can then be imported into another module.

The member that needs to be exposed is just prefixed with the `export` keyword, as shown here for our `BoardService` class:

```
export class BoardService{
    url:string;
    getBoardInformation(){
        return "No boards available";
    }
}
```

With the `export` keyword added, we can now import the `BoardService` class into a separate module.

Importing a module

To be able to use the exported module and its members, we need to explicitly import them into another module. Once we import the members, we can then use them in our modules, just like the local members of the modules.

The following is the syntax of the import statement:

```
import {BoardService} from './Modules/service';
```

This import statement is added to a new file (app.ts), which is itself a module. Let's go through each part of the import statement and understand how the import module works:

- To import any module members, we start with the import keyword, followed by the members that would be imported inside the curly braces.
- After the members, we define the path where the module resides. As we know, the module is just a physical file; hence, the path will be the relative path of the module where we are importing. It's important to note that we do not end the path with the file extension, as it is implicitly known to the compiler. Here we had our service.ts file inside the modules keyword; hence, the path was defined as ./Modules/service.
- Inside the curly braces, we define all the members that we want to import from the module. It's important to understand that we don't need to import all the exported members of the module; we can just selectively import what we need. So, in our example, we have a class and an interface inside the service.ts file and both are exported. However, in our new module, we just need the BoardService class; hence, we imported just that.

Once imported, we can now use BoardService as a local class member in app.ts, as follows:

```
import {BoardService} from './Modules/service';
let board = new BoardService();
board.getBoardInformation();
```

There are a couple of other features that TypeScript provides while importing a module, which can help us write a more robust and manageable code:

- We can change the name (add an alias) of the member while importing, which would allow us to use the alias when referencing the imported member, as follows:

  ```
  import {BoardService as Service} from './Modules/service';
  ```

```
let board = new Service();
board.getBoardInformation();
```

So, here we added an alias, `Service`, for `BoardService` and used this alias when accessing the imported member.

- Let's assume that we have many members in a module that need to be imported, and rather than defining all the members inside the curly braces, we can use an asterisk to import all. This allows us to write more compact code.

The following is the modified example of our `BoardService` class:

```
import * as Service from './Modules/service';

let board = new Service.BoardService();
board.getBoardInformation();
let interface: Service.iBoardService;
```

Here, we used an asterisk followed by the alias of the imported module, that is, `Service`. So, when using the imported module, we refer to its members by prefixing them with `Service`.

We will see the use of imports extensively in our sample *Trello* application, where we will import Angular modules as well as our own custom modules to be referenced in other modules.

TypeScript Generics

Traditional programming languages had generics for a long time. Microsoft introduced generics in C# in 2005; Java also has generics. JavaScript itself does not have any explicit concept of generics but TypeScript does.

Generics, in layman's terms, is a concept that allows developers to define functions or classes without explicitly defining the types that the said function or class expects but rather allowing a generic definition, which would then be consumed by the calling functions as they see fit.

We have been using generics in our last application and we will be using it again, extensively, in our current application.

Generics allow us to create reusable and consistent component definitions. For example, we can have a function that accepts a string or a number and adds it to a collection.

So, we can either define two functions, each with their parameter type as string and number, respectively, and perform a similar operation in the function body, or we can define the function as generic and let the caller define what type of parameter it wants to send.

As you can imagine, apart from reusing the code with generics, we have reduced the code complexity and the maintainability overhead. If our requirement grows in the future and we need to support another type for the same functionality, the generic function would not need any change.

Definition

A function or a class is defined generic by introducing a type parameter. Type parameter defines what type the function parameters or class instance should be. Type parameter is not the regular parameter that is passed to a function but a special kind of parameter, which lets us define the type. The type parameter is defined inside angle brackets after the function or class name. In generics, a type parameter is normally defined as T, but it's just a convention and you can define it with any letter. The actual type a function or class will be used is defined at the time of calling the said function or class instance.

Functions

Generic functions are very similar to normal functions, except for how we specify the types used in a function. Let's take a standard function, and see how it can be converted to a generic function.

The following function takes a number as the input parameter and pushes that number into an array:

```
data = [];
pushNumberToArray(item: number){
this.data.push(item);
}
```

Now, let's say that we get another requirement in the future of pushing a string into the same array. To handle this requirement, we will write another function, which takes a string as the input, as follows:

```
pushStringToArray(item: string){
this.data.push(item);
}
```

As you can see, this is not the best practice to manage the array. Every time we have a new requirement, we would need a new function. This is where generics comes to the rescue. We can create a generic function, which can accept any type and, then, push it into the array.

The best part of having a generic function is that the caller gets to decide the type it wants to send. The following generic function replaces the preceding two functions:

```
pushGenericToArray<T> (item:T){
  this.data.push(item);
}
```

As you can see, in the generic function, we have a type parameter defined as T, which is the type mentioned for the input parameter, item. This tells the compiler that the pushGenericToArray function will take one parameter as input and that the type of the parameter will be defined by the caller function.

The following example shows how this function can be called with different data types:

```
this.pushGenericToArray<string>("10");
this.pushGenericToArray<number>(10);
```

Here, we passed the types when calling the function, which will let the compiler know what type is expected.

Classes

Generic classes are very similar to generic functions in the fact that they also use type parameters to specify the generic type. Let's suppose we want a class whose purpose is to manage the data in a collection, with operations such as adding the data to a collection and, then, retrieving the data from a collection. Now, a collection can be of any type, be it a string or a number.

This becomes a use case for generic classes, wherein we can define a class and assign a type parameter to the class. Then, we can use this type parameter as a concrete type in the different functions implemented in that class. Check out the following example:

```
class GenericClass <T>{
  items :T[] = [];
  pushData(val: T){
  this.items.push(val);
  }

  getData(index: number):T{
```

```
    return this.items[index];
  }
}
```

Here, in this example, we defined a class with the type parameter, `T`, and this type parameter is then used to define the `items` variable. With generics, this class can now be used with multiple types, as shown in the following code snippet where we create an instance of the class with `number` as our type parameter:

```
let numClass = new GenericClass<number>();
numClass.pushData(10);
numClass.pushData(20);
let num:number = numClass.getData(0);
```

Once we create an instance of the class, we will get TypeScript compiler support when calling any function on the instance to let us know that `number` is the type expected. If we try to call the `pushData` function with a type other than `number`, the TypeScript compiler will warn us with an error message. This allows consistency, with respect to the types used, and flexibility, with respect to defining the types by the caller.

Classes allows us to create custom types as we can see in the following example. Here we defined a class `Person` which is then used as a type when declaring a object `personClass`.

```
class Person{
  firstName: string;
  lastName: string;
}
let personClass = new GenericClass<Person>();
personClass.pushData({firstName: 'Homer', lastName:'Simpson'});
personClass.pushData({firstName: 'Marge', lastName:'Simpson'});
let person:Person = personClass.getData[0];
```

Now, the TypeScript compiler knows that the `pushData` function will only accept a parameter of the `Person` type and the `getData` function will return the value of the `Person` type.

Generic constraints

In the previous example, we can assign any type as a type parameter and, then, use that type to call the functions. This does provide us with flexibility but it also opens the door to various scenarios where our code may not behave consistently.

For example, if we add a new function `getSpecificItem` to our `GenericClass` which takes-in a string and then returns a value associated with that string as shown here:

```
getSpecificItem (title: string): T{
for(let value of this.items){
if(value.title == title){
return value;
}
}
}
```

In this case, the preceding function, when added to our class, will highlight an error that the `title` property does not exist on the type `T`. This is because `T` can be of any type and not all types have the `title` property.

In this case, it's useful to add some constraints to the type parameter we define so that we can use the specific properties based on the constraint. In generics, constraints are defined by the `extends` keyword, followed by the constraint. So, in the preceding case, we will want a constraint on type `T` such that it should be of a type that, in some way or form, derives from a type that has the `title` property.

Check out the following code change to our class to add the constraint:

```
interface iTitle{
 title: string;
}
class GenericClass <T extends iTitle>{
 items :T[] = [];
 pushData(val: T){
 this.items.push(val);
 }

 getData(index: number):T{
 return this.items[index];
 }
getSpecificItem (title: string): T{
 for(let value of this.items){
 if(value.title == title){
 return value;
 }
 }
 }
}
```

The first change is to define a type that has the `title` property in it; for this, we defined an interface, but you can use a class as well. Then, we added this interface as a constraint to our class type parameter. This lets the compiler know that only the types that derive from the `iTitle` interface can use this class, which would mean that in the previous example, the instance of the class defined with the `number` type is no longer valid.

As you can see, adding constraints to generics helps us to define a more specific implementation of the generic classes and, hence, provides better code consistency.

Sample Trello application

Now is the time for us to start building a sample *Trello* application. In the next few sections, we will focus on getting our application up and running and, along the way, visit some TypeScript and Angular concepts. We will start with understanding the application architecture and the application feature set. Then, we will delve into creating components with Angular and TypeScript.

On a high level, we will focus on the following features of *Trello* in our application:

- We will look at how to use TypeScript modules to organize our code.
- In our application, we will have multiple components and the communication between the components will vary between using services to manage the data and direct data communication. We will look at the communication features provided by Angular.
- While creating our models and using observables, we will look at the use of TypeScript generics.
- We will also take a brief look at the life cycle of components in Angular to understand the actual flow of how a component is created and destroyed, and how we can intercept these events to add our custom logic.

Application Architecture

The following is the high-level architecture diagram for our application:

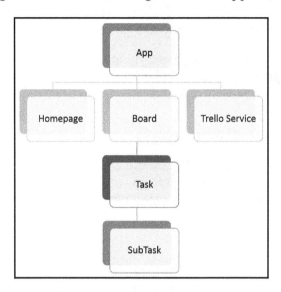

As you can see in the diagram, the application is comprised of four components, namely **Homepage**, **Board**, **Task**, and **SubTask**. Along with the components, we have a service class, which communicates with the **Homepage** and **Board** components. **Task** and **SubTask** are the child components of **Board**. So, the communication between the **Homepage** and **Board** components is achieved using services and the communication between **Board** and **Task/SubTask** will be achieved through the @Input and @Output properties.

In our application, we are not hitting any external web service to fetch the initial data but we have a JSON file in our API folder, which will be used to populate the data. We can create new boards, tasks, and subtasks but for the simplicity of the application, the data will not be persisted.

Code setup

We will use the Angular CLI to help us do the initial setup of the project, as we did in our previous application. We saw in Chapter 2, *Our First Application – Sports News Combinator*, how easy it is to set up the project with the Angular CLI. With just one command, we will have all the necessary files added to our project, downloaded packages, and a local server configured.

Let's run the following command to set up our project:

```
ng new SampleTrelloApplication
```

You can even go to our GitHub page, at `https://github.com/sachinohri/SampleTrelloApplication.git`, and download the entire code if you are interested.

The preceding command will create the initial components and configure the packages as required. Once the command is executed, you will have the basic skeleton created and you can even run this application using the following command:

```
ng serve
```

As of now, our application does not have any code with respect to our feature set but generic code that has one page showing an Angular icon and a couple of links. We will start now by creating our components in the application. In `Chapter 2`, *Our First Application – Sports News Combinator,* we discussed the folder structure of an application created by the Angular CLI, so we will not revisit that here. However, note that the folder structure is exactly the same as we had initially in `Chapter 2`, *Our First Application – Sports News Combinator.*

We will start now by creating our components in the application.

The Trello homepage

Our homepage will be the landing screen for our application. On this page, we will show all the boards that are available in our application. Along with the board name, we'll also show the number of tasks on that board.

We will also provide an option for the user to add new boards to the application using the *Create a new board* link. Once a user creates a new board, he/she will be able to go to the board and add tasks and subtasks there.

To create a new component, use the following command:

```
ng generate component homepage
```

This command will generate our `Homepage` component, its specific template file, and a style sheet file. The functionality on our homepage is limited to displaying the board data and the total number of tasks, so the first thing that we should do is define the data models to be used in our application.

Models

Our application's primary data structure is a board that consists of an array of tasks, and each task, in turn, contains an array of subtasks. So, let's create our three models: `Board`, `Task`, and `SubTask`.

Each of these models will be defined with TypeScript modules, meaning that they will be in a separate file and each class will be exported so that they can be imported into the `Homepage` component.

First, create a new file, `subtask.ts`, in the `model` folder with the following code:

```
export class SubTask {
id: string;
 title: string;
}
```

As you can see, we have added the `export` keyword in front of the class so that the `SubTask` class can then be imported.

Next, we will create a `task.ts` file, which would have a reference to subtasks, as follows:

```
export class Task {
  id: number;
  title: string;
  subtask: SubTask[];
  taskheaderId:string
}
```

With the preceding code, an error will be reported by the TypeScript compiler on the line where we added a property of `SubTask`. This is because we are using a different module, `SubTask`, in this case but we have not imported it. As you learned in an earlier section of the TypeScript module, in order to use a module, we need to import the same. Hence, we will add the following line to the `Task.ts` file:

```
import {SubTask} from './subtask'
```

Last, we will create our `Board.ts` module, which will refer to the `Task` module, as follows:

```
import {Task} from './task'
export class Board {
  id: number;
  title: string;
  task: Task[];
}
```

As you can see, all these models are pretty straightforward with `id` and `title` as their primary members. Now, let's use these models in our `Homepage` component.

The homepage component

In our `Homepage` component file, we will implement two functionalities:

- Fetch the initial board and task list to be displayed on the UI
- Handle the `Create a new Board` event to add a new board to our UI

In our initial set, we will be fetching the data hardcoded into our services file. In the next chapter, where we'll discuss services and HTTP, we will change this logic to fetch the data from an HTTP call.

So, let's first create our method in a service file, which will return a single board with a task and a subtask.

Board service

Create a new file, `trello.service.ts`, in the `services` folder with the following code:

```
Injectable()
export class TrelloService {
  public Boards: Board[];
  constructor() {}
  public seedData(){
    let temptask: Task = new Task();
    let tempSubTask:SubTask = new SubTask();
    let board:Board= new Board();

    temptask.id = 1;
    temptask.title = "Hello Task!!";
    temptask.taskheaderId = "1";

    tempSubTask.id="1";
    tempSubTask.title = "Hello Task Header!!";

    temptask.subtask = Array();
    temptask.subtask.push(tempSubTask);

    board.id=1;
    board.title = "Hello Seed Board";
    board.task = new Array();
```

```
            board.task.push(temptask);
            this.Boards = new Array();
            this.Boards.push(board);
            return board;

        }
    }
```

Here, we create a `TrelloService` class module, which has one method, `seedData`, which returns a board object populated with `Task` and `SubTask`. We will use this method to populate our homepage.

Don't forget to add the `import` statements for the `Board`, `Task`, and `SubTask` modules, as follows:

```
import { Board } from '../model/board';
import { Task } from '../model/task';
import { SubTask } from '../model/subtask';
```

Don't forget to add the service file in the `app` module under the `provider` array.

Homepage – initialize the data

Populating the data into our homepage is now simply a matter of calling the `seedData` method and assigning the value to the local `Board` object. To do this, we will call `TrelloService`.

Angular provides life cycle hooks for us to manage the component workflows. These life cycle hooks are the events exposed by Angular, which signify a specific action performed, such as when Angular creates a component, when it initializes the components, when it renders the component, and, in the end, when it destroys the component.

All the life cycle hooks are exposed by Angular in its `core` module with the most common hooks, which are used.

OnInit

As the name suggests, `onInit` is called when Angular initializes the component and displays the data-bound properties. This event is the recommended place to perform any specific initialization that needs to be performed for the component and to set any input properties on the component.

So, if you want to make a service call anytime to fetch the initial set of data, or perform some complex calculations required for the component display, this is the event to use.

OnDestroy

Angular calls the `onDestroy` event when it's about to destroy the component. This is a good place to have a logic for cleaning up our resources, stop any timers or actions happening automatically, and clean up the memory.

Sometimes, we also use this event to let the other components or other parts of the application know that the component is being destroyed, and they may want to update or perform some specific action, as required by the business logic.

OnChange

Angular has an event to identify any changes happening on the bounded properties of the component. So, whenever a property is modified, Angular will fire an `OnChange` event and pass the properties that are bound in the template.

In the `OnChange` event for each property, Angular will have a current and previous value which can then be used to identify the change and add logic. This event is mostly used when we want to handle some validations to the properties or any changes in the workflow, based on the value of the property.

In our `Homepage` component, we will use the `OnInit` life cycle hook to fetch the data for boards and bind that to the property. To be able to use the `OnInit` method, we first need to import the `OnInit` module from `angular/core` and, then, implement the `OnInit` interface on our `Homepage` component class. The following is the code for these two steps:

```
import { Component, OnInit } from '@angular/core';
@Component({
  selector: 'app-homepage',
  templateUrl: './homepage.component.html',
  styleUrls: ['./homepage.component.css']
})
export class HomepageComponent implements OnInit {
}
```

The `OnInit` interface exposes only one method, `ngOnInit`, which is called by Angular when the initialize event is fired. Hence, we will write our logic inside this method. You may remember from the previous section that we have a `seedData` method in our service class, which will return the board object.

So, we will refer `BoardService` in our constructor and then call the `seedData` method to fetch the records. The following is the full code of the `Homepage` controller class:

```
import { Component, OnInit } from '@angular/core';
import {Board} from '../model/board'
import {SubTask} from '../model/subtask';
import {Task} from '../model/task'
import{TrelloService} from '../services/trello.service'
@Component({
  selector: 'app-homepage',
  templateUrl: './homepage.component.html',
  styleUrls: ['./homepage.component.css']
})
export class HomepageComponent implements OnInit {
  boards: Board[]= Array();
  errorMessage: string;
constructor(private _trelloService:TrelloService) { }
ngOnInit() {

  this.boards.push (this._trelloService.seedData());

  }
}
```

Here, we saw the use of features such as Angular life cycle hooks, services, and components. With this code, we can fetch records and assign them to the local property boards. The next step is to bind this value to the UI.

Homepage – template

Our homepage template is pretty straightforward with only two blocks: one to display all the available boards and one to allow users to add a new board to our application.

Check out the following code snippet:

```
<div class="boards-wrapper">
  <h2>Boards</h2>
  <div id="boards">
  <a class="board" *ngFor="let board of boards" [routerLink]="['/board',
board.id]"
>
  <span class="title">{{board?.title}}:
  <label style="font-size: smaller">Total Task:
{{board?.task.length}}</label>
  </span>
```

```
</a>
<a href="#" class="board add-board" (click)="addBoard()">
<span class="title">Create a new board...</span>
</a>
</div>
</div>
```

We will not discuss the styling of our application; you can refer to CSS from the GitHub code.

As you can see, to fetch the records, we use the *ngFor Angular directive, which will loop through all the available boards and create an anchor tag for each of them. In each loop, we'll print the board title and the total number of tasks that are on that board. We also have a router link defined to our anchor tag, which will be used to navigate to the boards component.

After the boards are printed, we have another tag to allow the users to create a new board. It calls an addBoard method in HomepageComponent, which would create a new board object and add to the Boards array.

Homepage – add a new board

Adding a board involves creating a new board object, assigning it to the ID and title, and, then, adding the object to the global Boards object. Check out the following code:

```
public addBoard(){
  console.log('Adding new board');
  let newBoard:Board= new Board;
  newBoard.id = this.boards.length + 1
  newBoard.task = Array();
  newBoard.title = "New Board";
  this.boards.push(newBoard);
  console.log('new board added');

}
```

Running the application

Now, it is time for us to run the application and see our progress so far. To run the code, we just execute the following command in the Terminal window:

```
ng serve
```

If everything works fine, we will have our code built and hosted on `localhost:4200`, which should look like the following screenshot:

The header on our application was created in the `app` component file and you can refer it to see the code.

Now it's time to add some other components to our application. We will add the `Board`, `Task`, and `SubTask` components, which will be used to show our second screen. In this process, we will look at the concepts of data sharing between Angular components using `Services` and `@Input`/`@Output`.

Trello – the board component

When we select any of our boards on the homepage, the application will redirect us to the selected board page. On the board page, we will have the board title and all the tasks and subtasks associated with the board.

To achieve this functionality, the following tasks need to be implemented:

- We need to route to the board page for which we will use Angular routing.
- Once routed, we need to know which board was selected on the homepage; this will be achieved by passing a parameter in routing.
- On the board page, we need to fetch the respective tasks and subtasks. We will share `Trello` service to achieve this.
- With the required data, we will need to display the tasks and their respective subtasks. For this, we will create the `Task` and `SubTask` components and pass the required data to them.
- The communication between `Task` and `SubTask` will be handled by the `@Input` and `@Output` properties.

Let's delve deeper into each of these tasks and build our components.

Routing

We learned about routing in the previous chapter, so we will not discuss it here in much detail. Our routing is defined in the `app.module.ts` file. We only have two routes for our application—one for our default route for the homepage and the other route for `BoardComponent`.

The route for our `Board` component will take one parameter, `id`, which will be the ID of the board selected on the homepage. The following is the code of the `app.module.ts` file, where we have defined the routes and imported them into `NgModule`:

```
const appRoutes: Routes = [
  { path: 'board/:id', component: BoardComponent,pathMatch:"full" },

  { path: '', component: HomepageComponent },
];
imports: [
 BrowserModule,
 HttpModule,
 FormsModule,
 RouterModule.forRoot(appRoutes)
 ],
```

As we discussed, we just have two routes. Next, let's look at the code of the `Homepage` component where we use routing to route to the `Board` component:

```
. .
<a class="board" *ngFor="let board of boards" [routerLink]="['/board',
board.id]">
. .
```

Here, we can see that we create a unique route for each board based on the board ID. So, whenever the user clicks on one of the boards, Angular creates a URL with the page as `board` and the parameter as the board ID.

Once routed, we will land on the `Board` component, so let's look at its code with respect to identifying the ID that was passed in routing.

Routing in the Board component

To be able to use routing we need to import the `Route` module from `angular/router`, and that's what we do as the first step in our new component:

```
import { Params, ActivatedRoute } from '@angular/router';
```

Once we have imported the modules, the next step is to refer them in our constructor so that Angular takes care of passing the reference to the router:

```
constructor(private _route: ActivatedRoute, private_trelloService:
TrelloService) { }
```

We have another parameter in our constructor for referencing `TrelloService`. We will discuss its purpose in the next section.

As we discussed in the previous section about the Angular life cycle hooks, here also we will use the `init` method to initialize the data for our board template. Hence, we will have our code to fetch the ID from the route and get the data specific to that route logic in the `OnInit` method.

```
ngOnInit() {
  let boardId = this._route.snapshot.params['id'];
}
```

Board component – populating the data

Once we have the `id`, we can then use `TrelloService` to fetch all the boards and then filter the board based on the `id`, as shown in the following code:

```
ngOnInit() {
let boardId = this._route.snapshot.params['id'];
console.log(boardId);
this.board = this._trelloService.Boards.find(x=> x.id == boardId);
}
```

You can see in the preceding code that we used `TrelloService` to fetch all the records and then just filtered to get the board for which the ID was passed. With this, we now have the selected board and its tasks and subtasks in our component.

One interesting thing to note here is how we used the same service in the `Homepage` component and in the board component to share the data. In the `Homepage` component, we called the `seedData` method, which initializes the data and saves it in the `boards` property in the `TrelloService` class. The board component just uses the same property to fetch the boards.

But how did the `Board` component receive the data persisted by the `Homepage` component? This is because Angular creates a singleton for the service and the instance is shared between components. Angular takes the responsibility of managing the state of the service and passes the single instance to any component that has referenced the said service in its constructor.

Board component – passing data to child components

In the board component, we have the data based on the `id` selected, next step is to have our Task and SubTask component and populate the data in them.

As we saw in our architecture diagram, the `task` component is the child of the `Board` component and the `subtask` component is the child of `task` component. So, it's a hierarchical structure wherein the data is passed back and forth between parent and child.

In this chapter we will focus on how data can be passed between master/child component; the functionalities of these three components will be looked in next chapter.

We can very well have all our data on our `Board` component, but that would not be the best solution wherein we will have all the logic in one component. The best practice is to always follow the single responsibility principle, wherein we have one component responsible for only one feature so that if in case we need to modify or add any new functionality, we would not need to worry about the impact on other features in the same component.

For this case, we would create two components, `Task` and `SubTask` and divide the responsibilities. This also helps us to create reusable components which can span across the application. Angular provides a mechanism for us to share data between parent and child components using the concept of input and output.

Passing data to child components with @Input

Angular provides an @Input decorator which a child component can use to expose a property to the parent component. This can be any property that a child component wants to be available to the parent so that parent can assign values to it.

In our application, we will have a task property which will be exposed to the Task.ts component. The board component will then assign the specific task to this property that will then be used to populate the task template.

We start by marking the property task in our Task component with a @Input decorator as shown in the following code snippet:

```
@Component({
  selector: 'app-task',
  templateUrl: './task.component.html',
  styleUrls: ['./task.component.css']
})
export class TaskComponent implements OnInit {
  @Input()
  task: Task;
  @Input()
  subTasks: SubTask[];

}
```

Now, the Board component will be able to pass the data to the task component by setting the task and subtask properties using the property binding technique. Property binding is achieved by setting the binding target within square brackets, as we can see in the following code:

```
<div *ngFor="let task of board.task " class="sortable-task">
<app-task [task]="task"
[subTasks]="board.subTasks">
</app-task>

</div>
```

Here we are looping through all the tasks in a board and creating a child task component instance for each task. On creating the child task, we pass the values to the task and subtask properties, marked with a square bracket. Every time we change any value of the task or subtask property in the Board component, the change will be reflected in the task component.

For the sake of brevity, we have not shown the whole `Board` component template at this time. You can download the code from GitHub. We will be looking at all the events in our `Board` component template in the next chapter.

Similarly, in our `subtask` component, we will have a `subTask` property decorated with the input property, which will then be populated by the `task` component, as follows:

```
<li *ngFor="let subTask of subTasks ">
<app-subtask [subTask]="subTask"></app-subtask>
</li>
```

The preceding code in the `task` component template loops through all the subtasks and attaches the value to the `subTask` property. We can look at the `subtask` component as follows:

```
@Component({
selector: 'app-subtask',
templateUrl: './subtask.component.html',
styleUrls: ['./subtask.component.css']
})
export class SubtaskComponent implements OnInit {
@Input()
subTask: SubTask;
}
```

As you can see, this code is very similar to what we saw in the task component for `task` and `subtask` binding.

Passing data from a child component to the parent component

We saw that, using `@Input`, Angular allows us to pass data from parent to child; similarly, we have the `@Output` decorator to pass the data back from the child to the parent. The main difference is that we can output only one event from the child component to the parent component.

The child component exposes an event and decorates it with the `@Output` property. In Angular, an event is exposed using `EventEmitter`, as shown in the following code snippet:

```
@Output()
public onAddsubTask: EventEmitter<SubTask>;
```

Here we created an output parameter of the `EventEmitter` type in our `task` component. Here, we can also see how the generics are used by Angular.

`EventEmitter` is of a generic type and, when using it, we need to mention the type of property that will be used. In our case, it is `SubTask`. This generic parameter tells the event emitter that when the event will be fired, the type of object passed will be of the `subtask` type.

To use the output event, we bind the named event in the parent component, which is our board component, using parentheses, as follows:

```
(onAddsubTask)="addsubTask($event)"
```

Here, we identified an `onAddSubTask` event from the child component to the parent component, and when the said event is fired, we will call a method in our parent component called `addSubTask` and pass the event payload as the parameter.

To fire an event from the child component, we use the following line of code in our `addSubTask` method in the `task` component:

```
this.onAddsubTask.emit(newsubTask);
```

All the event emitters in Angular provide an `emit` function, which will be called by the child component to notify that an event needs to be raised, which will then be propagated to the parent component.

The following code listens to the `onAddSubTask` and logs the response:

```
addsubTask(event){
   console.log("Event Fired");
   console.log(event);
}
```

By now, we have an application with the homepage, board, task, and subtask components. We have the ability to fetch the data in the `Homepage` and `Board` components and pass the data between the board, task, and subtask components using the `@Input` property, and between the homepage and the board using shared services.

Summary

In this chapter, we started on our second application and made a lot of strides in implementing the feature set. You learned about TypeScript modules and generics. Then, we started creating our application and implemented most of the core functionalities using Angular features, such as components, services, multiple component communication, and life cycle hooks.

In the next chapter, we will make changes to our application to fetch data from HTTP. You will learn about TypeScript features, which helps us make web service calls.

6
Trello - Adding Features

We have divided our sample Trello application into three parts: in the first one, covered in Chapter 5, *Application 2 - Trello*, we handled the basic flow with features such as data communication between components and TypeScript modules, and reached a stage where we had a homepage and board page that would display the data.

Our focus in this chapter will be on implementing all the remaining functionalities of our application, such as allowing the user to add a new task and subtask and change the data via HTTP instead of our current hardcoded method.

We will be covering the following topics in this chapter:

- We will start by looking at what iterators are and how they are implemented in TypeScript
- We will focus on async programming and the options available to us for writing async code
- We will look at how Angular uses TypeScript to provide us with the features of asynchronous programming
- We will also briefly look at custom pipes provided by Angular, which allows us the flexibility to format the data at runtime
- In the end, we will discuss dependency injection, which will be a preface for us for adding testing features to our application

Iterators

Iterators are found all over the place in TypeScript and JavaScript. Iterators are the reason we can access values in a sequential manner. Iterators allow us to use functions such as `for...of` and `for...in` to access the data in an array.

Some common iterators in TypeScript are arrays, maps, sets, and strings, which allow us to access elements in a linear fashion. For any object to be iteratable, they need to have a `Symbol.iterator` property. The `Symbol.iterator` property is a function with methods that allow us to iterate over the elements of an object.

Iterators in JavaScript

First, let's look at a simple example of how we can access the elements of an object in an iterative fashion:

```
let stringArray = "Learning TypeScript";
for(let c of stringArray){
console.log(stringArray);
}
```

Here, we are looping through each character in a string and printing it. This is possible because the string has a `Symbol.iterator` property and the `for...of` loop works on the iteratable objects to print their values. The preceding example can be rewritten by explicitly using the `Symbol.iterator` property, as shown in the following code snippet:

```
let stringArray = "Learning TypeScript";
let iter = stringArray[Symbol.iterator]();
console.log(iter.next().value);
```

Here, we access the property in a string and then call its `next` function. The `next` function returns an object with two values, `done` and `value`. The `done` value signifies whether the iterator has iterated over all the elements and `value` is the value of the iterated element.

Iterators in TypeScript

Similar to JavaScript, TypeScript also provides the data types that have iteratable properties in them. In fact, they are the same data types, that is, arrays, string, maps, and sets, in TypeScript as well. If we look at the definition of a string or an array in TypeScript, we will see the `Symbol.Iterator` property defined in them, as shown in the following screenshot in the case of an array:

```
31    interface IteratorResult<T> {
32        done: boolean;
33        value: T;
34    }
35
36    interface Iterator<T> {
37        next(value?: any): IteratorResult<T>;
38        return?(value?: any): IteratorResult<T>;
39        throw?(e?: any): IteratorResult<T>;
40    }
41
42    interface Iterable<T> {
43        [Symbol.iterator](): Iterator<T>;
44    }
45
46    interface IterableIterator<T> extends Iterator<T> {
47        [Symbol.iterator](): IterableIterator<T>;
48    }
49
50    interface Array<T> {
51        /** Iterator */
52        [Symbol.iterator](): IterableIterator<T>;
53
54        /**
55         * Returns an array of key, value pairs for every entry in the array
56         */
57        entries(): IterableIterator<[number, T]>;
```

The `Array` interface has a `Symbol.iterator` property of
the `IterableIterator` interface. This `IterableIterator` interface implements an
iterator interface with three methods: `next`, `return`, and `throw`. As you can see in lines
number **38** and **39**, `return` and `throw` are optional while `next` is a mandatory method.
These methods are of the `IteratorResult` type, which has two properties: `done` and
`value`.

It's important to understand this implementation because, then, we can easily create our
own custom iterators by implementing these interfaces. You can check this same
implementation for `Strings` as well.

Custom iterators in TypeScript

Let's create a function that could be used as a counter; the custom logic we'd have for our counter will be that after the counter reaches 100, it should reset to 0 and then continue again.

To implement this, we will create a `customCounter` class which will implement the `Iterator` interface. In the `next` method, we will implement our custom logic. Let's look at the following code and then discuss how to implement the `Iterator` interface:

```
class customCounter implements Iterator<number>{
 private calculatedVal:number=0;
 next(value?: any): IteratorResult<number>{
 this.calculatedVal = this.calculatedVal >
   99 ? 0 : ++this.calculatedVal;
 return{
 done: false,
 value: this.calculatedVal
 }
 }
}
let c = new customCounter();
for(let i = 0; i < 101;i++){
 console.log(c.next().value);
}
```

Here, we have a `customCounter` class, which implements the `Iterator` interface. The class has only one private property named `calculatedVal`, which is initialized to 0 and is the value that will be returned from the iterator.

As we discussed the `Iterator` interface has three methods out of which only `next` is mandatory, so we have implemented this method. The `next` method returns an object of type `IteratorResult` interface which has two properties. So, we need to return these two properties as shown on lines number 6-8. In the function `next` we have implemented our custom logic to check if the current value is more than 99, then we add one and return that value. Once the value is 100, we reset the value to 0 and continue.

Then we created an object of the class and just called the `next` method 101 times to see how the values were printed. If you run this code you will see the that the values 1 to 100 are printed and the back to 0.

So, anytime you want to access the properties of an object in sequential fashion, check if the object implements the `Iterator` interface or has a property of `Symbol.iterator`. If they do, then we can access the properties using `for...of` or `for...in` functions.

For...of and for...in loops in TypeScript

We used `for...of` loop earlier to loop through all the elements of a string, because the string implemented the `Iterator` interface. We have another function available for us by TypeScript, that is, `for...in`.

The major difference between both these functions is what they return as the value. The `for...of` will return the value of each element and the `for...in` will return the index of each element. The following is the example of both these functions.

```
let sampleArry = ["TypeScript","Angular","Node"];
for(let val of sampleArry){
  console.log(val);
}
for(let val in sampleArry){
  console.log(val);
}
```

The output of the `for...of` a loop will be `TypeScript`, `Angular`, and `Node`. The output for the `for...in` a loop will be 0, 1, 2.

These both functions iterate over the objects using the `Iterator` interface with just the distinction of the value returned. If we compare the JavaScript generated for both these functions, it will provide us with details on how the values are printed. The following is the JavaScript generated for both:

```
var sampleArry = ["TypeScript", "Angular", "Node"];
 for (var _i = 0, sampleArry_1 = sampleArry; _i < sampleArry_1.length;
_i++) {
 var val = sampleArry_1[_i];
 console.log(val);
 }
 for (var val in sampleArry) {
 console.log(val);
 }
```

As we can see for the case of `for...of`, JavaScript basically fetches the item in an array using the square bracket notation, where we pass the index of the array and get the value of the element at that index. In case of for:in we just print the index of the array.

Asynchronous programming using TypeScript

Asynchronous programming is one of those concepts which are little tricky to understand but mandatory to know if you are building a responsive application. JavaScript is a single-threaded application so if we do all our work on that thread, then any time we have a task that is time-consuming, such as a web service call, we will end up making our user wait until the application returns back from the call.

To be able to manage these expensive tasks we have asynchronous programming. As you would imagine TypeScript makes it easier for us to write and manage asynchronous code. Today, there are multiple ways to write efficient, asynchronous code with each new version of JavaScript. TypeScript supports all these approaches and we will go through them here to better understand the asynchronous programming.

Callback functions

A `callback` function is a function which is scheduled to be called after some asynchronous processing is completed. The `callback` functions are passed to another function as parameters which allows them to be called when the async processing is completed.

If you have used JavaScript before, then you will have definitely used `callback` functions in the form of timeout functions or interval functions, or even when you make a web service call. For example, if we write a `setTimeout` function, it calls another function after a specific period of time. This other function is a `callback` function. Take a look at the following code:

```
setTimeout(callback, 2000);
function callback() {
 alert("Callback function called");
}
```

In this code, we are calling a JavaScript function `setTimeout` which will wait for 2 seconds and then call another function named `callback`. This is very similar to how asynchronous processing works, where we call a web service or a long-running task and on completion of that task we call a callback function to process the response.

With this mechanism, we make sure our JavaScript code does not have to wait to process user requests until the long-running task comes to an end. The `callback` function can be any function with any type of definition which fits your need. So, how does TypeScript allows us to write `callback` functions?

Callback in TypeScript

Let's assume you have a function which makes a web service call and once the response comes back, we want to process the response and show the data to the user. And all this should be done in an asynchronous way. The following is the code for one such function:

```
function doWork(clientName: string, callback: (boards: Board[], status:
string)=> void): void{
  let response:Board[];
  // web service call based on id and in response we get list of Boards
  // then we call our function passing required values
  callback(response, "Success");
}
```

This function takes two parameters as input, one being the name of the client for whom we will fetch all the boards and the other being the callback function. As we can see in the function signature we have defined the type of callback as well. The `callback` function will take two parameters, an array of boards and the status of the web service call. So, once this method is called, it will internally call a web service, and after the web service response, it will call the `callback` method. Now, let's look at the `callback` method we defined:

```
function callBack(boads: Board[], status: string){
  if(status != "Success"){
    console.log(status);
  }
  else{
    boads.forEach(x=>console.log(x.title));
  }
}
```

This method here is pretty simple; it checks the status, and if the status is not `success`, then it prints the status; else, it will print all the board titles.

This flow would allow us to process the response asynchronously while the application is responsive.

CleanUp the function

We can modify our callback signature in `doWork` to be more concise by using TypeScript interfaces as shown here:

```
interface ICallBack{
  (boards: Board[], status: string) : void;
}
function doWork(clientName: string, callback: ICallBack): void{
  let response:Board[];
  // web service call based on id and in response we get list of Boards
  // then we call our function passing required values
  callback(response, "Success");
}
```

Here we defined an interface with our callback signature and used the interface type to mention the type of the second parameter in the `doWork` method.

This way we just made our code more concise and clean; additionally, now we can use the same callback signature in multiple places.

Promises

Callbacks are good, they solve our problem of writing asynchronous code. But, as you may have noticed in the preceding code examples, callbacks are very verbose and have one too many handshakes. Additionally, if you want to write multiple callbacks wherein the response of one async operation triggers another async operation, we would have a very complex looking code with callbacks chaining to other callbacks.

To solve these problems we have promises. The promises are now part of native JavaScript since ES2015, so if we write a TypeScript code with promises, we would want to set our target compilation to ES2015 in `tsConfig.json`.

So, what are promises? A promise is an object which is returned by the asynchronous call and which represents the value that would be eventually returned from the call. So, a promise is a placeholder which is returned and when the real value is returned, this placeholder will have that value. The main difference here with respect to callbacks is that in promises you don't pass callbacks to the functions but instead attach the callback to the promises using its API. Promises help us write more concise code that is easier to understand when compared with callbacks.

Promise API

The signature of the promise takes a function which will do some asynchronous work. This function itself takes two parameters, `resolve` and `reject`. These parameters allow the function to inform a promise if the operation was a success or a failure. If the operation was successful, we call the `resolve` function, which informs the promise of the success, and we can pass the return value from our async operation to the `resolve` function. The following is the code snippet of a promise:

```
let p:Promise<Board[]> = new Promise((resolve, reject) =>{
// do some asyn work
if(success){
resolve(result);
}
else{
reject(errorMsg);
}
});
```

Here we are creating a new `Promise` object and passing an arrow function to it. This arrow function takes two parameters which are called based on our async task, and if successful calls `resolve`; else, it calls `reject`.

Another important point to notice here is the type of our variable p. The variable is of type `Promise` which has a generic signature. In our case, we assign the promise the type Board array, which means that if the promise is a success then it will return a result of type Board array.

Handling the response

The next step is to handle the response returned by the promise. The Promise API provides two functions, namely, `then` and `catch`. The `then` function handles the successful completion of the promise and it takes another function which should be called when the promise is resolved, as seen in the following line of code:

```
p.then(boards=>boards.forEach(board=>console.log(board.title)));
```

Here, we fetch the boards array and then loop through each element to print the title of each board. This method will be called if the promise returned successfully. To handle the error scenario, the promise API has a `catch` function as shown here:

```
p.catch(msg=>console.log(msg));
```

Because our `reject` function was passing an error message, in catch we just print the error message.

Both, the `then` and `catch` functions return a promise, which allows us to chain multiple promises together.

Chaining the promises

One of the real-world scenarios you will face is to call multiple async operations one after the other. Promises provide chaining which allows us to manage multiple calls. The `then` function will return a new promise which is different from the initial promise object and represents the completion of the previous promise operation and its callback.

The following is an example of how we can chain the promises:

```
let p:Promise<Board[]> = new Promise((resolve, reject) =>{
// do some async work
if(success){
resolve(result);
}
else{
reject(errorMsg);
}
});
let newPromise = p.then(boards=>doSomeMoreAsyncWork(boards));
newPromise.then(result => console.log(result));
```

This code is an extension of our initial promise code where, after performing the initial async operation, we have a variable p that returns a promise of type `Boards` array. We extend that example by calling another async operation in the `then` function, which would then return a new promise that is resolved in a subsequent `then` function.

This allows us to chain multiple async operations, making sure that each operation is executed after the completion of the previous async operation. The chaining is not only allowed in the `then` function but works on the `catch` function, which means that we can chain multiple operations wherein if one operation fails then next can be executed. The preceding code modified to chain with the `catch` block is shown here:

```
let newPromise = p.catch(boards=>doSomeMoreAsyncWork(boards));
newPromise.then(result => console.log(result));
```

The code is same as we have for our `then` function chaining, except for the fact that we chained with the `catch` function.

Async-await

TypeScript introduced async-await in the 1.7.x version, but it was only available if your compiler version was ES2015. In the 2.x version, they made it backward-compatible to support ES5 and ES3 JavaScript versions as well.

In TypeScript async-await is built on top of promises and allows us to write asynchronous code in more linear fashion. The main advantage of async-await is that it provides developers with a way to write code, which is similar to writing synchronous code, thus providing better readability and cleaner code.

Let's look at the sample async-await code and go through the differences with promises:

```
async function callAsyncFunction(id:number) {
  console.log("before making a async call");
  await doAsyncWork(id);
  console.log("async work completed");
  return "success";
}
function doAsyncWork(id:number){
  //make a web service call
}
console.log("before calling async function");
let p = callAsyncFunction(1).then(x=>console.log(x));
console.log("after calling async function");
```

The following is the description of the async-await function:

- The first thing to know about async-await is that because they are built on top of promises, they end up returning the promises from the async function.
- As we can see on a line number **1** we have a function `callAsyncFunction` which is prefixed with `async` keyword. This tells the compiler that there is some execution inside the function which should be run separately from the main execution cycle.

- The method which we want to be executed in parallel is always prefixed with `await` keyword as with `doAsyncWork` call.
- If you look at the return type of `callAsyncFunction` method you will notice that the compiler has assigned the type as `Promise<string>`, which tells us that here the compiler will return the promise for the async operation.
- If we did not have any `return` statements in our function, `Promise` would have been of the `void` type.
- Because the function returns a promise, we use promise APIs to fetch the result of the async operation. We see this in the end, where we have used a `then` API to fetch the value returned by the function.

So, we can see that writing code in async-await fashion allows us to write code in a more linear fashion. The output of the preceding code will look as follows:

```
before calling async function
before making a async call
after calling async function
async work completed
success
```

This shows that the compiler continued processing after calling the async function rather than waiting for it to finish.

Error handling in async-await

As async-await are just promises, to handle any exception we can follow the same process we did in case of promises; that is, use the promise API's `catch` method to handle the failure scenarios. The following is the modified code for line number **13**, where now along with handling the success scenario we are also handling the failure case:

```
let p = callAsyncFunction(1).then(x=>console.log(x))
  .catch(errorMsg => console.log(errorMsg));
```

You can see we have chained the `catch` method to our `then` function. So, if the function `callAsyncFunction` returns an error case, the `catch` method will be called and we can handle the exception as required.

Adding features to Sample Trello app

Now, its time to integrate our learning into our *Sample Trello* application. In the previous chapter, we had implemented the following functionalities:

- **Homepage**: We developed our homepage which would show all the available Boards
- **Board data**: In the last chapter, we were fetching the data from a hardcoded method in our services file
- **Board**: We created our board component which would encompass our Task and SubTask component
- **Task and SubTask component**: These components were used to display the current task and subtask for a selected board
- **Hierarchical data communication**: With Board, Task, and SubTask component we learned about how Angular provides the mechanism for communicating with child components using @Input and @Output decorators

In this chapter, we will implement all the remaining functionalities for our application as listed here:

- **Data from HTTP**: Rather than fetching the data from a hardcoded method we will fetch the data from an HTTP call. This will be achieved using promises.
- **Functional implementation**: We will cover all our functional implementation, including adding a new task, a new subtask, and new boards to our application.
- **Data formatting**: Angular provides a mechanism called pipes which allows us to format specific data at the runtime. We would look at pipes and implement them in our application.

So, let's get started.

Using promises in sample Trello

In our last application, News Combinator, we had fetched the sports news articles from an external API link using observables. In this chapter, we will use promises to show how we can make an HTTP call. To fetch the data we have created a JSON file that has some boards and their respective tasks and subtasks.

Board JSON

You can download this JSON file from the GitHub; it's located under the `src/api` folder. The following is part of that JSON:

```json
{
    "id":1,
    "title":"Learn TypeScript",
    "task":[
        {
            "id":"1",
            "title":"Basics",
            "taskheaderId":"1",
            "subtask":[
                {
                    "id":"1",
                    "title":"Types"
                },
                {
                    "id":"2",
                    "title":"Classes and Interfaces"
                }
            ]
        },
        {
            "id":"2",
            "title":"Advanced",
            "taskheaderId":"2",
            "subtask":[
                {
                    "id":"1",
                    "title":"Generics"
                },
                {
                    "id":"2",
                    "title":"Modules"
                }
            ]
        }
    ]
}
```

As we saw in the previous chapter our `Board` class is made of three elements, `id`, `title`, and `array` of the task. The task is then made up of `id`, `title`, and an array of the subtask. The preceding JSON is designed in the same format. This JSON represents the first `Board` with a title `Learn TypeScript` and `id` as 1. Then it has an array of the task, with each task having an array of the subtask.

We will fetch this JSON using HTTP call and then pass the `Board` object to our Homepage component.

Implement promises

To implement promises we first need to add the required dependencies that are used to make the HTTP call and fetch the response in a promise object.

Add HTTP dependency

Angular provides us with the HTTP client to make the web services call. To be able to use the HTTP client we need to add the HTTP module to our application, which as we learned earlier is done in the `app.module` file. Here are the steps to add a reference to the HTTP module in our project:

1. Add the import statement in the `app.module` file for HTTP:

   ```
   import { HttpModule } from '@angular/http';
   ```

2. Reference the HTTP module in the imports array of NgModule:

   ```
   imports: [
       BrowserModule,
       HttpModule,...]
   ```

The preceding two steps inform the Angular compiler of the dependency which the host application requires. Angular is then responsible for managing this dependency and injecting the references wherever the application mentions.

Now, we will add the reference to HTTP in our services call as follows:

1. In the `trello.service` file, import the reference to HTTP as follows:

   ```
   import { Http, Response } from '@angular/http';
   ```

We have imported `Response` object along with the HTTP from the Angular HTTP module because to be able to access the return object from the web service call we need the `Response` object which is used to map the response.

2. Add a reference to HTTP in the constructor of the service class as

```
constructor(private _http: Http) {}
```

This reference defines the dependency which needs to be injected into the service class when the object of service class is created. The dependency injection of the reference is then the responsibility of the Angular compiler. We will discuss dependency injection at the end of this chapter. For now, just remember that we have created a private _http object of type HTTP which would be automatically initialized when the service class is created.

Logic for HTTP call

Now, we can use the _http object to make a web service call. We will create a function, getBoardsWithPromises where we will make a GET call to our JSON file and return the promise to the Homepage component.

The following is our code for the function:

```
getBoardsWithPromises(): Promise<Board[]> {
        if(this.Boards == undefined){
        return this._http.get(this._boardUrl).toPromise()
            .then((response: Response) => {
                this.Boards = <Board[]>response.json();
                return <Board[]> response.json()    ;         } );
        }
        else {
            return Promise.resolve(this.Boards);
        }
    }
```

Let's go through each line of the function to understand the implementation:

- On the first line, we have the function name with the return type of the function. As we know that we are returning the `Boards` object from the HTTP call; hence, our promise is of the `Boards` type.
- On line **2**, we just have a logical validation to see if we have already fetched the boards, if not then we will make the HTTP call; else, we will return a promise with the already saved board's array object as seen in the last line.

- Next, we make an HTTP GET call using our local HTTP object. Now, we know from our last example that in Angular the HTTP by default returns the observable object, so we need a way to convert this observable to a promise.
- We do that by using a rxJS API, `toPromise` which will convert the response into a promise.
- The promise API comes with two methods, `then` and `catch`. To resolve the API result we use the `then` function which would take another function with one parameter; that is, the response from the HTTP call:

```
.then((response: Response) => {
            this.Boards = <Board[]>response.json();
            return <Board[]> response.json()   ;          } );
```

Here, we used the arrow function to resolve the `then` response and set our local variable of boards array to the response. And that's it, we have implemented the promises to fetch the data and assign that to the local variable as well as pass the response to the caller.

Call from the Homepage component

In the last chapter, we were fetching the data in the `Homepage` component by calling the `seedData` method in our services call. Now, we will replace that with the call to this new method and fetch the data using promises. The following is the code we will use to make the call:

```
this._trelloService.getBoardsWithPromises()
                .then(boards => this.boards = boards,
                    error => this.errorMessage = <any>error);
```

This code will be called from the `ngOnInit` method when the `Homepage` component is initialized. Here we are just making a call to the method `getBoardsWithPromises` and then resolve the response using the `then` function.

One thing to note here is that we are using the `then` function to handle both success and failure scenarios. The `then` function takes two parameters, with the first one for the promise getting fulfilled and the second one for the promise getting rejected.

If `getBordsWithPromises` throws an exception, the `then` function will execute the second parameter. The following is the signature of the `then` function:

```
then<TResult1 = T, TResult2 = never>(onfulfilled?: ((value: T) => TResult1
| PromiseLike<TResult1>) | undefined | null, onrejected?: ((reason: any) =>
TResult2 | PromiseLike<TResult2>) | undefined | null): Promise<TResult1 |
TResult2>;
```

As we can see here, it has two parameters and both are not mandatory: `onfulfilled` and `onrejected`. We can even rewrite this logic by using both the `then` and `catch` functions, as follows:

```
this._trelloService.getBoardsWithPromises()
    .then(boards => this.boards = boards)
    .catch(error => this.errorMessage = <any>error);
```

The only difference is that here we have explicitly used the `catch` function, but the behavior of both code pieces will be exactly same.

This implements the promises and now we will be able to fetch the data from our JSON file. Next, up, functional implementation of *Trello*.

Functional implementation

Currently, our *Trello* application does not do much except for showing the already existed data.

In this section, we will implement the following functionalities:

- The ability to add a new task
- The ability to add a new subtask to a specific task
- The ability to change the title of board, task, and subtask
- When a new task is added, reflect the change on homepage

Because we are fetching data from our local JSON file, we will not be implementing the logic to persist the changes. So, let's say that if you refresh your application after making a change to the title of a Board, that change will not be reflected after the application refresh.

Implement – adding a new task

To be able to add a new task we will need to implement the following actions:

- When a user clicks on the *add a task* section, the application should focus on the input area for the user to type in.
- Once the user is done typing and presses *Enter*, the application should add the new task to the board
- If a user does not press *Enter* but moves the focus from the input area, then also the the application should add a new task to the board

Let's look at the code for each step defined here.

Board component

First up will be the Board template. The following is the code snippet for adding a new task:

```
<div class="add-task"
        (click)="enableAddtask()" >

    <input
            (keyup)="addtaskOnEnter($event)"
        (blur)="addtaskOnBlur()"
        [(ngModel)]="addtaskText"
placeholder="Add a task" />
    </div>
```

Here we have a div which encapsulates the *add a task* input area. We have three functions defined in this template namely, `enableAddTask`, `addtaskonEnter` and `addtaskonBlur`. Then we have a `addTaskText` property, which will represent the text entered by the user.

The enableAddTask function

This function is pretty simple; it will just set the property identifying that we are going to add a new task and set the focus on the input element as shown below.

```
enableAddtask() {
    let input = this.el.nativeElement
      .getElementsByClassName('add-task')[0]
      .getElementsByTagName('input')[0];
    setTimeout(function () { input.focus(); }, 0);
  }
```

The addtaskonEnter function

This function will be called when the user is done typing in the input area and presses *Enter*. The purpose of this function would be to add a new task to our list of tasks for the board. The following is the code for the same:

```
addtaskOnEnter(event: KeyboardEvent) {
    if (event.keyCode === 13) {
      if (this.addtaskText && this.addtaskText.trim() !== '') {
        this.addtask();
      } else {
        this.clearAddtask();
      }
    }
    else if (event.keyCode === 27) {
      this.clearAddtask();
    }
  }
```

This method internally calls a couple of other functions, `addtask` and `clearAddtask`.

In a call to this method, we pass an event of type `KeyBoardEvent` from the UI, which will provide the information of the key pressed by the user.

If the key pressed is enter (keycode 13) and the input area is not blank, we call `addtask`, if the key pressed is ESC (keycode 27), the application assumes that the user canceled their previous action and the application will not add a new task.

The addTask method

The `addTask` method is the one responsible for adding the task to the `Board` array, which will then be reflected in the UI. The following is the code for doing so:

```
addtask() {
  let newID = this.board.task.length + 1;
  let newtask = <Task>{
    title: this.addtaskText,
    id: newID
  };
  this.board.task.push(newtask);
  this.updateBoardWidth();
  this.addtaskText = '';
}
```

Here, first we create a new id for the task by just incrementing on the existing number of the task by 1. Then we create a new object of `Task` class and assign the `id` and the task text to the object.

This new object is then added to the board object we have in our `Board` component.

Because of the two way binding, the UI is updated to reflect the new task on the board.

The clearTask method

This method simply clears the `task` property, `addtaskText` so that the UI can again reflect the *add a task* text on the input area.

The addtaskonBlur method

The `addtaskonBlur` method simply check if the text area has any text, and if so, calls the add `task` function; else, it calls the clear task as shown here:

```
addtaskOnBlur() {
    if (this.addtaskText && this.addtaskText.trim() !== '') {
      this.addtask();
    }
    this.clearAddtask();
  }
```

Implement – adding a new subTask

The implementation of adding a new `subTask` is very similar to adding a new task, with a major difference in the data object we work on. When adding a new task, we just make sure we add the task to the list of tasks for the selected board.

When adding a new subtask, we have to identify the parent task to which this subtask will belong and then make sure we update the task to reflect the changes. Because the majority of the implementation is similar we will just go through the code and not get into the details of each line.

Task template

The following is the code we have in our `task` template which provides the user interface for adding the new `subTask`:

```
<div class="add-subTask"
        (click)="enableAddsubTask()" >
      <input
        (keyup)="addsubTaskOnEnter($event)"
        (blur)="addsubTaskOnBlur()"
        [(ngModel)]="addsubTaskText"
        placeholder="Add a new SubTask" />
    </div>
```

As we can see we are handling the same events we handled when adding a new task. We have a click event `enableAddsubTask`, which will add the focus on the input area as shown in the code here:

```
enableAddsubTask() {
  let input = this.el.nativeElement
    .getElementsByClassName('add-subTask')[0]
    .getElementsByTagName('input')[0];
  setTimeout(function () { input.focus(); }, 0);
}
```

Then we have a property in the input area `addSubTaskText` which will represent the subtask entered by the user. We have two events to handle the adding of subtask, namely `addSubTaskOnEnter` and `addsubTaskOnBlur`.

The functional aspect of both these methods is the same, that is, to identify the subtask and add that to the task list. They both have basic logical validations like checking if there is text entered by the user and the keypress. The following is the code for both these functions:

```
addsubTaskOnEnter(event: KeyboardEvent) {
  if (event.keyCode === 13) {
    if (this.addsubTaskText && this.addsubTaskText.trim() !== '') {
      this.addsubTask();
      this.addsubTaskText = '';
    } else {
      this.clearAddsubTask();
    }
  } else if (event.keyCode === 27) {
    this.clearAddsubTask();
  }
}
addsubTaskOnBlur() {
```

```
    if (this.addsubTaskText && this.addsubTaskText.trim() !== '') {
      this.addsubTask();
    }
    this.clearAddsubTask();
  }
```

Both these method call the addSubTask method shown here:

```
addsubTask() {
    this.subTasks = this.subTasks || [];
    let newsubTask = <SubTask>{
      title: this.addsubTaskText
    };
    let selectedtask: Task;
    for (let v of this.board.task) {
      if (v.id == this.task.id) {
        selectedtask = v;
        break;
      }
    }
    if (selectedtask.subtask == undefined) {
      selectedtask.subtask = new Array();
    }
    selectedtask.subtask.push(newsubTask);
    this.subTasks = selectedtask.subtask;
    this.onAddsubTask.emit(newsubTask);
  }
```

Here we are creating a new subtask object and assigning the text to the property of the said object. Then we loop through all the tasks we have on our board and identify the selected task. We check if the selected task has a subtask array or not; if not, we initialize the array. Then we finally add this subtask to the selected task.

In the last line of code, we are firing an event to let the parent component know about the change and passing the new subtask property. The parent component, in this case, is the Board component. We looked at this logic in the previous chapter where we discussed @Input and @Output decorators.

Change title of board, task, and subTask

In this section, we will add the ability of the application to allow the user to edit the text of the board, tasks, and subtasks. The implementation is similar to all three components where we just handle the events and update the respective properties.

So, we will go through the code for one of them, and you can as a practice implement similarly for the other two, or use the code on GitHub as the reference.

Modify the title of a board

On our board page, we show the board title at the top, which is editable, as shown in the following screenshot:

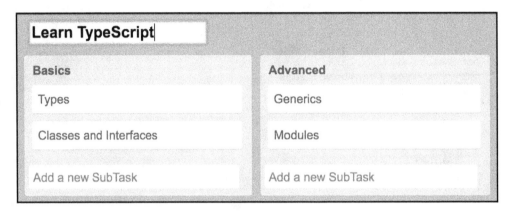

The user can edit the title on the board and then press *Enter* to see the changes reflected. And similar to adding a task, if the user presses escape, the changes will be canceled and original title will persist.

The following is the template code for the Board component that handles the board title:

```
<div *ngIf="board" class="board-title">
  <span [style.display]="editingTitle ? 'none' : ''"
(click)="editTitle()">{{ board?.title }}</span>
    <input
    [style.display]="editingTitle ? '' : 'none' "
    (keyup)="blurOnEnter($event)"
    (blur)="updateBoard()"
    [(ngModel)]="board.title" />
</div>
```

If you look carefully, this code is very similar to the code we wrote for adding task and subtask.

We call a click method editTitle which will set the focus on the board title input area when the user clicks.

Then we have a couple of functions for keyup and blur which will internally update the board title when the user presses enter or move the focus to some other part of the screen.

Let's look at the following `updateBoard` method to understand how we are editing and updating the board title:

```
updateBoard() {
    this.editingTitle = false;
    document.title = this.board.title + " | Generic Task Manager";
    this._trelloService.Boards.find(
        x=>x.id == this.board.id).title = this.board.title;
}
```

Here we see that we are just updating the board title in the `Trello` service class by identifying the selected board. We are not updating any other property inside the board component and that is because of the following line:

```
[(ngModel)]="board.title"
```

Here we have mentioned that we are binding directly to the `title` property of the board object in our `Board` component. So whenever the title is updated, this property is also updated, which reflects in the `board` object.

Reflecting the changes on the Homepage

We have implemented the functionality to add a new task or even change the title of the Board. Our `Homepage` component shows both these content with the board name followed by the number of tasks. So, how do the changes that happen in the `Board` component or in the `Task` component reflect on the `Homepage` component?

This is achieved using the Angular binding, which allows us to make a change in property and Angular takes care of reflecting the changes where all that property is accessed. Angular keeps a track of all the properties binded to the UI and if any change happens it propagates those changes by comparing the older value to the new value and reflecting the new value.

As we saw in the earlier code, when we modified the title of the `Board` we updated the service object which contains all the boards fetched from the HTTP call:

```
this._trelloService.Boards.find(x=>x.id == this.board.id).title =
this.board.title;
```

Once we have updated that property in the service class, the homepage uses this property to bind all the boards to the UI.

Thus with Angular's binding and reference checking we don't need to worry about how the data object and UI will be in sync. This is one of the major benefits of Angular, which helps us focus more on implementing our application logic.

Data formatting in Angular

In real-world applications, we always have a scenario where the data returned by the backend web service call is not in the format we would like to present on the user interface. Angular provides us with a feature called pipes which allows us to format the data as per the needs while processing it to be shown on the user interface.

Angular pipes allow us to format the data before they are displayed which helps us make the values more user interactive. Angular provides some built-in pipes for us to handle some common operations such as `upperCase` and `lowerCase`, which allow us to change the case of a text or date, allowing us to format the date as desired, or even currency pipe, which helps us to format our data by defining any specific currency we want to display and the number of decimal places.

Built-in pipes

Let's look at one such pipe and use that in our application. We would want to make sure we display our task title always in `upperCase` even if the user entered it in lowercase. To use the built-in pipes we don't need to do anything extra for referencing, just add the pipe symbol follow it with the pipe name to a binding where we want that pipe to take effect.

In our case, we would just add the `upperCase` pipe to our task template where we bind the task title as shown here:

```
<h4
        [style.display]="editingtask ?'none' : '' "
        (click)="edittask()" >{{task.title | uppercase}}</h4>
```

As we can see in the preceding code we just add the pipe symbol to the `task.title` and followed by the pipe name. This will make sure that when Angular is binding the title property for each task, it calls the built-in `upperCase` pipe function and pass the title value to it.

The `upperCase` pipe function will then convert the title to uppercase and return the updated result, which will then be binned to the UI.

Some pipe functions allow us to pass parameters which define how we want the pipe function to behave. One such example is currency pipe. The parameters are specified by adding the colon and then the parameter value after the pipe name, as shown here:

```
{{book.price | currency: 'USD':true:'1.1-2'}}
```

The first parameter in currency symbol indicates the currency we want to show. In this case, its USD. The second parameter, which again is prefixed by a colon, identifies whether we want to show the current symbol, and the last parameter indicates the format of the currency, which in our case states that we will have at least 1 digit before the decimal and, at least, 1 digit after the decimal and a maximum of 2 digits after the decimal.

Custom pipes

Angular provides us with an interface to create our own custom pipes. This helps us in customizing our business logic to format the data on the user interface.

Creating our custom pipes is very similar to creating a new service or a new component. In our *Trello* application, let's suppose we have a requirement to always display the task and subtask in alphabetical order. So, let's create a custom pipe named `custom-sort.pipe` and implement the logic of sorting.

Sorting pipe for Trello

To create a custom pipe, we will add a new file to a shared folder with the name `custom-sort.pipe.ts`. The following is the code for the pipe:

```
import { PipeTransform, Pipe } from '@angular/core';
import { Task } from '../model/task';
@Pipe({
  name: 'customSort'
})
export class CustomSort implements PipeTransform {
  transform(value: Task[], sort: boolean): Task[] {
    if(sort){
      return value.sort(this.compare);
    }
    else{
      return value;
```

```
    }
  }
  private compare(a,b) {
    if (a.title < b.title)
      return -1;
    if (a.title > b.title)
      return 1;
      return 0;
  }
}
```

Let's look at the following code and understand the significance of each line:

- To be able to use pipes we need a reference to pipes from Angular and in line number **1** we import the required pipe modules.
- On the first line after the import statements, we decorate our class with the @Pipe decorator which is very similar to what we do for our component and services. This helps Angular identify that the class is a pipe.
- To be able to implement pipe we need to implement an interface PipeTransform, which Angular provides.
- The PipeTransform interface exposes only one method, transform:
  - The first parameter to our pipe function is the value which is passed to the pipe function. In our case, this will be the Task array. Passing a value to this parameter is handled by Angular by itself; hence, when we use the pipe, we don't need to explicitly pass any parameters.
  - The second parameter we have defined as Boolean, which signifies whether we need to sort or not. If the value is passed as false then the pipe function will just return the same value in the same order as it was received.
  - Then the return type, as we are just reordering the content our return type is same as task array.
  - The logic inside the pipe function is a standard code to format any string in an object array.

Adding pipe dependency

Before we can use the pipe function we need to add the class to our module so that Angular can identify and load the pipe function and its dependency.

To do that we just need to add the dependency in our `app.module` file as follows:

```
import {CustomSort } from './shared/custom-sort.pipe'
declarations: [
    AppComponent,
    HomepageComponent,
    ...
    CustomSort]
```

And that's it, now Angular knows about the pipe and loads it when it loads other components.

Using the custom pipe

Using the custom pipe is exactly the same as using the built-in pipe. We will use the custom pipe in our board component template where we loop through all the tasks as follows:

```
<div *ngFor="let task of board.task  | customSort: true" class="sortable-task">
```

Here we are calling our custom pipe and passing the value of the parameter as `true`, signifying that we want the values to be sorted. If we had passed the value as `false`, the tasks would have been displayed as they are in the JSON file.

Understanding dependency injection in Angular

Dependency injection is one of the most fundamental aspects of Angular. The Angular team has been very careful in using dependency injection since its first release of the Angular 1.x version and this has been the primary reason that Angular applications are easy to test.

The ability to write good, robust tests for an application largely depends on how the application manages dependencies. If the application creates concrete dependencies in its classes than it becomes very difficult to write test cases for individual classes, whereas if the dependencies are not the primary responsibility of a class, then writing test cases for that class becomes so much simpler.

We have been implicitly relying on dependency injection since our first application, and some of the code examples in our *Trello* application where we use Angular's dependency injection are shown here.

The constructor of the `Homepage` component will look like this:

```
constructor(private _trelloService:TrelloService,private _router: Router) {
}
```

The constructor of the `Trello` service will look like this:

```
constructor(private _http: Http) {}
```

In both these examples, we defined the dependency of the class on a couple of other objects, for example, in the `Homepage` component, we have a dependency on the `Trello` service and router and in `Trello` service class we have a dependency on the HTTP module.

So, how do these classes get the object of these dependencies?

Managing the dependencies

In Angular, the framework determines what dependencies a specific class has and then injects those dependencies into the class at the time of object creation. So, taking from the above example, when Angular is creating an object of the `Trello` service class, it checks the constructor signature and identifies the dependencies that the `Trello` service needs.

In our case, it's only one, the HTTP module. Here Angular checks where the HTTP module resides, which it finds out from the definition in the `app.module` file. It then either creates a new instance or uses the existing instance and passes that to the `Trello` service constructor.

This allows us to not have the responsibility of identifying the dependency and creating that in our class, which in turn allows us to write code which is easily testable.

So, if we want to test a specific class, we don't need to worry about the dependencies the said class has, but in fact, we can stub the dependencies when creating the object of the class, which allows us to provide exact dependency values from outside the class when writing test cases.

We will look at writing test cases in the next chapter, and there we will see the advantage of having dependencies injected into our classes by Angular rather than creating them inside our classes.

Summary

In this chapter, our focus was on implementing the remaining functionalities of our *Sample Trello* application. In doing so, we learned about async programming in TypeScript and Angular using callbacks, promises, and async-await. We also looked at iterators, pipes and dependency injection. By the end of this chapter, we had implemented all the features of our application and it's still not in full working condition.

In the next chapter, we will discuss testing and how we can write test cases for our application. We will continue to build our application by adding a few test cases to showcase the features provided by Angular and some third-party frameworks.

7
Testing the Trello Application

Does your application work as intended? Are there any scenarios where your application behaves unexpectedly? To confidently answer these questions, we need to test our application. Now, we can manually test all our features and functionalities and try to unearth any bugs in our application, or we can write test cases in our application. Which approach is better?

In this chapter, we will focus on testing, and how writing test cases provides us with a better application than solely relying on manual testing. In this chapter, we will be covering the following topics:

- We will start by looking at what it means to be writing test cases in comparison to manual testing
- Then we will also talk about test-driven development, and how to go about implementing that in software development
- After these, we will start implementing our test cases in the *Sample Trello* application
- We will look at Jasmine and Karma to write and run our test cases

Because we created our application using the Angular CLI, we already have the test case set up, but we will also briefly look at how to set up the dependencies to be able to set up the test project in our application.

Fundamentals

Before we start digging deeper into testing our application and the respective testing tools, it would be useful if we take a look at why we should write test cases, and what advantages we have in comparison to relying on manual testing.

How many times has it happened where you have put in hours of effort to develop an application, and when it's about to go into production, or worse, it is launched in production, you discover a blocking issue? You and your team have done exhaustive testing; but still, how did this bug skip through?

You do the retrospection and identify that there was one scenario that was never part of your testing, and that's what caused this problem. Now, you add that scenario into your test cases but, six months down the line, the cycle repeats.

Challenges in testing

One way to solve this cycle of having bugs reported in production, or close to production, is to write test cases in your application. Most of the developers I have worked with at some point have had a diversion to writing test cases in their applications. It felt like wasted time in writing this extra piece of code on top of their own logic to test, and one of the reasons was that it was way too complex to just set up the testing framework.

Angular is brilliant in identifying this pain point, and that is the reason they created the Angular in a way that allows developers to write testable code without going out of their way. This is achieved through dependency injection in Angular. The Angular team made sure all the modules are loosely designed and the framework supports injecting the dependencies at runtime, which allows us to mock the dependencies and test every component in isolation.

Test-driven development

In the software industry, there are two schools of thought with respect to when to write the test cases. One is **test-driven development** (**TDD**), and the other is to write tests when implementing the function flow.

In TDD, we first write a test and then write code to pass the test. Once the code passes the test, we refactor the code to make it optimized, and then use the test to make sure that the code does not break. With this approach, we are forced to think of all the conditions and alternate flows that can happen in our code, which in turn helps us write code that satisfies all the scenarios. But, it can become an overhead if you are developing an application that has a frequent change in requirements, because every time there is a requirement change, you would have to modify or even discard the earlier test cases and write the new one.

Another approach is to write test cases when implementing the code. The main difference of this approach from TDD is that you don't restrict your development based on the test cases, but both go hand in hand. The disadvantage of this approach is you lose the opportunity to follow a failure to success development, which we get in TDD. On the other hand, the advantage is that we don't have to do a lot of rework if the requirements change later.

Taking an approach of writing test cases is more of a personal and an organizational decision; there is no one right way of doing it. But, everyone does agree that there should be test cases for any application to help make sure that there are no bugs.

Unit testing versus end-to-end testing

There are two forms of testing that we can achieve in an Angular app. They are as follows:

- Unit testing
- End-to-end testing

Both these tests provide unique advantages, and help us cover our application from different perspectives.

Unit testing

The purpose of the unit test is to confirm the correctness of a *specific piece of code* independent of its dependencies. Here, the phrase *specific piece of code* can imply different things, and is based on how your application code is structured.

Typically, *a specific piece of code* can be a class that follows a **single responsibility principle**, or can be a component. The most important factor of the unit test is that we only test the code inside the class, and not the dependencies that the said class has. This means that if a class is dependent on another class for some data, some web service response, we stub those out and just test the logic of the class.

This approach allows us to confirm the behavior of the class in isolation, thus providing a confidence that the logic implemented is correct.

The following are some of the key features of a unit test:

- **Single piece of code**: As we discussed earlier, a unit test should focus on a small piece of code rather than the whole module.
- **Fast**: The unit test should be fast to execute and quick to write. Because we are just testing a specific piece of code, the test should not be complex.
- **No dependencies**: The code to be tested should not have any dependencies that can allow the behavior of the code to change.
- **All code paths**: Because with the unit test we are focused on a small piece of code, we need to make sure we cover all code paths for the said piece.
- **Assert one thing**: The unit test should be asserting only one thing, rather than checking multiple things in a single step.

These features allow us to write more clear and concise unit tests with the focus on the code to be tested rather than the whole functionality of the application.

End-to-end testing

In contrast to the unit test, the focus of the end-to-end test is on testing the whole system working together. In an end-to-end test, we don't worry about each line of code and don't focus on writing test cases for code coverage, but insteat we look at the system as an end user and write test cases to simulate that behavior.

End-to-end testing does focus on dependencies, and how the application will behave based on these dependencies. Think of the end-to-end test as the next step in the unit test. If you have tested all your code in isolation that confirms that the code works fine independently, but for the user, that piece of code may be dependent on a web service, or a database call, or another piece of code, which is where these tests come in.

With all the advantages of end-to-end test there are couple of drawbacks as well.

- **Slower**: They tend to be slower to execute and write in comparison to the unit test because they are testing the system
- **Complex**: Because the end-to-end test is focused on user-level testing, writing these tests is more complex when compared to unit tests

Structure of a test

There is a definite structure of any test we write. This structure is based on the process that needs to be followed for us to write effective tests. The structure is defined with the acronym **AAA**, as explained in the following list:

- **Arrange**: As the name suggests, this is the part where we write the initial state of the unit test. The initial state here means the setup that is required for us to write the test. The setup can be initializing the class, or even setting up the initial set of data.
- **Act**: This is the step where we act in our class and make a change that is to be tested. So, this can be like calling a function in a class, or changing some property in a class.
- **Assert**: This is the step where we validate our test. After we have to change the state of our code in the act step, in the assert step we validate if the state change is as expected. This is the place where we determine if our test case succeeds or fails.

Mocking

Mocking is a concept of stubbing the dependencies so as to test the piece of code in isolation. Mocking is an important concept for unit testing because most of our code would, in one way or another, depend on the external piece of code. So, if we want to test our code and just our code logic without worrying about the impact of dependencies, we need to mock those dependencies.

Mocking allows us to create a dummy object of the dependencies, and pass this dummy object to our code so as to make sure that the dependency has no impact on the execution of our code.

For example, we have to test a customer class, but the customer class also calls external dependencies such as an HTTP or database. So, to be able to test the customer class without worrying about how the HTTP or database behave, we mock these objects and pass the mock object to the customer class. This way, we can ensure that we only test the code we want, and also that the test does not alter the state of the object permanently.

Tools for testing

We will be using two primary tools for writing our test cases: Jasmine and Karma. Because we created our application using the Angular CLI, the CLI already adds these dependencies to our solution. The Angular CLI also creates sample test for our application including services and components, which include the initial setup work required to start writing the test. This is very useful for us because we avoid doing the setup work, and can therefore be more productive on what matters most: writing the test for our application.

Though we already have these (Jasmine and Karma) installed in our application, it would be good to look at these tools in isolation and understand them, so that if you would want to develop an application without the Angular CLI, you can use these tools.

Jasmine

Jasmine is a testing framework that is widely used with Angular. Jasmine provides functions for us to write and manage our test cases. These functions are described as follows:

- `describe()`: This function acts as a container for our suite of tests. Jasmine identifies the describe function as the root of the test case, and uses that as the start of running the test case.
- `beforeEach()`: The `beforeEach` function acts as an *arrange* in our test case. This is where we write our common code, which is required to set up our test case.
- `it()`: This is a function where we *act* on our code. We will normally have multiple `it()` functions inside our `describe()` function. Each `it()` function acts as a separate unit test.
- `expect()`: The `expect()` function is where we *assert*. It's here we validate our test case. The `expect()` function has associated matcher functions that allow us to write the *asserts* we need. Some of the matchers are as follows:
  - `toBe`: This specifies the value `toBe` expected in our *assert*
  - `toContain`: As the name suggests, this allows us to check if a specific value is contained in the return from the asset
  - `toBeLessThan`, `toBeGreaterThan`: To check the range of a value

Karma

Once you have written your test cases using Jasmine, the next step is to run these test cases. Karma does exactly that: it allows us to run our test cases. It's a command-line tool that identifies our test cases and then executes them, and shows the result of the execution.

Karma is a configurable tool that allows us to launch the browser and then execute the test case in that browser. We can configure the type of browser to run our test cases, we can configure the test cases to be executed, and much more.

Karma comes with its Karma-CLI package, which allows us to configure it quickly and easily and provides us with a faster execution environment.

Installing and configuring Jasmine and Karma

As I mentioned earlier, because we are using the Angular CLI, we already have Jasmine and Karma installed in our application, and you can check that by looking into the `package.json` file present in the root of our application, as shown in the following code snippet:

```
"devDependencies": {
"@angular/cli": "1.2.0",
"@angular/compiler-cli": "^4.0.0",
"@angular/language-service": "^4.0.0",
"@types/jasmine": "~2.5.53",
"@types/jasminewd2": "~2.0.2",
"@types/node": "~6.0.60",
"codelyzer": "~3.0.1",
"jasmine-core": "~2.6.2",
"jasmine-spec-reporter": "~4.1.0",
"karma": "~1.7.0",
"karma-chrome-launcher": "~2.1.1",
"karma-cli": "~1.0.1",
"karma-coverage-istanbul-reporter": "^1.2.1",
"karma-jasmine": "~1.1.0",
"karma-jasmine-html-reporter": "^0.2.2",
"protractor": "~5.1.2",
"ts-node": "~3.0.4",
"tslint": "~5.3.2",
"typescript": "~2.3.3"
}
```

As we can see in the preceding code snippet, we have multiple packages for Jasmine and Karma in our application, and all this is taken care of by Angular CLI.

But, it will be useful if we learn how to install and configure these tools independently so as to have a better understanding of these tools.

Installation

As we saw earlier, there are quite a few libraries that are needed for us to write and execute the test cases, so let's start looking at them one by one.

Karma-CLI

Let's first install the Karma-CLI by using the following command:

```
npm i -g karma-cli
```

This will install the Karma-CLI in global scope from `npm`. `karma-cli` allows us to run Karma from the command line.

Other dev dependencies

Apart from the Karma-CLI, we also want to install dependencies such as `karma`, `karma-chrome-launcher`, `karma-jasmine`, and `jasmine-core`. We can do so by using the following command:

```
npm i karma karma-chrome-launcher karma-jasmine jasmine-core -D
```

This command installs all the dependencies in the dev dependencies section, which we saw in our `package.json`.

Jasmine typing

Because we are working in TypeScript, we want to write our test cases in TypeScript format, and to do that we want the Jasmine TypeScript typings installed.

We can do so by running the following command:

```
npm i @types/jasmine
```

Configuration

To configure Karma for our application after installing all the dependencies, we first verify the `package.json` to confirm all the dependencies are installed.

Next, we will create a new file called `Karma.conf.js` in our `root` folder. You can copy the file from our `https://github.com/sachinohri/SampleTrelloApplication`, or from the following code snippet:

```
module.exports = function (config) {
  config.set({
  basePath: '',
  frameworks: ['jasmine', '@angular/cli'],
  plugins: [
  require('karma-jasmine'),
  require('karma-chrome-launcher'),
  require('karma-jasmine-html-reporter'),
  require('karma-coverage-istanbul-reporter'),
  require('@angular/cli/plugins/karma')
  ],
  client:{
  clearContext: false // leave Jasmine Spec Runner output visible in browser
  },
  coverageIstanbulReporter: {
  reports: [ 'html', 'lcovonly' ],
  fixWebpackSourcePaths: true
  },
  angularCli: {
  environment: 'dev'
  },
  reporters: ['progress', 'kjhtml'],
  port: 9876,
  colors: true,
  logLevel: config.LOG_INFO,
  autoWatch: true,
  browsers: ['Chrome'],
  singleRun: false
  });
};
```

Let's look at the main components of this file:

- `basePath`: This defines the base path for our application, which Karma uses to start looking for the test cases
- `frameworks`: This tells Karma which other frameworks it should look for while running the test cases; in our case, it's Jasmine

- `plugins`: This provides an array of dependencies that Karma needs to load for executing the tests
- `reporters`: This allows us to configure whether we want to see the progress of our test case execution
- `autoWatch`: The `autoWatch` flag tells Karma whether to keep on looking at the files, and as and when a change happens, to run the test again
- `browsers`: This provides the browser details for Karma as to where it should run the test cases

Folder and file structure for the test project

The common convention we have for naming the file for our test is a file that is suffixed with `spec.ts`. So, if you have a file named `homepage.component.ts`, your test file will be named `homepage.component.spec.ts`.

Karma does not use the filenaming conventions to find the test cases, it just scans through all the transpiled files and executes the test cases it finds in any file. This naming convention is specifically for us to manage our code in a more logical fashion.

As we are using the Angular CLI, it creates the respective test file when we generate a component or a service with the same naming convention. So, if we look at our current folder structure, you will see the files with names as `*.spec.ts` in your respective folders, as shown in the following screenshot:

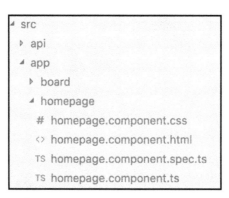

Writing test for pipes

Writing test cases for pipes is one of the easiest examples we can use to get started. The primary reason for this is that normally, pipes don't have external dependencies, which allows us to easily test the code logic without the worry of mocking.

We have one pipe function in our *Sample Trello* application, *custom sort*, so we will be writing test cases for this. You can review the custom sort code from our previous chapter, or look it up in `https://github.com/sachinohri/SampleTrelloApplication`.

Creating a new file

To write our test case, let's first create a new file in the same folder where we have the custom sort code. Let's name our file `custom-sort.pipe.spec.ts`. The logic in our `pipe` function is based on two parameters: `task` array, and the `sort` boolean property. Based on the `sort` boolean property, we identify whether we should sort our `task` array or not. The sorting is based on the `title` property in our `task` object.

So, here's a list of some of the unit test cases we can use for our `pipe` function:

- Expected `task` array sent to the `pipe` function with the `sort` property as `true`
- Expected `task` array sent to the `pipe` function with the `sort` property as `false`
- If we pass a blank `task` array
- If the `task` array has a task with a blank title
- If the `task` array has more than one task with the same title

We will not write test cases for each of the preceding scenarios, but we will focus on the first two and then you can build on top of it and write more test cases.

Writing the test case

To start off, before we write any test case, the first step is to import the dependencies for the test case. Every test case will have the dependencies on its respective component/pipe/services and any model data. In our case, that would be the custom `pipe` class and the `task` object. The following is the code for the import:

```
import { CustomSort} from './custom-sort.pipe';
import { Task } from '../model/task';
```

Next up is the logic for the test case. The following is the code for both of our test cases; we will go through each step in detail:

```
describe('Custom Sort pipe', () => {
  let pipe:CustomSort;
  let tasks: Task[];
  beforeEach(() => {
  pipe = new CustomSort();
  tasks = [{title:"Basic",id:0,subtask:[],taskheaderId:"1"},
  {title:"Advance",id:0,subtask:[],taskheaderId:"1"},
  {title:"Complex",id:0,subtask:[],taskheaderId:"1"}];
  });
  it('should sort the task array', () => {
  let expectedTask: Task[] = [
  {title:"Advance",id:0,subtask:[],taskheaderId:"1"},
  {title:"Basic",id:0,subtask:[],taskheaderId:"1"},
  {title:"Complex",id:0,subtask:[],taskheaderId:"1"}]
  expect(pipe.transform(tasks,true)).toEqual(expectedTask);

  });
  it('should not sort the task array', () => {
  let expectedTask: Task[] = [
  {title:"Basic",id:0,subtask:[],taskheaderId:"1"},
  {title:"Advance",id:0,subtask:[],taskheaderId:"1"},
  {title:"Complex",id:0,subtask:[],taskheaderId:"1"}]
  expect(pipe.transform(tasks,false)).toEqual(expectedTask);

  });
});
```

As we discussed earlier, writing test cases has three steps; let's look at those in our code.

Describe function

First up is the `describe` function, which acts as the container for our test case. The signature of a `describe` function is shown in the following screenshot:

As we can see, the describe function takes two parameters. The first one is the description, which is just a string and defines our test case, and the second is the callback function that will be executed. In our case, we have declared a couple of objects that we will use in our test case.

 We are able to see the definition of the describe function because we have installed the typings file for Jasmine.

The beforeEach function

This is the function where we prepare our data to run the test. In our case, that means initializing the custom sort object and creating a task array, which is passed to the transform function.

The important thing to note about the beforeEach function is that, as the name suggests, this function is called before each of the it functions. This helps in making sure that when we execute multiple test cases, the data from a previous test case does not modify the data for the next test case.

The it function

This is where we execute our test, and this is where we expect to assert our test results. Let's look at our first test case, *should sort the task array*. This test case will pass the task array that we created in our beforeEach function and expect the array to get sorted by the title. This function also defines the expected array output, which is then compared with the returned value from the transform function using a toEqual matcher.

And that's it. This is all we have to do to write a test case. Isn't it simple?

Executing the test cases

Using the Angular CLI is fairly easy to execute our test case. We just run the following command in our Terminal, and Karma will launch the browser and execute all the test cases in our application:

```
ng test
```

If we now run our test case, we should see two test cases executed and passed, as shown in the following screenshot:

```
Custom Sort pipe
  should sort the task array
  should not sort the task array
```

These titles are clickable, which means that we can run our test case again by just selecting the specific test case.

Also, if you remember, we had an autoWatch flag set to true in our karma.config.js file, which means that now if you change anything in your test case, Karma will automatically execute the test cases.

Writing test cases for the services class

Next up, let's look at our service class, and see how we can write a test for it. Every project you work on that will require data from some other system will have a service class, which will be using HTTP to make the web service call.

So, if we want to write a unit test for our service class, we would need to mock the HTTP and any other external dependencies our service class would have.

Creating a new file

Let's first create a new file, trello.service.spec.ts, in our services folder. All our test cases for the Trello service will be written in this file.

Our Trello service has only one function right now, that is, to fetch the boards from the JSON file using the HTTP GET method. We use promises here to fetch the response and return a success or a failed promise. If we look in our function, we have two code flows that would require testing: one to check if we already have boards in our public variable, and the second to make an HTTP call if we did not have the boards.

Again, there can be multiple unit tests that can be written for this class, but we will focus on two test cases: one to check if we do not have a board object and HTTP also does not return any board objects, and the second would be where we already have a board object and we will check that we receive the same object back.

Writing the test case

The first step being the `import` statements, we will be importing the `Trello` service and `Board` class. Also, because we know that our HTTP returns a promise, which is basically a wrapper around the observables, we will import those as well, as shown in the following snippet:

```
import {TrelloService} from './trello.service';
import { Observable } from 'rxjs/Observable';
import { Board } from '../model/board';
```

The describe function

In our `describe` function, we will create properties for `Trello` service, `Board` array, which we expect to be returned from the function. Also, we will need to mock the `Trello` service class dependencies, which in this case is HTTP. The following is our `describe` function:

```
describe('Trello HTTP Service',() =>{
  let trelloService: TrelloService;
  let mockHTTP;
  let fakeBoards:Board[];
});
```

As we can see here, we are just declaring the properties, and not initializing them. That will be done inside the `beforeEach` function.

The beforeEach function

By now, we know that the primary purpose of the `beforeEach` function is to provide us with the place where we write the code that we want to be executed after every test. This allows us to make sure that each test is performed in isolation, and not affected by the result of the previous step.

In our `Trello` service test, the `beforeEach` function would mock the HTTP object and create an instance of the `Trello` service class, as shown in the following code:

```
beforeEach(()=>{
  mockHTTP = jasmine.createSpyObj('mockHTTP',['get']);
  trelloService = new TrelloService(mockHTTP);
});
```

The first line of the `beforeEach` function is interesting.

To be able to mock the HTTP object, we would need a way to also mock the methods inside the object. Else, when we call the function, the test case would not be able to return the expected result.

Jasmine provides us with a `createSpyObject` function, which basically creates a dummy object of the type we define, and also provides a dummy function to it so that when the parent method uses the dummy object, `mockHTTP` in this case, it is able to find the `GET` method. But, what about returning the result from a `GET` method? We will look at this inside the `it` function.

The second line is straightforward, where we just create an instance of the `Trello` service class and pass the `mockHTTPP` object to it.

The it function

Our first `it` function is pretty straightforward, where we check if there is no JSON object, do we get the board object as undefined? As we know in our `Trello` service code, if the `Board` array object is undefined, we would make an HTTP call. That's what we will do in our test case.

The following is our code for the first test case:

```
it('get Boards undefined', ()=>{
mockHTTP.get.and.returnValue(Observable.of(fakeBoards));
trelloService.getBoardsWithPromises().then(boards => this.boards =
boards);
expect(fakeBoards).toBeUndefined();
});
```

The first line inside our `it` function is another feature of Jasmine. In our `beforeEach` function, we had created the `mockHTTP` object using Jasmine's `createspy` object. There, we also define that our `mockHTTP` object will have a `GET` function. But, we still need to tell Jasmine what this `GET` function should return when we call the `mockHTTP` function.

This is what we are doing on our first line. We tell Jasmine that when the `GET` function is called, return a value of type boards array wrapper in an observable. So, when the second line of our `it` function executes and we call the `getBoardsWithPromises` function, Jasmine makes sure that it returns an observable of type `Board` array on the HTTP call.

As we have not initialized this board array, the returned value would be undefined, which is what we tested in our third line inside the `expect` statement.

If we had initialized our `fakeBoards` object before, we would have set that as the return value, then our `expect` statement would have received a defined boards array object, as shown in the following code:

```
it('get Boards undefined',()=>{
fakeBoards = new Array();
mockHTTP.get.and.returnValue(Observable.of(fakeBoards));
trelloService.getBoardsWithPromises().then(boards => this.boards =
boards);
expect(fakeBoards).toBeDefined();
});
```

This shows that with Jasmine we have the flexibility to not only mock an object, but also let that mocked object return a value that we can use in our unit test.

The next test case we have is where we assign a board object to the property of the `Trello` service. In this case, the expected behavior would be that we will go through the `else` code flow of our `getBoardsWithPromises` function. The following is the code for our `it` function, in this case:

```
it('get Boards',()=>{
trelloService.Boards = new Array();
trelloService.Boards.push({
id:0,
title:'Test Board',
task:[]
});
mockHTTP.get.and.returnValue(Observable.of(trelloService.Boards));
trelloService.getBoardsWithPromises().then(boards => {
fakeBoards = boards;
expect(fakeBoards).toBeDefined();
expect(fakeBoards[0].title).toEqual('Test Board');
});
})
```

Here, we first create a new board array object and assign that to the `Trello` service board object. Next, we call our function, and inside the `then` promise function we have our `expect` statements to check if we received the correct object back.

It's important to note that the `expect` function, in this case, is inside the `then` function of the promise because we want to make sure our `expect` is only executed after we have the promise returned from the calling function. If we had our `expect` function outside the `then` promise function, then the `expect` function would be called before the promise would have returned, which would cause the test case to always fail.

Writing test cases for isolated component

The unique thing about components with respect to services and pipes is that the components interact with the user interface. Components have a template that can alter the state of the component and its properties, and in the similar fashion, components may alter the content of the user interface.

So, to test components, we can employ two different strategies:

- Test components in isolation, which means we test components in a similar fashion as the services and pipes. We do not consider the template part of the component and neither test those. This approach is useful if we just want to test the logic that resides in the component. But this way, we may not get the comprehensive test cases for our components.
- Test components end-to-end. In this case, we test components in conjunction with their template. This way, we can test the impact of a change happening in component logic on its template.

In this section, we have looked at the first point where we test the component in isolation. In the next section, we will focus on testing the component end-to-end.

Creating a new file

For this test, we will use our board component. If you created the board component using the Angular CLI, then you will already have a corresponding `spec` file in your folder, as shown in the following screenshot:

```
    ◢ board
      # board.component.css
      <> board.component.html
      TS board.component.spec.ts
      TS board.component.ts
```

If not, create a new file called `board.component.spec.ts`, where we will add our test cases.

Our board component performs a lot of operations, such as adding a new task, modifying the board title, modifying existing tasks, and much more. We can create many test cases for each of these functionalities, but for our purposes, we will focus on the `addTask` functionality and write a couple of test cases around that.

Writing the test case

If you review the `addTask` method, you will notice that the logic we have is to fetch the total length of the already existing task, and increment it by 1 to create a new ID for a new task. Then we add this new task to the list of existing tasks in our board object.

So, we will write two test cases. One will be to add the first task in our board object, and the other will add a task to the already existing list. These test cases are very simple, and the purpose of us choosing these test cases is to make sure we focus on how to write test cases, rather than focusing on the content of the test case itself.

By now, we know that the first step is adding the required `import` statements, and the following is the code for our board component `spec` file:

```
import { BoardComponent } from './board.component';
import { Board } from '../model/board'
```

Because we are creating isolated test cases, our imports are restricted to classes for which we want to create the object.

Implementing the test cases

The board component has multiple dependencies, namely:

- Element reference to refer to the HTML elements
- `ActivatesRoute` to fetch the routing values
- `Trello` service to `GET` and `Update` the board object

So, we would need to mock all these for us to effectively test the board component. Because we are only focused on testing the add task functionality, which does not use any of these dependencies, we will just create the mocks of these dependencies, but not the spy objects like we did in our testing of the `Trello` service class.

Similarly, in the `beforeEach` function, the only thing we will do is create an instance of the board component and pass these mock dependencies, as shown in the following code:

```
describe('BoardComponent', () => {
 let boardComponent: BoardComponent;
 let mockElementRef,mockRoute,mockTrelloService;
 beforeEach(() => {
 boardComponent = new BoardComponent(mockElementRef, mockRoute,
mockTrelloService);
 });
});
```

Next up are our two test cases where we test the add task functionality. The following is the code for both `it` functions we implemented:

```
it('test add new task to existing task', ()=>{
   boardComponent.addtaskText = "Dummy";
   boardComponent.board = new Board();
   boardComponent.board.id = 1;
   boardComponent.board.title = "Board 1";
   boardComponent.board.task = new Array();
   boardComponent.board.task.push({
   id:1,
   title:'task1',
   subtask: [],
   taskheaderId:"1"});
   boardComponent.addtask();
   expect(boardComponent.board.task.length).toBe(2);
});
it('test add first task ', ()=>{
   boardComponent.addtaskText = "Dummy";
   boardComponent.board = new Board();
```

```
boardComponent.board.id = 1;
boardComponent.board.title = "Board 1";
boardComponent.board.task = new Array();
boardComponent.addtask();
expect(boardComponent.board.task.length).toBe(1);
expect(boardComponent.board.task[0].id).toBe(1);
expect(boardComponent.board.task[0].title).toBe('Dummy');
});
```

As we can see in the first `it` function, *test add new task to existing task*, we first initialize the existing board object in our board component class and also define a new task as *test task*, then we just call the `addTask` function. Our `expect` in this case only checks for the length of the `task` array in our board component. We can very well have multiple `expects` here to check the `title`, `id`, or any other criterion.

In the second test case, we assume that the board does not have any existing tasks, and that we are creating a new task. The test case is very similar to the first one, with the exception that we check the length is `1`. This test case allows us to make sure there are no exceptions in our code if we are creating the first task. Also, you will see that we have multiple `expect` statements in this test case to verify multiple parameters.

Writing the test cases for integrated components

In this section, we will focus on writing our component end-to-end test. We will look at how we can integrate the template into our testing of components. Integrated tests are complex to write when compared to the isolated test, primarily because now we don't just want a standard component object like we created in the previous section, but we also need a component object that is integrated to the template so that both can be tested together.

The most complex thing in implementing the integrated test is the setup part, because it is here we do the initialization of our component and its dependencies.

Though complex, integrated tests provide us with some unique advantages, as follows:

- Testing the bindings, which is not possible in the isolated test. Some of the bindings may be very simple, and it may not add value to create an integrated test for them. For the components where we have complex bindings, having the integrated test is very useful.

- Identifying issues when writing tests rather than later. If we test the components isolated, we are assuming that the respective templates are working fine, which may pose a problem for a medium to large-scale application. In these types of applications, it's important that we have integrated tests because they can help us make sure that if any logic in a component changes, it does not break any bindings on the template.
- Having integrated tests allows us to write code where we can identify and fix template-related bugs quickly and efficiently.

Setting up the integrated test

In the case of an integrated test, we don't need an instance of a component—the one that we had created in the last section. Here, we need a component that has an associated template and is included in a module so that we can load the component and test its binding as well.

To be able to create such an instance of a component, we will have a very different setup compared to the setup we had earlier for `BoardComponent`, when we wrote an isolated test. We will be writing our integrated test cases for the home page component.

The first step is the `import` statements, which we need for our test cases. The following is the first `import` statement that we need:

```
import { async, ComponentFixture, TestBed } from '@angular/core/testing';
```

Angular provides us with a special library for testing under the `angular/core/testing` module. We import the following items from this library:

- `TestBed`: For Angular to create our component, it uses this utility. The `TestBed` has a responsibility of creating a template and associating that with the respective component. It also creates a module that holds the component we are testing.
- `async`: This is a helper function that we use to convert our asynchronous operation into asynchronous operation in the `beforeEach` method. We will look at it when we write our `beforeEach` function.
- `ComponentFixture`: The `ComponentFixture` is a type that is used by the tested function. When we create our component using `TestBed`, it returns the component of type `ComponentFixture`.

Next, we will include the import for our `Homepage` component that we are going to test. Let's look at the `Homepage` component's constructor, as shown in the following line of code:

```
constructor(private _trelloService:TrelloService,private _router: Router) {
}
```

As we can see, the `Homepage` component is dependent on two services:

- `Trello` service, so we will import the `Trello` service as well
- Router service, which is an Angular service, so we will import that also

All these imports are shown together in the following code snippet:

```
import { async, ComponentFixture, TestBed } from '@angular/core/testing';
import { RouterModule } from '@angular/router';
import { HomepageComponent } from './homepage.component';
import{TrelloService} from '../services/trello.service';
```

At this point, these are the minimum imports that we require for our integrated test. We will be adding a few more imports as we start working on our test case.

Implementing the test cases

Our `HomeComponent` has the following functionalities:

- `ngOnInit` to fetch all the boards available and bind them to our local board array object
- Add new board functionality, where we create a new board with zero tasks and the board title as `New Board`

So, we will write three test cases to cover basic scenarios for these two functionalities. Our test cases will cover the following things:

- Check if the component is created successfully
- Add two boards and check if those boards have been added in the component and displayed on the template
- Create a new board and check if the board is displayed on the UI

Here, we see that in an integrated test we can also check the UI to confirm if the bindings are working as expected.

The integrated test cases require a few extra steps to get an instance of a component, and we will look at those steps now.

The describe function

In our `describe` function we just have two lines of code, as follows:

```
let component: HomepageComponent;
let fixture: ComponentFixture<HomepageComponent>;
```

The first one is just a definition for our `Homepage` component; the second line is interesting.

We create a fixture for our component and pass in the type, which, in this case, is `HomepageComponent`. The fixture is basically a wrapper around the component that provides additional features that we would not otherwise have if we just create an instance of the component. These features include change detection and access to the HTML elements of the component template.

First beforeEach function

The `beforeEach` function will be the one where we will create our component and its module. We will also define the dependencies and their behavior. In the case of an integrated test, we normally have two `beforeEach` functions: one to initialize the module, and another to create the component. The following is the code for the former one:

```
beforeEach(async(() => {
  let mockTrelloService={
    getBoardsWithPromises:()=>Observable.of([]).toPromise()};
  TestBed.configureTestingModule({
    declarations: [ HomepageComponent ],
    imports:[RouterModule.forRoot([])],
      providers: [{provide: APP_BASE_HREF, useValue: '/'},
      {provide: TrelloService, useValue:mockTrelloService}]
  })
  .compileComponents();
}));
```

Let's first look at the second line inside the `beforeEach` function. Here, we use a function of the `TestBed` utility to create the module. The `configureTestingModule` function is responsible for creating a module and defining the dependencies to the module. If you remember the `app.module` file, there we had `ngModule`; this function also creates a similar module.

The module will have same properties, as we see in the code:

- Declarations that define the component that will be associated with the module.
- Imports, which identify the modules that we import here. In this case, it's `Router` module, because our `Homepage` component has a dependency on the `Router` module. We have just added the blank route in our imports because we are not really testing the routing, and the component would be satisfied with just the route object.
- Providers, which define the external dependencies such as services and the base `href` link. Each provider object has two properties, `provide` and `useValue`. The `provide` property tells us which dependency is needed, and `useValue` tells us which object or value should replace this dependency.

The `configureTestingModule` function is an asynchronous function, but we want it to be executed synchronously because we want to make sure that the module is created before our test cases are executed. To be able to do that, we wrap this function inside another function, as we saw in the definition of `beforeEach`. The `async` function allows us to convert the asynchronous to a synchronous operation, which is why we imported `async` in the first place.

Now, let's look at the first line of code in our `beforeEach`. Here, we are creating a `mockTrelloService` object, which would be used in place of the original one. We know that from this service class we use one method, `getBoardsWithPromises`, which returns a promise of board type. So, to make sure that when the `Homepage` component ends up making a call to this method in `mockTrelloService` we return a promise of type board array, we assigned a blank array as the return value of this method.

To handle these changes, we also need to include a couple more imports for the base; HREF, `Observables`, and a promise wrapper, as shown in the following code:

```
import { APP_BASE_HREF } from '@angular/common';
import { Observable } from 'rxjs/Observable';
import 'rxjs/add/operator/toPromise';
```

The last line in our `beforeEach` function is a chained function to our `TestBed`, `compileComponents`, which has to be called to compile to a component with the template and add to the module.

Second beforeEach function

Now, we have created our module and added the component and its dependencies. The next step is to create the component and get an instance of it. For this, we write a second `beforeEach` function, as shown in the following code:

```
beforeEach(() => {
fixture = TestBed.createComponent(HomepageComponent);
component = fixture.componentInstance;
fixture.detectChanges();
});
```

Here, we see that we are doing three things:

- Creating the `Homepage` component and assigning that to the component fixture.
- Then, accessing the component object from the component fixture and assigning it to the component variable.
- Calling the `detectChanges` method in the component fixture. As we mentioned earlier, the component fixture provides extra features, and one of them is to detect the changes. We always need to call the `detectChanges` method after we make any change to refresh the UI of the component while testing, because Angular cannot detect the changes directly.

The it functions

As we mentioned earlier, we will have three test cases for our `Homepage` component. The first one will just check if we were able to create the component successfully. The code for this is shown here:

```
it('should be created', () => {
expect(component).toBeTruthy();
});
```

As you can see, it just checks if the component exists using the `toBeTruthy` matcher. Whenever we write an integrated test, this test case should always be executed. This test case allows us to make sure that the component instance we have created and the dependencies we have defined are all correct and nothing is missing.

Check boards on the user interface

In this test case, we will see how we test end-to-end from component to the template. The purpose of this test is to have a couple of boards and then we check if the boards are available on the user interface and also in the component property.

The following is the code for this test case:

```
it('should have 2 boards', () => {
    component.boards= new Array();
    component.boards.push({
        id:1,
        task:[],
        title:'Board 1'
    },
    {
        id:2,
        task:[],
        title:'Board 2'
    })

    fixture.detectChanges();
    const compiled = fixture.debugElement.nativeElement;

    let title = compiled.querySelectorAll('.title') ;
    expect(title[1].textContent).toContain('Board 2');

    expect(component.boards.length).toBe(2);
});
```

The first thing we do is create a board array inside the component object and populate it with two boards. For our current testing purpose, we did not add any tasks to them, but you can try to add a task and check those as well.

Next, we call the detectChanges method because we need to make sure these new boards are reflected in the UI as well. The detectChanges method will call Angular to refresh its binding for all the properties.

In the next line, we use the functions of the component fixture object to fetch the elements from the template. The debugElement is the root element that is associated with the component template, and the nativeElement provides the handle to the template from the root.

Once we have the handle to the template, we can call the standard UI APIs to fetch any element, and look inside for its value. Here, first we check for the HTML elements that have `title` as a class property and fetch all. Once we have those, we can loop through and check for the `textContent` property of those elements to confirm if our boards were bound successfully.

In the last line, we are checking to make sure that the board object in our component class has two boards.

Test new board creation

The last test case we have is to test the *add board* functionality. Here, we will check if a new board is added to the UI successfully. The following is the code for the test case:

```
it('create a new board',()=>{
  component.addBoard();
  fixture.detectChanges();
  expect(component.boards.length).toBe(1);
  const compiled = fixture.debugElement.nativeElement;
  let title = compiled.querySelectorAll('.title') ;
  expect(title.length).toBe(2);
  expect(title[0].textContent).toContain('New Board');
});
```

Here, we first call the `addBoard` method on our component, and then to make sure that Angular refreshes its bindings, we call the `detectChanges` method.

Once done, we assert the `expect` statements to check if the number of boards is equal to `1`, and that there are two elements with class type `title`.

One of them will have the content as *new board,* which will be the board we added.

Test cases for other components

In the previous section, we focused on writing the integrated test for the `Homepage` component, and isolated test cases for the board component. But, we have made sure for other components, namely `Task` and `Subtask`, that we have baseline integrated test cases.

Both the `Task` and `Subtask` components have their respective test files with all the required test fixtures and integration steps implemented.

Also, these components have one standard test case to check if the component is created successfully. We encourage you to use the learning from this chapter and create more test cases as a practice.

You can find all the code on our GitHub link at `https://github.com/sachinohri/SampleTrelloApplication`.

Summary

In this chapter, we learned about writing test cases in our Angular application. All these test cases were written on top of our *Sample Trello* application. We wrote test cases for pipes, services, isolated components, and integrated components. We learned about the library support Angular provides for us to write test cases.

We looked at the tools that are used to write the test cases, Jasmine and Karma. We also looked at how we can set up these tools, although by using the Angular CLI we get all the tools automatically set up and configured. We will be looking at the Angular CLI and its features extensively in the next chapter.

8
Trello - Using Angular CLI

In Chapter 2, *Our First Application – Sports News Combinator*, we discussed how to create an application without Angular CLI, and it had multiple steps that needed to go perfectly for us to have a bare minimum application up and running. Angular CLI does that for us and does it in the easiest possible manner. For both our applications, *Sports News Combinator* and *Trello*, we used Angular CLI to get the application off the ground.

The Angular CLI can do much more than what we have seen so far in the preceding chapters. It can be used for creating a new project and adding components, services, and modules, and provides features such as building, testing, and linting your application, all of which we will see in this chapter.

We will focus on the following topics in this chapter:

- An introduction to Angular CLI, where we'll learn what Angular CLI is and why it should be used
- We will then look at how to create an application using Angular CLI and the files that it generates
- Then we will look at the option of generating components, services, pipes, modules, and routing
- From there, we will focus our attention on how Angular CLI provides options for linting, building, and serving the application
- At the end, we will look at the testing features of Angular CLI

So, let's get started!

Introducing Angular CLI

Developing a web application is a challenging task in itself and making sure that the application follows best practices and is consistent puts additional load on the developer. Angular CLI tries to solve the latter part of these challenges. It's a command-line interface which helps in building, managing, and enforcing the best practices for an Angular application.

Whether you are part of a 1-2 member team or a 10-20 member team, the challenges of creating and managing an application exist for all. We need to make sure that everyone, including us, uses the following:

- Predefined best practices
- Correct naming conventions for our code
- Optimized build scripts
- Folder structure
- Test structure

The Angular team answered and solved these problems by developing Angular CLI.

Apart from Angular CLI, there are many seed projects which can help you get started with developing an Angular application. These projects will have a basic folder structure, some may have a build configuration as well, but one problem they present is that all of them will have different ways to generate and develop an Angular application.

Angular CLI from the Angular team tries to make sure that it integrates all the accepted industry best practices and allows an interface to develop applications efficiently. Angular CLI provides features such as the following:

- Creating an application with a recommended style guide
- Building and serving the application in both dev and prod mode
- Integrating tests for each component, services, and pipes
- Allowing linting to make sure the application is consistent with the design

Setting up Angular CLI

Before we start using Angular CLI, we need to install it from npm. Angular CLI is a node module, hence to install CLI we need node.

If you don't have Node.js on your machine, you can easily install it from the official Node.js website, `https://nodejs.org/en/`.

You can confirm that the node has been installed properly by using the following command:

```
node -v
```

This command will output the current version of node installed.

Once you have Node.js, next you need to run following command to install the Angular CLI:

```
npm install -g @angular/cli
```

This command will install the Angular CLI globally (based on the -g flag) on our machine. Once installed, like Node.js, you can check the version of Angular CLI installed on your machine by using the following command:

```
ng -v
```

`ng` is a command for Angular and v will provide the current version installed. You should have an output similar to the following:

```
     _                      _                 ____ _     ___
    / \   _ __   __ _ _   _| | __ _ _ __     / ___| |   |_ _|
   / △ \ | '_ \ / _` | | | | |/ _` | '__|   | |   | |    | |
  / ___ \| | | | (_| | |_| | | (_| | |      | |___| |___ | |
 /_/   \_\_| |_|\__, |\__,_|_|\__,_|_|       \____|_____|___|
                |___/
@angular/cli: 1.2.0
node: 6.11.0
os: darwin x64
```

Angular CLI help command

When you are starting to use Angular CLI for the first time , the `help` command is one of the most useful commands available.

This command provides you with a list of all the options that are available in Angular CLI and their default values as well. The `help` command is as follows:

```
ng --help
```

The result of this command will not fit on a page, so the following is just a snapshot of it:

```
ng build <options...>
  Builds your app and places it into the output path (dist/ by default).
  aliases: b
  --target (String) (Default: development) Defines the build target.
    aliases: -t <value>, -dev (--target=development), -prod (--target=production), --target <value>
  --environment (String) Defines the build environment.
    aliases: -e <value>, --environment <value>
  --output-path (Path) Path where output will be placed.
    aliases: -op <value>, --outputPath <value>
  --aot (Boolean) Build using Ahead of Time compilation.
    aliases: -aot
```

You will notice the `help` command listed all the options, such as `ng build`, `ng generate`, `ng new`, `ng test`, and many more. We will be looking at of all these in this chapter.

We can then even delve into a specific option and look at its help, such as using the following command for `ng new`:

```
ng new --help
```

This command will only show the help for the `ng new` command. The `ng new` command is used for generating the initial application, as shown in the following screenshot:

```
ng new <options...>
  Creates a new directory and a new Angular app eg. "ng new [name]".
  aliases: n
  --dry-run (Boolean) (Default: false) Run through without making any changes. Will list all files that would have been created when running "ng new".
    aliases: -d, --dryRun
  --verbose (Boolean) (Default: false) Adds more details to output logging.
    aliases: -v, --verbose
  --skip-install (Boolean) (Default: false) Skip installing packages.
    aliases: -si, --skipInstall
  --skip-git (Boolean) (Default: false) Skip initializing a git repository.
    aliases: -sg, --skipGit
  --skip-tests (Boolean) (Default: false) Skip creating spec files.
    aliases: -st, --skipTests
  --skip-commit (Boolean) (Default: false) Skip committing the first commit to git.
    aliases: -sc, --skipCommit
  --directory (String) The directory name to create the app in.
    aliases: -dir <value>, --directory <value>
  --source-dir (String) (Default: src) The name of the source directory. You can later change the value in ".angular-cli.json" (apps[0].root).
    aliases: -sd <value>, --sourceDir <value>
  --style (String) (Default: css) The style file default extension. Possible values: css, scss, less, sass, styl(stylus). You can later change the value in ".angular-cli.json" (defaults.styleExt).
    aliases: --style <value>
  --prefix (String) (Default: app) The prefix to use for all component selectors. You can later change the value in ".angular-cli.json" (apps[0].prefix).
    aliases: -p <value>, --prefix <value>
  --routing (Boolean) (Default: false) Generate a routing module.
    aliases: --routing
  --inline-style (Boolean) (Default: false) Should have an inline style.
    aliases: -is, --inlineStyle
  --inline-template (Boolean) (Default: false) Should have an inline template.
    aliases: -it, --inlineTemplate
  --minimal (Boolean) (Default: false) Should create a minimal app.
    aliases: --minimal
```

Generating an application with Angular CLI

Let's first start by creating an Angular application using Angular CLI by using the following command:

```
ng new trello-app --skip-install
```

This command will create a new folder on your machine with the name `trello-app`, as shown in the following screenshot:

```
installing ng
  create .editorconfig
  create README.md
  create src/app/app.component.css
  create src/app/app.component.html
  create src/app/app.component.spec.ts
  create src/app/app.component.ts
  create src/app/app.module.ts
  create src/assets/.gitkeep
  create src/environments/environment.prod.ts
  create src/environments/environment.ts
  create src/favicon.ico
  create src/index.html
  create src/main.ts
  create src/polyfills.ts
  create src/styles.css
  create src/test.ts
  create src/tsconfig.app.json
  create src/tsconfig.spec.json
  create src/typings.d.ts
  create .angular-cli.json
  create e2e/app.e2e-spec.ts
  create e2e/app.po.ts
  create e2e/tsconfig.e2e.json
  create .gitignore
  create karma.conf.js
  create package.json
  create protractor.conf.js
  create tsconfig.json
  create tslint.json
Project 'trello-app' successfully created.
```

As the preceding screenshot shows, Angular CLI created a bunch of files for our application, including the `app` files and configuration files.

`flag --skip-install`, which we used in the above command, informs the Angular CLI that we don't want to run the `npm install` command to download all the `node` modules. We will look at this and other flags in the next section.

File overview

Let's now open our application in Visual Studio Code and look at the files that were generated:

As we can see, there are a bunch of files which were generated by Angular CLI. There is an `src` folder that contains our application code under the `app` folder, the application-level files such as `main.ts`, `style.css`, `tsconfig`, and `typing` files. The following are some of the important files and their significance:

- **Editor config**: This file provides us with configuration for how we want our code structured with respect to spacing. We can configure the indent size to be based on the style guide we want to follow in our application.
- **git ignore**: This file provides rules on which files and folders need to be checked in to the Git and which not. We would not want to check in our `node` module folder in the Git and would prefer that the user installs the packages when they download the code.
- **Karma config**: We saw this file in the last chapter when we discussed testing our *Trello* application. The Karma config file allows us to configure our test case framework.
- **Package JSON**: This file will have a list of all dependencies that we need to run our application. If we had not used the `--skip-install` flag, the Angular CLI would have used `npm install` to install all the dependencies defined in this file. The dependency version would normally be the latest, most stable version of those packages. If you add or modify any package information in this file, you can then run the `npm install` command to install that package in our `node` module.
- **Protractor**: This file is used by Angular CLI to run the end-to-end test cases.
- **tsconfig:** This file is a used by TypeScript to configure the compiler options. We can configure things such as base URL, target compilation, and much more.
- **tsLint:** This file defines the rules for linting, which can help in enforcing standard code conventions and the style guide.
- **Angular CLI JSON:** This file is used by Angular CLI to configure the rules which we want to follow when generating our application components. We will look at this in-depth in the next section.
- **src\index.html:** This is our launch file. In Angular applications, the `index.html` file serves as the base file on which all the components are loaded.
- **src\main.ts:** The `main.ts` file serves as the entry point of the application. Angular defines the bootstrapping logic in this file.
- **src\tsconfig:** There are a couple of `tsconfig` files(`tsconfig.app` and `tsconfig.spec`) which are used to define the local TypeScript compiler options.

ng new – flags and customization

In the previous section, we created our *Trello* app with the default flag. Apart from a `skip-install` flag which tells the CLI not to run `npm` install the packages, all other flags were taken with a default value. If you run the `ng new --help` command, you will see there are many flags which can be configured when generating an application. Let's look briefly at these flags:

- `dry run`: This tells the CLI whether we want to generate the files or just list the files which would be generated. This command is very helpful if we just want to check which files and folders will be created by the CLI rather than actually creating them. This command is normally used when you are trying multiple configurations to see which suits your need.
- `skip install`: We saw this flag earlier; it makes sure that the application files are generated, but not the `node` module, and no packages are downloaded.
- `skip git`: Angular CLI, by default, initializes the local Git for the project. If we don't want that then we can set the value of this flag to `true`.
- `skip tests`: As the name suggests, this flag make sure that CLI does not generate any content/files related to tests. Ideally, you should never turn off this flag and have the test cases validate the function behavior.
- `style`: This flag defines the extension of the style files; by default, it's CSS but we can change it to Sass or LESS.
- `prefix`: By default, when we generate any component, the component selector is named as `app-*`, where * is the name of the component. In production, this may not be the convention you want to follow. You may want to make sure all your component selectors have a specific prefix; for example, in our application, we would want all our components to have a prefix of `trello-*`. Using this flag, we can assign the value and whenever CLI generates a component, it will use this prefix for the selector.
- `routing`: When we created our application above, there was no routing information generated by Angular CLI, just the app component and the module files. But, most of the time, we will need the routing logic in our application to be able to navigate between components. The Angular CLI provides the `routing` flag, which is `false` by default but when set to `true` generates the respective files for routing and stitches them with the default `NgModule`.

Customizing the app

Now, let's create our app again using the CLI with the flags which we discussed earlier.

We will create our application with routing enabled, a component selector as `trello`, and the style defined with sass rather than CSS. The following is the command which we will use:

```
ng new trello-app --skip-git true --style sass --prefix trello --routing
true --dry-run
```

Here, we used `dry-run` so that we can see what Angular CLI will generate rather than creating it on the HDD. Also, note that because we have used the `dry-run` flag, the CLI also does not run `npm` install. The following is the output of the command:

```
You specified the dry-run flag, so no changes will be written.
  create .editorconfig
  create README.md
  create src/app/app-routing.module.ts
  create src/app/app.component.sass
  create src/app/app.component.html
  create src/app/app.component.spec.ts
  create src/app/app.component.ts
  create src/app/app.module.ts
  create src/assets/.gitkeep
  create src/environments/environment.prod.ts
  create src/environments/environment.ts
  create src/favicon.ico
  create src/index.html
  create src/main.ts
  create src/polyfills.ts
  create src/styles.sass
  create src/test.ts
  create src/tsconfig.app.json
  create src/tsconfig.spec.json
  create src/typings.d.ts
  create .angular-cli.json
  create e2e/app.e2e-spec.ts
  create e2e/app.po.ts
  create e2e/tsconfig.e2e.json
  create karma.conf.js
  create package.json
  create protractor.conf.js
  create tsconfig.json
  create tslint.json
Project 'trello-app' successfully created.
```

As we see in the first line, the CLI gives a warning that `no changes will written`. Another thing which you can notice right away is the `app-routing.module.ts` file; we will look at this file but understand that this file was generated because we have the routing flag turned ON. Also, you can see that the style files we have are of the extension `sass` and not `css`. Angular CLI uses webpack as a build system and it takes care of building the `sass` files into `css` and bundling them together for rendering.

Now, let's run the same command again but without the `dry-run` flag. This time, the CLI will generate the files on the hard drive and we can open our `Trello-App` folder in Visual Studio Code. If you want, you can add the `skip-install` flag to avoid running npm `install` and can later run npm install.

Let's look at `app-routing.module.ts` in the next section.

App routing file

The following is the code for the `app-routing.module.ts` file which was generated by Angular CLI:

```
import { NgModule } from '@angular/core';
import { Routes, RouterModule } from '@angular/router';
const routes: Routes = [
  {
  path: '',
  children: []
  }
];
@NgModule({
  imports: [RouterModule.forRoot(routes)],
  exports: [RouterModule]
})
export class AppRoutingModule { }
```

As we can see, Angular CLI created an `App` routing module and added route paths. Now, the CLI does not know which routes you want to define, hence the path is blank. But the CLI has done all the basic work for you to set up the routing and plug it into the `app` module, as can be seen in the following code from `app.module.ts`:

```
import { BrowserModule } from '@angular/platform-browser';
import { NgModule } from '@angular/core';

import { AppRoutingModule } from './app-routing.module';
import { AppComponent } from './app.component';
@NgModule({
```

```
declarations: [
AppComponent
],
imports: [</span>
BrowserModule,
AppRoutingModule
],
providers: [],
bootstrap: [AppComponent]
})
export class AppModule { }
```

Here, in the app module, we imported the routing module in the imports array. This has allowed us to have a basic minimum application up and running with the CLI.

Angular CLI file

The Angular CLI maintains all its configurations in the .angular-cli.json file found in the root folder. All the configurations we defined in the previous section when creating trello-app will be stored here. Let's look at some of the configurations in this file.

We start with the project name, which in our case is trello-app; this was the name we gave when we ran the ng new command.

Then we have an array of apps in the JSON file, as shown in the following code:

```
"apps": [
{
"root": "src",
"outDir": "dist",
"assets": [
"assets",
"favicon.ico"
],
"index": "index.html",
"main": "main.ts",
"polyfills": "polyfills.ts",
"test": "test.ts",
"tsconfig": "tsconfig.app.json",
"testTsconfig": "tsconfig.spec.json",
"prefix": "trello",
"styles": [
"styles.sass"
],
"scripts": [],
```

```
"environmentSource": "environments/environment.ts",
"environments": {
"dev": "environments/environment.ts",
"prod": "environments/environment.prod.ts"
}
}
],
```

Let's go through these tags:

- `Root`: This tag provides the configuration of where we want our code to be located. By default, it's the `src` folder, but you can configure it based on your preference.
- `outDir`: This provides the folder name where the code, when built, will be stored. So, if you run the `ng build` command, Angular CLI will build the application and put the files in the `dist` folder as defined in `outDir`. Then we can use the files in this folder and deploy the same.
- `Assets`: Here, we list the assets which we want to serve with the application.
- `Prefix`: This signifies the value which we used in our `ng new` command. Angular CLI uses this to prefix the component selector name.
- `Styles`: In our `ng new` command, we associated the `sass` file extension with our styles and that value is reflected here.
- `Environment`: This provides the path of the environment files we have to the dev and prod versions.

We have other tags, such as main, test, polyfills, and config; all these tags signify the path where the respective files will be placed.

As we can see, all the flags which we looked at in the `ng new` command can also be configured in the Angular CLI JSON file. This provides us with the flexibility to configure our application so that we can follow predefined best practices.

Generating files for the application

Once we have generated our application, the next step is to add features to our application. The feature can be a component or service or pipe, and Angular CLI provides us with the command, to generate these easily. As with the `generate` command for the application, these commands also have options for us to configure how we want to generate the files.

The Angular CLI provides one main command for generating the components, pipes, services, and classes as follows:

```
ng generate <<featureName>> <<fileName>> <<options>>
```

As we can see, the command is `ng generate` followed by the feature name, which can be a component, class, service, or pipe, followed by the name of the feature that we want, and then, at the end, the options. It is not mandatory to specify the options and if not specified, Angular CLI will take the default values of the options.

The `ng generate` command also has the same option of `dry-run` that we saw while generating the application, which can help us first see what we are generating before writing it to the hard drive.

Generating a component

The most common thing that is required in an Angular application is components. The following is the command for generating a component:

```
ng generate component homepage --dry-run
```

The output of the command is shown here:

```
You specified the dry-run flag, so no changes will be written.
  create src/app/homepage/homepage.component.css
  create src/app/homepage/homepage.component.html
  create src/app/homepage/homepage.component.spec.ts
  create src/app/homepage/homepage.component.ts
  update src/app/app.module.ts
```

As we can see, Angular CLI would create four files under the `src\app\homepage` folder: one for the component, another for the style, then one for the template, and lastly one for the test. Angular CLI would also create a `homepage` folder which would contain these files.

Also, we see that Angular CLI would update an existing file, `app.module.ts`. This is the `main` module file which has reference to all the files that Angular would need to load. Now you can run the same command again, this time without the `dry-run` flag, and generate the component.

Angular CLI also provide aliases for some of the commands just like the shorthand. For generating a component, we can use the following command for the same result:

```
ng g c homepage
```

g is an alias for generate and c is an alias for component.

Component options in Angular CLI

Let's look at the options provided by Angular CLI when generating the component. Remember that these options are not mandatory and if not specified, Angular CLI will use the default values.

The flat option

The flat option informs the Angular CLI whether the files to be created should reside in a separate folder or not. The default behavior is to have a folder for each component as we saw when we generated the component for Homepage. If we set the flag as true, Angular CLI will not create a folder and generate the files in the parent folder itself.

The recommended practice is to always have a separate folder for each component.

The inline-template option

There will be times when we may not want a separate template file for a component. Normally, we would want otherwise. This type of behavior should only be considered if you are writing a component that is very small in size with a minimal template associated with it.

The Angular CLI provides an inline-template option for us to configure this behavior. If set to true, we will have a component with a template defined in the component ts file.

The inline style option

The inline style option is similar to the inline-template option and is used to determine whether we want our style inline or in a separate file. The default behavior is that the styles are generated in a separate file.

The spec option

The `spec` option is used to configure whether we want to generate the test files along with the component files. By default, it is set to true, meaning the Angular CLI will generate a `*.spec.ts` file for writing test cases for the component.

Again, the recommended practice is to have the `spec` files and always write the test cases for our components.

Generating a service

For generating services using Angular CLI, we use the same command, `ng generate`, but rather than the component, we use the service as the command option as shown here:

```
ng generate service trello.service
```

If we want to write this command using an alias, it will come out as shown here:

```
ng g s trello.service
```

Here, `g` stands for `generate` and `s` for `service`.

If we run this command, we will see two files generated by Angular CLI, one for the service and the other for the `spec` file as shown here:

```
create src/app/trello.service.spec.ts
create src/app/trello.service.ts
WARNING Service is generated but not provided, it must be provided to be used
```

As we can see, there are two things that are different in the case of a service as compared to generating a component:

- The files were generated in the `root` folder rather in a separate folder as with components
- There is a warning at the last line; `Service is generated but not provided, it must be provided to be used`

Let's look at this in more detail.

Service options in Angular CLI

Similar to components, Angular CLI provides some options to configure when generating services.

The flat option

The `flat` option has the same meaning as in the case of components, the only difference being that the default value is `true`. That was the reason, when we ran the preceding command to generate the service, that the files were generated in the parent folder rather than in a new folder.

Normally, we would not want this behavior so it's better to have the flag set to `false` as shown here:

```
ng generate service trello.service --flat false
```

The spec option

The `spec` option is the same as we have in components. When turned off, Angular CLI will not generate the `spec` files for the service.

The module option

As we see on the previous page Angular CLI returned a warning when we generated the service. The warning states that "Service is generated but not provided, it must be provided to be used" which implies that the service we created is not referenced in any module and hence Angular may not be able to find it at runtime.

In Angular, we need to refer the service we create to either a component or a module to be able to access and use them. The Angular CLI does not know where you want to provide the said service; hence the warning message.

The `module` option is used to inform the CLI where to add the service reference, so if you want to add the service to the `app` module, we will add the following flag:

```
ng generate service trello.service --flat false --module app.module
```

When we run this command, Angular CLI will generate the service file in a separate folder and modify the `app.module` file to include the reference of the service in the `provider` tag as shown here:

```
create  src/app/trello/trello.service.spec.ts
create  src/app/trello/trello.service.ts
update  src/app/app.module.ts
```

Generating a pipe

Generating a pipe is similar to generating the component, as shown here:

```
ng generate pipe custom-sort.pipe --flat false
```

This command will generate the pipe and add the reference in the `app.module` file as well. Here also, if we don't specify the `flat` flag, Angular CLI will generate the pipe in the parent folder. If you have a separate folder, such as the `shared` folder in our case, where you will keep all your pipes, then you can navigate to that folder in the command line and then run the `generate` command without the `flat` flag.

We can use the `spec` and `module` flags similar to the way we saw in the cases of services and components.

Generating a module

In large-scale applications, we want to have multiple modules, with each module enclosing some related functionalities. Modules help us organize our code better and provide more reuse.

Angular CLI provides us with a command to generate a module as shown here:

```
ng generate module login
```

This command will create a new folder named `login` and generate a module in it with the name `login.module.ts`. In the output, you will see a similar warning to the one we saw when generating the services.

Providing the login module in the app module

We can very easily add the reference to our `login` module in the `app` module in the `imports` array. This is required for Angular to have a reference to the `login` module to load at the start of the application. The following is the code for `app.module`, to which we have added a reference to the `login` module:

```
import {LoginModule} from './login/login.module';
....
@NgModule({
 declarations: [
 AppComponent,
 HomepageComponent,
 CustomSortPipe
 ],
 imports: [
 BrowserModule,
 AppRoutingModule,
 LoginModule
 ],
 providers: [],
 bootstrap: [AppComponent]
})
```

As you can see, we have added the `LoginModule` into the `import` array.

Adding components, services, and more in the login module

Once we have our `login` module, if we generate a component or a service or a pipe that we want to be associated with this module, we can easily do that by providing the `module` flag.

So, if we want to create an `appLogin` component which should be registered with the `login` module, we can use the following command:

```
ng generate component appLogin --module login --dry-run
```

This will generate four files associated with `appLogin` as shown in the following screenshot:

```
create  src/app/app-login/app-login.component.css
create  src/app/app-login/app-login.component.html
create  src/app/app-login/app-login.component.spec.ts
create  src/app/app-login/app-login.component.ts
update  src/app/login/login.module.ts
```

The files are the `appLogin` component and its template, style, and test files. Also, we will see that the `login.module` file is updated with the reference to the `appLogin` component.

This allows us to segregate different features and functionalities in the module and keep all the changes consistent with the application.

Adding routing to the modules

When we created our application using the `ng new` command, we used a `routing` flag to add routing by default in our application. The Angular CLI looks at this flag and determines to generate a file for routing and adds a reference to that in the `app` module file.

Now, when we create a new module in our existing application, we have two options:

- Use the existing routing file to define routes for the components inside this new module
- Create separate routes for modules so that the code is cleaner and easier to manage

The Angular CLI provides us with a `routing` flag when generating the module, which informs the CLI to define separate routes for the said module.

Let's look at the command to generate the module with routing:

```
ng generate module login --routing true --dry-run
```

We can also write it using an alias as follows:

```
ng g m login -r true -d
```

Here, `r` signifies the routing and `d` signifies the dry run.

Both these commands will return the following result:

```
You specified the dry-run flag, so no changes will be written.
  create src/app/login/login-routing.module.ts
  create src/app/login/login.module.ts
  WARNING Module is generated but not provided, it must be provided to be used
```

Here, we see that, apart from the `login.module` file, we have one more file that will be generated, that is, `login-routing.module`.

This file will define all the routes for the `login` module, which will help keep the code maintainable.

Generating TypeScript files

So far, we have seen how we can generate Angular-related files such as components, services, modules, and pipes. Apart from these files, we also want to generate some standalone TypeScript files, such as our models and interfaces.

The Angular CLI provides us with options for creating such files as well.

Generating a class

The Angular CLI provides the following command to generate a class:

```
ng generate class board
```

This command will create the `board.ts` file in the parent folder, which we may not want in our case because our board class may represent a model or a business logic class to be placed in a specific folder. So, to be able to generate a class in a specific folder, we need to create a folder, navigate to said folder on our command line, and then run the command.

Generating an interface

Generating an interface is same as generating a class, with the difference being the command for `interface` rather than `class` as shown here:

```
ng generate interface IBoard
```

We can also use the alias for `generate` and `interface` as shown in the following command, which will result in the same output as the preceding command:

```
ng g i IBoard
```

Generating an enum

Similar to class and interface, we can generate an enum in a separate file with the following command:

```
ng generate enum taskEnum
```

This will generate a class with a blank enum defined, as shown here:

```
export enum taskEnum{
}
```

Normally, you will have multiple enums defined in a single class, for which you will then manually create a file.

Building an Angular app

The first step in application development is the setup, which we achieved using Angular CLI. Then comes writing the code, which we did in earlier chapters for our *Trello* application. Next up is building our code, for which Angular CLI provides some neat APIs.

The Angular CLI provides a host of options to build the application, such as building in the dev environment versus building in a production environment. Angular CLI uses webpack for building the application and we will see how webpack helps in managing the application and its dependencies.

The build process

There are a lot of steps that are executed when Angular CLI builds an application, steps which may differ based on whether we are building an application in dev mode or production mode. We may want to consider bundling, minification, and tree-shaking (the process of removing all the dead code when building) as some of the aspects when building in production mode, whereas when in dev mode, our focus will be on debugging and code efficiency.

Building an application consists of compiling the application to an output directory, bundling the application, and optimizing in the case of production builds.

The Angular CLI provide options to manage these differences.

The build command

The Angular CLI provides the following command to build our application:

```
ng build <<options>>
```

We can check all the options available with `ng build` by using the `help` option as shown in the following command:

```
ng build --help
```

When you run this command, you will see many options available; we will look at some of them in the following list:

- `Target`: This option defines the target of the build, meaning whether we want to build in development mode or in production mode. In the following section, we will look at how these two differ in more detail. For now, remember that there are quite a few things that Angular CLI does based on the target selected. The possible values are `development` and `production`.

- `Environment`: This flag informs Angular CLI which file to use for environment variables. So, we may have different URLs for our web services for dev and prod environments. These configurations can be persisted in the respective environment files under the environments folder in our application. By default, if we build our application in dev mode, then the CLI uses the `environment.ts` file, and in prod mode it uses the `environment.prod.ts` file. The possible values are `dev` and `prod`.

- `Output-Path`: The Angular CLI uses the path defined in the Angular CLI JSON file to copy the build files. If you look at our JSON file, there will be an `outDir` tag with a value of `dist`. This informs the Angular CLI to copy all the build files in the `dist` folder. But, with the `Output-Path` flag, we can change the path where we want to copy the files.

- `AOT`: Angular CLI handles the **Ahead-of-Time** (**AoT**) compilation for our application based on the target of the build. If we are building the application in dev mode, the value for AoT will be `false`, and `true` for prod target. But, with the `AOT` flag, we can configure the value for both build targets.

- Sourcemaps: The `sourcemap` files are used for debugging our TypeScript code. Browsers don't understand TypeScript, they just run the JavaScript that is transpiled for our TypeScript code. But, it may be a pain for us to debug the JavaScript when running an application on the browser. `sourcemaps` helps us solve this problem. With `sourcemaps` in our build, we will be able to debug the TypeScript file in the browser, which will then use the JavaScript generated to execute the code. `sourcemaps` is, by default, enabled in dev mode, but we can enable it in prod mode as well by setting the flag as `true`. The recommendation is to not turn on this flag in production mode because we may end up deploying `sourcemaps`, which may cause security issues.

- `Watch`: This flag allows the Angular CLI to run an automated build when there is any change in any of the source files. If set to `true`, whenever we modify our code, the CLI will detect the changes and run the build for us. This feature is very useful, especially in a large application code base, where we can get immediate feedback on the changes we do.

There are many more flags that we don't really use frequently; you can explore them using the `help` command.

Building the application in dev mode

Now, let's build our *Trello* application and see what Angular CLI does. To build our application, from the command line, navigate to the path where you have the code. Building an application in dev mode is the default behavior of the `ng build` command so we can just run the following command in our Terminal:

```
ng build
```

When you run this command, you will see Angular CLI building the code and then the result of the build as shown here:

```
Hash: d19423fc119a16741544
Time: 9607ms
chunk    {0} polyfills.bundle.js, polyfills.bundle.js.map (polyfills) 183 kB {4} [initial] [rendered]
chunk    {1} main.bundle.js, main.bundle.js.map (main) 34.9 kB {3} [initial] [rendered]
chunk    {2} styles.bundle.js, styles.bundle.js.map (styles) 11.7 kB {4} [initial] [rendered]
chunk    {3} vendor.bundle.js, vendor.bundle.js.map (vendor) 2.47 MB [initial] [rendered]
chunk    {4} inline.bundle.js, inline.bundle.js.map (inline) 0 bytes [entry] [rendered]
```

The Angular CLI created 10 files, 2 each for the inline, vendor, main, polyfill, and style bundles. One file is associated with the bundle and the second is for `sourcemaps`. If we had built the code in production mode, the source map files would not have been generated.

As we discussed earlier, the Angular CLI will place all the build files in the folder that is defined in the Angular CLI JSON file, which in our case is the `dist` folder.

Dist folder details

Let's navigate to the `dist` folder in our explorer and check the files that were generated by Angular CLI during the build process. The following is a screenshot of the `dist` folder:

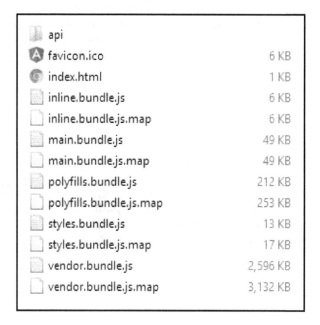

We will go through each file and understand the purpose of these files when running the application.

The API folder

In our *Trello* application, we are fetching the Boards and Tasks from a JSON file inside the API folder. To successfully run the application, we want to make sure that the file is served by Angular. This is done by defining the assets in the `assets` tag of the Angular CLI JSON file as shown in the following code snippet:

```
"assets": [
  "assets",
  "favicon.ico",
  "api/board/boards.json"
],
```

Here, we see in the last line that we have defined the path where our JSON file is placed. Apart from that, we have two more entries, one for the `assets` folder and one for the favicon. The Angular CLI uses this entry in the assets tag to determine which static files need to be served, which in our case is the `board.json` file.

Favicon

Similar to the API folder, Angular CLI served the favicon in the build because that was defined in the `assets` tag.

The index.html file

The `index.html` file is our launch file, which loads all the components when the application is executed. This file is also based on the `index` tag we have in our Angular CLI JSON file as shown here:

```
"index": "index.html",
```

If we had a different filename, Angular CLI would pick that file.

The inline bundle file

The inline bundle file is a webpack code which contains its runtime. This file is required because we use webpack to load our application and stitch everything together. The Angular CLI compiles the webpack into this one file, which is then used by the browser to render the application.

The main bundle file

This is the heart of our application. This file contains all our application code. The Angular CLI compiles all our code files and concatenates them together in the main bundle file. If you open this file, you will be able to see all our code, the `Board` component, the `Task` component, the `SubTask` component, and even our `Trello` service, and custom sort pipe as shown in the following snippet:

```
....
var BoardComponent = (function () {
  function BoardComponent(el, _route, _trelloService) {
  this.el = el;
  this._route = _route;
  this._trelloService = _trelloService;
  this.board = new __WEBPACK_IMPORTED_MODULE_3__model_board__["a" /* Board
  */];
  this.tasksAdded = 0;
  this.editingTitle = false;
  }
  ....
```

There are a couple of differences that you will notice in this code. First, this is not TypeScript code but JavaScript code, compiled by Angular CLI. Second, there is a reference to `__WebPack`; this is integrated with the webpack API and is then used to load the application.

The polyfill bundle file

The purpose of the polyfill is to handle the quirks of different browsers when running our application. Angular uses polyfill to make sure that there is support in each browser for the actions we are performing.

Some browsers may not have a specific functionality implemented and, to be able to handle the behavior consistently, the polyfill code helps.

The style bundle file

This file will consist of all the styles we have used in our application. The Angular CLI bundles all the styles in one file for easy download on the browser to avoid multiple network calls.

The vendor bundle file

This is the bundle where Angular resides. All the Angular base code and any other third-party libraries are clubbed in the vendor bundle file. So, if we use JQuery or rxJs or any other file, all these will be placed in this bundle.

The map files

Each of the preceding bundle files is accompanied by its respective `sourcemap` file, which allows us to be able to debug and access the code in a browser when running the application.

Building the application in production mode

In the preceding section, we saw how to build the application in development mode. There are not many differences when building the application in production mode. Just add the `prod` flag and Angular CLI will build the code in production mode as shown in the following command:

```
ng build --prod
```

This will result in the following output from the Angular CLI:

```
Hash: a9653d03296f70093e2c
Time: 9148ms
chunk    {0} polyfills.c9b879328f3396b2bbe8.bundle.js (polyfills) 183 kB {4} [initial] [rendered]
chunk    {1} main.e81f19d3f6b27a436c79.bundle.js (main) 1.09 kB {3} [initial] [rendered]
chunk    {2} styles.33a8c6ba6eafb36ebd16.bundle.css (styles) 69 bytes {4} [initial] [rendered]
chunk    {3} vendor.f7b8387390dd9e2ea53e.bundle.js (vendor) 851 kB [initial] [rendered]
chunk    {4} inline.211469f44e29d3f16648.bundle.js (inline) 0 bytes [entry] [rendered]
```

As we can see, the main difference here with respect to dev build is the removal of the `sourcemap` files from the list. We saw in the preceding section, where we discussed the flags available with `ng build` and their default values in dev and prod mode, that Angular CLI uses those values to build the application, with flags such as the following:

- `AOT` set to `true`
- `Sourcemap` set to `false`
- Uglification enabled
- Tree-shaking was done

- Styles extracted from CSS file rather than the bundle
- Using the prod environment file for any configurations required for the application

Now, let's look at the `dist` folder and see the differences in the file generated with the production flag.

Dist folder details

Let's start by looking our `dist` folder and the files generated by Angular CLI:

So, there are a few differences in this `dist` folder when compared to the folder we had in the dev build configuration.

The bundle files

We see that there are bundle files for inline, main, polyfill, and vendor but they have a weird naming convention. When Angular CLI builds the code in production mode, it uglifies the content and adds the unique GUID to the filename.

If you open any of these files, you will see the content is compressed and most likely you will not be able to identify your code in the main file.

During minification process, Angular CLI performs following actions: renames all the variables with single character names, removes comments, and trims the whitespaces, all of which reduces the size of the file. The lower the size of the file, the faster the browser will be able to download and render the content. This allows an application to be faster with the cost of reading the content of the file.

You can see the difference in the file sizes when generated in dev mode versus prod mode. The vendor file, which was around 2.5 MB in dev mode, is now only ~400 KB in prod mode. This happens because in prod mode, we do ahead-of-time compilation and remove the part of the Angular compiler code which we don't need.

Similarly, the main file was reduced from 49 KB to 29 KB.

Serving an Angular app

We have been running our application using the ng serve command since Chapter 2, *Our First Application – Sports News Combinator,* so we have some understanding of the command. Let's now look at it in more detail.

The Angular CLI uses webpack to serve up the built application. Webpack does not go to the dist folder to fetch the files for rendering but in fact uses the in-memory files. This allows the application's rendering to be fast as well as helping with live-reload of the application when changes are done at runtime.

Let's start looking at our serve command as shown here:

```
ng serve
```

When Angular CLI encounters the serve command, the first thing it does it ask webpack to build the code in-memory and then get the server up and running to host the application. This server is no physical server on any machine; it's a simple development server which webpack brings up to be used for the application. On running this command, you will see the following output:

```
** NG Live Development Server is listening on localhost:4200, open your browser on http://localhost:4200 **
Hash: fe538b5514c0330acb8b
Time: 10264ms
chunk    {0} polyfills.bundle.js, polyfills.bundle.js.map (polyfills) 183 kB {4} [initial] [rendered]
chunk    {1} main.bundle.js, main.bundle.js.map (main) 34.9 kB {3} [initial] [rendered]
chunk    {2} styles.bundle.js, styles.bundle.js.map (styles) 11.7 kB {4} [initial] [rendered]
chunk    {3} vendor.bundle.js, vendor.bundle.js.map (vendor) 2.77 MB [initial] [rendered]
chunk    {4} inline.bundle.js, inline.bundle.js.map (inline) 0 bytes [entry] [rendered]
webpack: Compiled successfully.
```

We notice that Angular CLI built the application and hosted that on the development server at port `4200`. So now, if you go to the browser of your choice and type `http://localhost:4200`, the application will be rendered. Also, notice the size of the files that were built; this shows that the code was built in development mode.

The ng serve options

The `ng serve` command has many of the same options we saw in the `ng build` command and that is because the `ng serve` command internally does the build of the application. Let's look at some of the frequently used options in `ng serve`:

- `open`: When we just run the `ng serve` command, it builds the code and deploys the same on the local development server, but we still need to go to the browser and open the application URL. To automate this step, we can use the `open` flag, which when set to true will, after building and hosting, open the default browser and load the application.

- `live-reload`: As the name suggests, this tells the Angular CLI whether to reload the application every time we make a change in our code. Now, this can be useful and productive for a small application, but if we have a large application, we may not want to automatically reload every time we make a change. If we set the value to `false` then we can just refresh the browser to see the latest changes to the application.

- `port`: By default, the application is hosted on port `4200` as we saw when we ran the `ng serve` command. But with the `port` flag, we can assign any other port which will be used to serve the application.

- `target`: The purpose of this flag is similar to what we saw in the `ng build` command for building the application in either development mode or production mode. One main difference is the warning that Angular CLI shows when we run the `ng serve` command with the target as production, as shown here:

```
*****************************************************************************
This is a simple server for use in testing or debugging Angular applications locally.
It hasn't been reviewed for security issues.

DON'T USE IT FOR PRODUCTION USE!
*****************************************************************************
** NG Live Development Server is listening on localhost:4200, open your browser on http://localhost:4200 **
Hash: d599de0b870e9118025f                                    t Time: 11396ms
chunk    {0} polyfills.c36d5e908a5c7f176ed9.bundle.js (polyfills) 183 kB {4} [initial] [rendered]
chunk    {1} main.0bfb175803120004eb04.bundle.js (main) 1.1 kB {3} [initial] [rendered]
chunk    {2} styles.33a8c6ba6eafb36ebd16.bundle.css (styles) 69 bytes {4} [initial] [rendered]
chunk    {3} vendor.00d803af3db4b5257d2a.bundle.js (vendor) 1.13 MB [initial] [rendered]
chunk    {4} inline.8f3d35497ee1ba7c4a19.bundle.js (inline) 0 bytes [entry] [rendered]
```

Angular CLI informs us that this is not a production server but a local server to host the files. It is always good to run the application in production mode once, to make sure that there are no issues before deploying it on the production servers.

Linting an Angular application

If there is one feature in Angular CLI which is my favorite, then linting is the one. Angular CLI integrates with the `tslint` JSON file and allows us to run the linting rules on our code base and help make sure we are following the style guides and the best practices defined for our project.

The command for running the linting on our code base is shown here:

```
ng lint
```

The Angular CLI on this command will run through our code base and check whether there are any violations based on the rules defined.

Linting rules

In an Angular CLI project, when the project is generated, the CLI adds a file with the name `tslint.json`. This file contains all the recommended rules for writing TypeScript code.

The following are some of the rules taken from the file; you can refer to the file for the comprehensive list of linting rules:

```
"arrow-return-shorthand": true,
 "callable-types": true,
 . . .
"curly": true,
"eofline": true,
. . . .
 "quotemark": [
 true,
 "single"
 ],
```

The preceding rules shown are just a small set defined in our file. Based on your team's preference, you can modify this file and have the rules defined. When Angular CLI runs the `ng lint` command, it will use this file as reference and flag any violations.

Linting options

To find the possible configurations that Angular CLI provides for linting, we can use the `help` command as follows:

```
ng lint --help
```

This will show all the options available with the `ng lint` command.

The two main options which are useful are as follows:

- `format`: This flag lets Angular CLI format the violations using color combination and grouping based on the files.
- `fix`: As the name suggests, Angular CLI will try to fix the linting violations. This command is very useful, but always be careful to check the code after having the linting rules fixed. Always make sure to review the changes to confirm that the changes are as expected.

Linting the Trello application

Let's run the `lint` command on our *Trello* code base and look at the violations we have. We will run the following command first:

```
ng lint
```

On running this command, we see multiple errors, as shown here:

```
ERROR: /Users/sachin/Documents/TypeScript_Book/Git/SampleTrelloApplication/src/app/model/subtask.ts[2, 1]: space
indentation expected
ERROR: /Users/sachin/Documents/TypeScript_Book/Git/SampleTrelloApplication/src/app/model/task.ts[7, 2]: file shou
ld end with a newline
ERROR: /Users/sachin/Documents/TypeScript_Book/Git/SampleTrelloApplication/src/app/model/task.ts[6, 18]: missing
whitespace
ERROR: /Users/sachin/Documents/TypeScript_Book/Git/SampleTrelloApplication/src/app/model/board.ts[7, 2]: file sho
uld end with a newline
ERROR: /Users/sachin/Documents/TypeScript_Book/Git/SampleTrelloApplication/src/app/services/trello.service.ts[53,
 15]: comment must start with a space
ERROR: /Users/sachin/Documents/TypeScript_Book/Git/SampleTrelloApplication/src/app/services/trello.service.ts[41,
 56]: trailing whitespace
```

As we can see, the errors are very difficult to read so let's run the command again and this time we will use the `format` flag as well, as shown here:

```
ng lint --format stylish
```

Now, the output is as shown in the following screenshot:

```
/Users/sachin/Documents/TypeScript_Book/Git/SampleTrelloApplication/src/app/model/subtask.ts
ERROR: 2:1      indent                  space indentation expected

/Users/sachin/Documents/TypeScript_Book/Git/SampleTrelloApplication/src/app/model/task.ts
ERROR: 7:2      eofline                 file should end with a newline
ERROR: 6:18     whitespace              missing whitespace

/Users/sachin/Documents/TypeScript_Book/Git/SampleTrelloApplication/src/app/model/board.ts
ERROR: 7:2      eofline                 file should end with a newline
                                    >
```

You can see the difference once we added the `format` flag. Now we can easily read the linting errors.

We can now try to fix these using the `fix` flag, where Angular CLI will try to fix as many issues as possible. The following is the command to run the lint with the `fix` flag:

```
ng lint --format stylish --fix true
```

Once you run this command, you will see that Angular CLI has fixed most of the issues and whatever is remaining is then shown as an error. As you can see, most of the errors are related to white space, end of the line, and comments, which can be configured as per the preference of the team working on the application.

But there are a few very interesting violations as well, which show the real value of using linting. Now, I have not fixed these errors in the code base we have on GitHub, so that you can look at these errors and fix them when working on the application. These errors are as follows:

- Use of == instead of ===: In JavaScript, we should always use === for the comparison so that the types are coerced properly. Our `tslint` file provides a rule to check the same.
- Use of `let` instead of `const`: The main difference between `let` and `const` is that if we have a variable which we know will not be reassigned then it is recommended to use `const` instead of `let`. Our linting rules provide us with this check.

Now you should be able to see the value of linting in providing a consistent coding environment for our teams to follow the best practices and have maintainable code. And because these rules are all configurable, this provides the necessary flexibility to manage and apply our own custom rules.

Code coverage using Angular CLI

We looked at testing our Angular application in Chapter 7, *Testing the Trello Application*, where we covered in detail how to write the unit test and how Angular CLI allows us to run and manage our test cases. We created multiple test cases in our components, services, and pipes and then, using the `ng test` command, were able to run the test in a separate browser.

The Angular CLI also provides some options to configure our test environment with `ng test`, such as a `watch` flag which informs the CLI that it should run the test cases automatically when there is some change in the code, or the `single-run` flag, which allows us to run the test cases only once and not have the test scripts running.

The `single-run` flag is most useful in CI scenarios where we want to validate our code and not keep running the test cases. We can also choose which browser we want to run the test cases on, or even change the port on which the application will be hosted to execute the test cases.

There is one flag, `code-coverage`, which is one of the most useful flags we have in our testing suite. This flag, when used, provides us with the code coverage of our application with respect to test cases written. The default value for code coverage is `false` but when turned to `true`, Angular CLI creates a new folder with the name `coverage` in the root of the application.

This folder has an `index.html` file which, when opened, will provide you with the current code coverage you have for your application. Let's look at the code coverage we have for our application.

Code coverage for the Trello application

In the Terminal window, navigate to the application folder and run the following command:

```
ng test --code-coverage true
```

This command will launch the web browser for running the unit test we have for our application, as shown here:

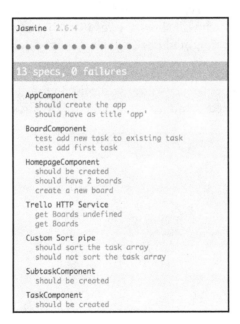

And, it will also create a folder with the name `coverage` in our application `root` directory, as shown in the following screenshot, which will have the details of the current code coverage of the application:

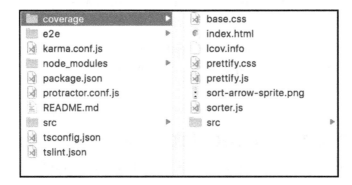

As you can see, we have a `coverage` folder which has a bunch of files in it. Angular CLI navigates through the whole code base and checks the functions, code flows, and code blocks to find out which ones have been covered by the test cases and which not. Under the `src` folder, inside the `coverage` folder, you will find the `app` folder, which will have the folder for all our components, services, and pipes. Each folder will then have two HTML files; one is `index.html`, which will show the result of that component, and the other file will have the code and the highlighted part, which shows which code flows have not been covered.

The `index.html` file in the `coverage` folder will contain the combination of all the code files and show the consolidated result, as seen in the following screenshot:

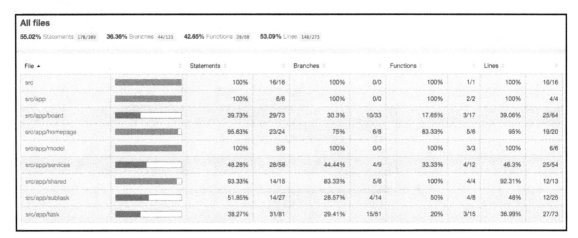

All files

55.02% Statements 170/309   36.36% Branches 44/121   42.65% Functions 29/68   53.09% Lines 146/275

File ▲	Statements		Branches		Functions		Lines	
src		100%	16/16	100%	0/0	100%	1/1	100%	16/16
src/app		100%	6/6	100%	0/0	100%	2/2	100%	4/4
src/app/board		39.73%	29/73	30.3%	10/33	17.65%	3/17	39.06%	25/64
src/app/homepage		95.83%	23/24	75%	6/8	83.33%	5/6	95%	19/20
src/app/model		100%	9/9	100%	0/0	100%	3/3	100%	6/6
src/app/services		48.28%	28/58	44.44%	4/9	33.33%	4/12	46.3%	25/54
src/app/shared		93.33%	14/15	83.33%	5/6	100%	4/4	92.31%	12/13
src/app/subtask		51.85%	14/27	28.57%	4/14	50%	4/8	48%	12/25
src/app/task		38.27%	31/81	29.41%	15/51	20%	3/15	36.99%	27/73

As we can see, some files have close to 100% and some just around 50% code coverage. As we discussed in Chapter 7, *Testing the Trello Application*, we created only some of the unit test cases rather than covering the whole code flow.

Code coverage is a very handy tool for identifying how well we have written our test cases and whether there are any specific code flows that are missing. In my experience, having 100% code coverage is not as important as making sure that we identify the critical and important code flows and have unit test cases for those, along with the end-to-end test cases for the application.

Summary

In this chapter, our focus was on learning about Angular CLI and how it helps us speed up application development in Angular. We saw how Angular CLI provides us with commands for generating an application and its components, services, pipes, and modules. We then delved deeper into the Angular CLI commands and looked at various optional flags which provide flexibility to configure our application.

We also saw the features of Angular CLI which help us manage the build for the application in both dev and production environments, serve the application on the local server for testing, linting to help us manage best practices, and testing, to provide us with tools to write and run a test on our application.

Our application is currently a web application which can be accessed on all platforms, but if we want to convert our application into a native mobile application, how can we achieve that? NativeScript is the answer. If you want to convert your current web application into a true native mobile platform application without rewriting the whole code base, you can achieve that using NativeScript. In the next chapter, we will do just that. We will take our *Sample Trello* application and convert it into a mobile application using NativeScript.

9
Trello Mobile – Using NativeScript

Our *Sample Trello* application is currently a web application that can be accessed in all browser formats, including mobile, desktop, and tablet. But web applications on the mobile platform have some limitations, such as not being able to access the native libraries that may help in better performance.

In this chapter, we will convert our *Sample Trello* application into a native mobile application. This will allow us to deploy our application on a mobile device and use it like a mobile app, rather than a web or a hybrid application.

We will achieve this using the NativeScript library, which allows us to create mobile applications using web technologies. In this chapter, we will cover the following topics:

- We will start with an introduction to NativeScript, and how NativeScript helps us convert web applications into mobile applications
- Then we will do a setup of NativeScript
- Once the setup is done, we will start converting our *Sample Trello* application into a mobile application
- We will look at some of the features of NativeScript as we convert our application

What is NativeScript?

NativeScript is the open source framework for building native Android and iOS applications with web technologies. This means we can develop native mobile applications with JavaScript, TypeScript, and/or Angular. NativeScript is based on the thinking of *write once and run everywhere*.

Applications developed with NativeScript are pure mobile apps when compared to applications developed with technologies such as PhoneGap. As they are native mobile applications, we can use all the richness of the mobile platform and provide the performance associated with that. We use native APIs and use native controls to render, which allows us to create more sophisticated applications compared to a hybrid approach. Hybrid applications do not provide the same level of flexibility or performance because they are hosted on a separate framework and do not get to interact with low-level mobile APIs directly.

The best part of NativeScript is that it does not require us to learn a new programming language, unlike developing an iOS-based application, for which you need to know objective C or Swift. So, we can use our existing skills to develop mobile applications.

NativeScript design

NativeScript is a runtime that sits on top of the native mobile operating system and uses the **JavaScript Virtual Machine (JVM)** V8 on Android and JavaScriptCore on iOS. Having access to these platforms allows NativeScript to expose a unified API system for developers, which is then converted into the native API at runtime.

This translation between the JavaScript APIs and the native platform APIs is possible through reflection, which NativeScript uses to create its own set of interfaces. Another advantage of using JavaScript by NativeScript is its independence from specific editors. You can use any of your favorite editors to develop a NativeScript application, and you will have access to all the native APIs rather than using Xcode for iOS-based apps and Android Studio for Android-based apps.

NativeScript architecture

The following is a high-level diagram of NativeScript and its interaction with the mobile platform:

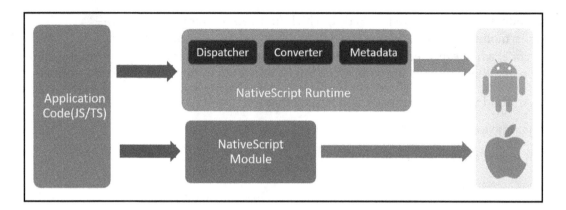

As we can see, the NativeScript runtime is responsible for converting JavaScript application code to the native platform code. It has various components that work together to convert and call the native APIs. Because NativeScript uses JVM and JavaScriptCore, it has access to all the latest ECMAScript language specifications for development, which allows us to use the latest ES6 feature set.

One of the main components that we need to understand in NativeScript design is NativeScript modules.

NativeScript modules

The NativeScript team made sure that the NativeScript platform was developed in a modular fashion, much like plugins, which allow us to include only the modules that we need in our development.

These modules provide us with the abstraction of native APIs, and allow us to write code that works on both platforms. NativeScript has separate APIs for each logical functionality. For example, if you want to use SQLite for your storage needs, there is a package for that; if you want to use a filesystem, there is a package for that.

Let's take one example to see how these NativeScript modules help us write consistent code for a multiplatform environment. If you want to access a filesystem on the native platform using NativeScript, you will write code similar to what you see in the following code snippet:

```
var filesystem = require("file-system");
new filesystem.file(path)
```

This code is written in pure JavaScript, which first gets a reference to a `file-system` module, and then, using the API of the `file-system` module, calls a `file` method. This code, when executed by the NativeScript runtime, first checks the platform it wants to run on and then converts the code accordingly, as shown in the following code snippets.

The Android version of the code will be as follows:

```
new java.io.file(path)
```

The iOS version of the code will be as follows:

```
nsFileManager.defaultManager();
fileManager.createFileAtPathContentsAttributes(path);
```

If you have worked on any of the mobile platforms before, you will recognize this code as using the native filesystem API to access the file path.

NativeScript versus web applications

Until now, we have been mentioning that we can use our web technologies to write mobile applications with the help of NativeScript. So, can we write a pure web application and use the NativeScript runtime to create a mobile application?

Yes and no. Yes, we can, and we will see with our application that we can use the same code base to write with NativeScript. No, because not all components of web applications can be directly used in NativeScript.

NativeScript allows us to use our existing JavaScript/TypeScript and CSS skills for developing the business logic and the design for our application. But because the native platforms are not web-based and do not have a DOM, we cannot use HTML as the template for our applications. Although you will see that the extension of our template files will be HTML, the element tags will be somewhat different.

To give you a brief example, NativeScript does not have UI elements such as `<div>` or `<span>`, but has elements such as `<StackLayout>` and `<DockLayout>`, which allow us to arrange our UI components.

Another thing to note here is that these UI elements are then converted into native elements based on the platform. So, if we use the `<Button>` control in NativeScript, it will get converted into `android.widget.Button` on the Android platform and `UIButton` on iOS.

Setting up your NativeScript environment

NativeScript provides very good documentation about installing and setting up your development environment. You can find the documentation at `https://docs.nativescript.org/angular/start/quick-setup`. We will briefly go through the setup process here, but recommend that you go through the NativeScript documentation to understand the process.

NativeScript CLI

The best way to use NativeScript is to through the NativeScript CLI. You can install the NativeScript CLI from `npm` using the following command:

```
npm install -g nativescript
```

This command will install the NativeScript library in your global scope. To confirm that the installation has been successful, you can try running the following command from the command-line window:

```
tns
```

The `tns` command is a short form for **Telerik NativeScript**, and will show the array of commands associated with NativeScript.

The NativeScript CLI comes with a host of commands to assist in our development, commands such as `create`, which helps us create a basic startup NativeScript project, and `deploy`, which informs the NativeScript CLI to deploy the application to the device (the device can be a connected device or an emulator). You can check all the commands available with the NativeScript CLI by using the `help` command as follows:

```
tns --help
```

Installing mobile platform dependencies

To build native applications using NativeScript, we need to install the dependencies for those mobile platforms. It is important to remember that if we want to build a NativeScript application for iOS and run it on an iOS-compatible device, we need to use macOS; for building Android applications, we can use both Windows and macOS.

NativeScript provides an easy single script for Windows and macOS that takes care of the responsibility to install all the tools and framework required.

The script for Windows is as shown in the following code:

```
@powershell -NoProfile -ExecutionPolicy Bypass -Command "iex ((new-object
net.webclient).DownloadString('https://www.nativescript.org/setup/win'))"
```

The script for iOS is as shown in the following code:

```
ruby -e "$(curl -fsSL https://www.nativescript.org/setup/mac)"
```

It's important to note that these scripts require administrator-level privileges, so you may need to run them using the `sudo` command. NativeScript also provides a step-by-step guide to installing all these dependencies manually; details can be found at `https://docs.nativescript.org/start/ns-setup-win`.

Once you have installed all the packages, you can check if the installation was successful by running the following command:

`tns doctor`

This command checks all the required prerequisites for building a NativeScript application, and if there are no issues identified, this command will return a success message, `No issues were detected`.

Installing an Android Virtual Device

Once you have installed all the dependencies, the next step is to install an Android emulator, which can be used for testing instead of connecting real devices. To be able to create an emulator, you need to have Android Studio on your machine.

You can install Android Studio from `https://developer.android.com/studio/index.html`. Once you have installed Android Studio, you can check whether you have the correct Android SDK version. The NativeScript CLI needs Android SDK version 25 or higher; if you see that you do not have the required Android SDK version, then you can install it either using the following command, or using the Android Studio IDE:

```
"%ANDROID_HOME%\tools\bin\sdkmanager" "tools" "platform-tools"
"platforms;android-25" "build-tools;25.0.2" "extras;android;m2repository"
"extras;google;m2repository"
```

To install the Android emulator, we use Android Studio, the details of which can be found at `https://docs.nativescript.org/tooling/android-virtual-devices`.

On macOS, we need to make sure we have hXcodeCode installed, or else, we will not be able to run iOS-based applications.

Again, you can use the `tns doctor` command to check if your installation was successful.

Developing the Sample Trello application using NativeScript

Now, let's look at how we can convert our *Sample Trello* application into a mobile platform application. Our *Sample Trello* application has the following functionalities:

- The home page, which shows all the Boards present and their task counts
- We can also create a new Board on the home page
- The Board page, which shows details of the tasks and subtasks
- We can add new tasks and subtasks on the Board page
- We can edit existing tasks, subtasks, and Board titles

For our native app, we will focus on a subset of these functionalities and will try to show the features of NativeScript. Our application will have the following functionalities:

- The home page, which will show all the Boards and their respective task counts
- On selecting a specific Board, we will see the list of tasks and subtasks

We have two options to develop our application: we can refactor our existing application and plug in the NativeScript components, or we can start from scratch and build our application on NativeScript. We will be following the latter approach because this will not only help us learn about using the Angular application in the NativeScript environment, but it will also provide us with the opportunity to understand the intricacies of NativeScript.

Creating the application skeleton

The NativeScript CLI provides a `create` command, which does the basic setup of the application with a couple of components. The `create` command has configurations that allow us to create an application with a pure JavaScript template, or a TypeScript template, or an Angular template. You can copy the startup project from an existing project as well. The following is the `help` command that provides all the configuration details for the `create` command:

```
tns create --help
```

We will be using the Angular template for our application, and hence our command will be as follows:

```
tns create SampleTrello --template ng
```

This command will create a folder named `SampleTrello` and set up the project with all the required dependencies of NativeScript and Angular.

Running the default NativeScript application

At this time, you can run your application and see the result of the default application created by the NativeScript CLI. To run the NativeScript application, we have two commands, one for Android and one for iOS, as shown in the following commands.

For Android, run the following command:

```
tns run android
```

For iOS, run the following command:

```
tns run ios
```

Like the `create` command, the `run` command also has multiple configurable parameters, and we can see all of them using the `help` command. So, if you want to check the configurations available for Android, you can run the following command:

```
tns run android --help
```

When you execute the `run` command, NativeScript does a bunch of things, such as the following:

- Identifying the device or the emulator on which to install the application
- If it is not running, starting the emulator
- Building the application with Gradle
- Installing the application on the emulator/device
- Starting the application
- Watching for any changes and refreshing the application

You should see an app with the name *Trello* installed on your device/emulator, which on opening will show a list of items.

Default folder structure for a NativeScript application

Let's try to understand what the NativeScript CLI did when we executed the `create` command.

In our `create` command, we had selected an option to create an app using an Angular template, which instructed the NativeScript CLI to create an application that has Angular components and routing, and Angular structure.

Along with the Angular structure, NativeScript also creates the files for platforms, and for managing resources for each platform.

Folder structure in Visual Studio Code

Let's open our *Sample Trello* application, which we just created in Visual Studio Code. You should have a folder structure similar to the following:

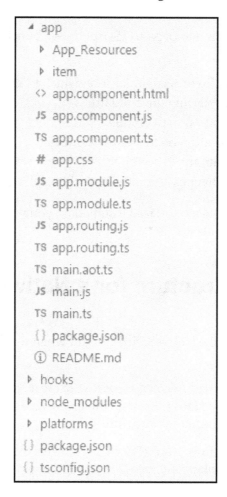

As we can see, the folder structure is quite similar to what we get when we run the Angular CLI command to create an Angular application. We will briefly go through the folder structure here.

The app folder

Similar to an Angular application, we have an `app` folder that contains all our application-specific and Angular startup files:

- We have `main.ts`, which acts as a bootstrap file similar to the one in the Angular application.
- The `main.ts` file bootstraps the `app.module` file, which will contain the `NgModule`.
- We have an `app.routing` file, where we will define our routes for the application. The default application already has some routing for the `item` component.
- Then we have our `main` component, `app.component`, which has an associated template.
- The `app.component` template right now just contains a `page-router-outlet` tag. This tag is similar to the `router-outlet` tag that we used in our Angular application. `page-router-outlet` is just a NativeScript wrapper on `router-outlet`, and is used by the Angular to manage the routing and display the HTML content inside the `app.component` template.
- The `app.css` file is the application-level style sheet file similar to what we had in our Angular application.
- The `item` folder contains the `item` component, `item` model, and `item` service-related files. These files should look very familiar to you, as these are same file types we created in our Angular application.
- Managing the resources or the assets for a mobile application is a bit different from managing those for a pure web application. Take the example of Android: there are many different Android devices with different resolutions, and you would not want to render the same image size and resolution on all Android devices. So, to handle such scenarios, we have different folders in the `App_resources` folder.

The node_modules folder

The `node_modules` folder contains all the node modules associated with our application. They are downloaded at the time of installation, and are managed in the `package.json` file.

The platforms folder

The platforms folder is a build folder that NativeScript uses to build an application for a specific platform. This folder will contain build configurations, build tools, and any libraries required.

Also, inside this folder will be the application under src/main; this folder is the one that is copied to the device when installation happens.

The hooks folder

The hooks folder is used by NativeScript to manage the live watch and syncing feature during runtime. As you may have noticed, when we ran our application in the Command Prompt, we got a message that said Looking for file changes. This feature is similar to the live update feature we have in Angular CLI, wherein the framework keeps track of the files, and if any of them changes, the framework automatically builds the project and deploys the latest code on the emulator/device.

Developing the Homepage component

We will start with our first component of the *Sample Trello* application. As we know, our Homepage component is responsible for displaying the existing Boards, and the task count for each Board. In the main application, we used to get this data from a JSON file we had in an API folder. We will follow the same logic here in our native application.

Cleaning up the existing content

Before we start making changes to the application by adding functionality to it, let's first clean up the code base and remove all the content that will not be required for our application.

This cleanup is required because when we created our application using the NativeScript CLI, the CLI did not just create a blank application, but instead created an application with some sample functionality. In this case, it was displaying the list items.

For our *Sample Trello* application, we do not need this functionality, so let's go through the following steps and remove all the content that is not required:

1. Remove the `item` folder, which contains the `item list` and `item detail` components, along with its service.
2. Once we have removed the component, we also need to remove the references to these components we have in our files.
3. Remove the references from the `app` module file for `ItemService`, `ItemComponent`, and `ItemDetailComponent`.
4. Remove the routes defined for these components from the `app.routing` file.

Trello Board models

So, before we start on the `Homepage` component, let's first migrate our models into our application. The models we had in our web application, namely `Board`, `Task`, and `subTask`, will remain the same in our native application as well.

We will create a new folder, `models`, under `app` and copy our model files from the web application.

 All the code that will be same as we had in our web application version of the *Sample Trello* app will not be listed here.

Implementing the Trello service

As we mentioned earlier, the best part of using NativeScript to develop a native mobile application with web technologies is that we can reuse the skills and code from JavaScript/TypeScript, Angular, and CSS.

Our `Homepage` component will be using the Trello service to fetch the Board information on the load. This Trello service will have the same code as we had in the web application.

So, first create a new folder, `services`, and add a file, `trello.service.ts`.

We will continue to use `Promises` as we did in our web application to fetch the data from our `board.JSON` file. This JSON file will reside under the `api/board` folder inside the `app` folder, and have exactly the same content.

Once we have our service code, the next step is to add a reference to the service in our `app.module` file.

Updating the app.module file with the Trello service

As was the case in our Angular web application, whenever we create a service, we need to provide that service to the module, or a component to consume. In NativeScript applications, the concept remains the same. If we do not provide the service, then the Angular `NgModule` will not be able to refer to the service and provide the instance to the respective components.

The following is the code from the `app.module` file with reference to `trello.service`:

```
import { TrelloService } from './services/trello.service';
....
providers:[TrelloService],
```

In the `app.module` file, you will have noticed another `import` statement that would not be there in an Angular web application, as shown in the following code snippet:

```
import { NativeScriptModule } from "nativescript-
angular/nativescript.module";
```

This `import` statement is specific to the NativeScript module. We need this module so as to access the NativeScript-specific elements and tags for our application, such as `<StackLayout>` or `<ListItem>`, which we will see in later sections. `NativeScriptModule` is not the only module that will be required; as we discussed earlier, the NativeScript framework is designed in a modular fashion, so when we need to use the HTTP module, we will need to import the respective `NativeScriptHTTPModule`, and similarly, if we need to access form elements then we will need to import `NativeScriptFormModule`.

Implementing the Homepage component

We have our models ready, we have our Trello service ready, now it's time to implement our `Homepage` component.

Start by creating a homepage folder under the app folder. Because it is an Angular-based application, our Homepage component will have three parts to it:

- homepage.component: This is the main component file
- homepage.component.html: This is the template file associated with the home page
- hompeage.component.css: This is the style sheet file associated with the home page

The Homepage component file

The responsibility of the Homepage component is twofold:

- To fetch all the Boards from the JSON file using the Trello service
- Routing to the Board component when the user selects any of the Boards on the home page

The following is the code for our Homepage component:

```
export class HomepageComponent implements OnInit {
boards: Board[] = Array();
errorMessage: string;
constructor(private _trelloService:TrelloService,private _router: Router)
{ }
ngOnInit() {
console.log("homepage");
this._trelloService.getBoardsWithPromises()
.then(boards => this.boards = boards,
error => this.errorMessage = <any>error);
}

public boardDetail(item: Board){
this._router.navigate(["board", item.id]);
}
}
```

As we can see, there are two methods in our `Homepage` component class:

- `ngOnInit`: The code in this method is exactly the same as what we had in our web application. Here, we are making an HTTP call to fetch all the Boards that are returned in `Promises`.
- `boardDetail`: This method is just responsible for routing the user to the `Board` component. We will be defining the `Board` component in a later section. Here, we are passing a parameter to the `Board` component that specifies the Board selected by the user.

Here, we saw how we could have code reused in our NativeScript application.

The Homepage style sheet file

NativeScript provides three ways of styling an application:

- `App.css`: As the name suggests, all the styles defined in `app.css` are global in nature and applicable for the whole application.
- `viewName.css`: The view name is the name of our component, so in the case of the homepage, it's `homepage.css`. This style sheet is the same as what we use in an Angular web application. The styles defined here are only applicable to the associated template.
- `viewName.platform.css`: In NativeScript, we target multiple mobile platforms, and sometimes we want a different style for an Android application versus an iOS application. In these cases, we can create separate styles using `viewname` followed by the platform, which can be Android or iOS. This way, NativeScript will package the correct styles for the specific platform.

As we mentioned earlier in the introduction to NativeScript, NativeScript supports CSS files as its style sheet file, so we do not need to make any changes to the CSS file that we had for our Angular web application.

The following is the CSS we have for our home page template:

```
.boards-wrapper {
padding: 10px;
background-color: rgb(147, 191, 192);
display: inline-block;
}

.label {
```

```
color: #333;
font-weight: 700;
line-height: 20px;
font-size: 25pt;
padding: 10pt;
}

.board {
background-color: rgb(173, 51, 102);
height: auto;
width: 500px;
color: white;
margin-right: 20px;
margin-bottom: 20px;
text-align: left;
padding: 9pt 8pt;
text-decoration: none;
}

.board .title {
font-weight: 700;
line-height: 20px;
font-size: 18pt;
}
```

You will notice that the CSS is much smaller in size to what we had in our web application, and that is because we are only focused on a subset of the functionalities here.

The Homepage HTML file

Up to now, we have looked at the `Homepage` component class and the `Homepage` style sheet, and both these files had similar code to the code we had in our web application.

 The minor code differences are mainly because we are focused on a subset of the main functionalities.

The main difference between a pure web application and a mobile application developed with NativeScript is the template definition. In native mobile platforms, we do not have the concept of DOM or DOM-related actions, thus NativeScript has a different set of UI elements that work the same as web-based UI elements. This is because these UI elements have to be rendered by the mobile platform natively, a Java-based compiler for Android and Objective-C based compiler for iOS.

These UI elements from NativeScript are common for both the platforms, and it is NativeScript's responsibility to convert them to UI elements for the respective platforms.

Let's look at the template code we have for our `Homepage` component, and in a later section, we will discuss some of the NativeScript features we used in our template:

```
<StackLayout class="boards-wrapper">
<label text="All Boards" class="label"></label>
<ListView [items]="boards" class="large-spacing">
<ng-template let-item="item">
<WrapLayout class="board" on-tap="boardDetail(item)">
<Label [text]="item.title" class="title"></Label>
<Label style="font-size: smaller" text="Total Task:
{{item.task.length}}"></Label>
</WrapLayout>
</ng-template>
</ListView>
</StackLayout>
```

As we can see, there are quite a few different UI elements when compared to our web application.

UI elements in the Homepage template

The way the page is laid out in our `Homepage` HTML file is different than what we had in our web application; we have different tags that have been used here.

StackLayout

As the name suggests, the `StackLayout` element allows us to stack the child UI elements. Using `StackLayout`, we can stack our child elements either horizontally, or vertically. `StackLayout` is one of the most common and frequently used UI elements. You will almost always use `StackLayout` elements as the outermost UI elements for a page similar to a `<div>` in a web application.

Label

The `label` control in a web application is a bit different than the label control in NativeScript, having a `text` property that does not exist in HTML. In our case, we have a `text` attribute that is bound to a `heading` property from the component. This label UI element is rendered as a `UILabel` element in iOS, and `android.widget.Textview` in the Android platform.

ListView

The `ListView` UI element is much like the `<li>` we have in the DOM world. This element is used to display the data in list format. In our web application, we used the `ngFor` directive, which will iterate through an array and display each element.

In the case of NativeScript, we have the `ListView` control, which has a property, `items`, which takes an array of objects that we want to be displayed. Inside `ListView`, we have a child control, `ng-template`, which is used to display each row of an object.

The `ng-template` has a property, `let-item`, which represents a single item in an array. Using this `item` property, we are able to access the object and display the required information.

In our case, we have a `boards` array that is bound to the `<ListView>` control, and the `ng-template` control then has access to each Board element.

Binding in a NativeScript Angular template

The binding in NativeScript when using Angular is the same as we have in pure Angular applications. We have one-way binding, two-way binding, and `Event` binding available to us.

As we can see in our home page template code, we have used one-way binding when binding the `label` control using the double curly braces.

Two-way binding is achieved similarly as in Angular with the `ngmodel` syntax.

The difference with Angular is the event to which we attach the binding. In a web application, this could be a `span`, a `label`, a `div`, or an `input` element; but in the case of NativeScript, the UI elements have their own properties. For example, in the case of `listview`, it is the items property, and in the case of `label`, it's the text property.

So, for example, if we have a textbox that needs two-way binding, we will be using the `ngModel` property on the text control similar to how we would use it in a web application, as shown in the following code.

The NativeScript code will look like this:

```
TextField [(ngModel)]="name" hint="Add a task" ></TextField>
```

The HTML code will look like this:

```
<input [(ngModel)]="addtaskText" placeholder="Add a task" />
```

Event binding

Like property binding, the syntax of event binding is also similar to HTML event binding, with the only difference being the event to which the binding happens.

So, in the case of HTML, you may have a `click` event which is then bound to a function in our component class. In NativeScript, there is a `tap` function, which does the same job as shown in the following code:

```
<WrapLayout class="board" on-tap="boardDetail(item)">
 <Label [text]="item.title" class="title"></Label>
 <Label style="font-size: smaller" text="Total Task:
{{item.task.length}}"></Label>
 </WrapLayout>
```

As we can see in the first line, we have an `on-tap` event which is then bound to a function `boardDetail` method in our component class. If this had been written in HTML, the code would be something like what we see here:

```
<span  (click)="boardDetail()"></span>
```

So, apart from the binding `tag` name, the concept of event binding is the same as we see in an Angular application.

Stitching the Homepage component

Now, our `Homepage` component is ready, but we still need to stitch it together with our app. As we know from our learning in Angular, we need to define a route to our `Homepage` component.

Because our `Homepage` is the default page of the application, the route defined will also be the default route. The following is the code we have in our `app.route` file:

```
import { HomepageComponent } from "./homepage/homepage.component";
export const appRoutes: any = [
 { path: "", component: HomepageComponent },
];
export const appComponents: any = [
 HomepageComponent,
];
```

This code is very similar to the routes that we defined in our web application, with one difference: a new constant, appComponents. This difference is just another way of defining the references to our components. We can very well not have this constant, and add the reference to the components in our app.module file like we did in our web application.

The following is the code for our app.module file with reference to the routing:

```
import { NgModule } from "@angular/core";
import { NativeScriptFormsModule } from "nativescript-angular/forms";
import { NativeScriptHttpModule } from "nativescript-angular/http";
import { NativeScriptModule } from "nativescript-
angular/nativescript.module";
import { NativeScriptRouterModule } from "nativescript-angular/router";
import { AppComponent } from "./app.component";
import { TrelloService } from './services/trello.service';
import { appRoutes, appComponents } from "./app.routing";
@NgModule({
 imports: [
 NativeScriptModule,
 NativeScriptFormsModule,
 NativeScriptHttpModule,
 NativeScriptRouterModule,
 NativeScriptRouterModule.forRoot(appRoutes)
 ],
 declarations: [AppComponent, ...appComponents],
 providers:[TrelloService],
 bootstrap: [AppComponent]
})
```

You can get the whole code from the GitHub link https://github.com/sachinohri/ SampleTrello-NativeScript. Here, we just want to show you how we used the appComponents constant to refer to the components of our application.

Later, when we add the BoardComponent to our routing array, we will just add the component name in the appComponent, and we will not be required to add the reference in the app.module file.

This approach helps us to keep our app.module file clean and not have all the references in this one file.

The application so far

We now have a basic version of our *Trello* application with the `Homepage` component and the `Trello` service integrated. So, now let's run our application and see the result.

As we saw in an earlier section, the NativeScript CLI provides us with the `run` command to build and execute the code and deploy it on the selected platform. We can execute the `run` command without specifying the platform, which will result in NativeScript running the application on all the connected devices. So, if you have iOS and Android devices connected, NativeScript will deploy the application on both and execute them.

We can configure a specific platform when executing the `run` command as well, and even mention a specific device ID on which we want NativeScript to install the code.

Executing the run command

Let's run the following command in our code and see the result:

```
tns run android
```

If you are using an iOS device for testing, then you can execute the following command:

```
tns run ios
```

This command will build the application and deploy it on your emulator/device. You should see the application running similar to the following screenshot:

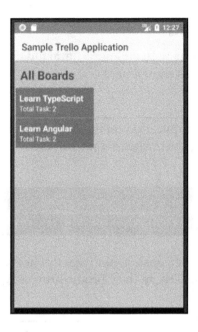

What we see here are the native elements of Android; the Label that we added is now converted to the Android Label widget, and the ListView is now an Android native listview control. Similarly, if you had executed the code on the iOS environment, these controls would be the native iOS controls.

This is a very important factor that helps NativeScript stand out from its peers. Other frameworks that have focused on code reuse and using the web application code to be hosted on a mobile platform have taken a hybrid approach that does not provide the same benefit of performance that we see when using the native controls.

Debugging the application

So, how do you debug an application that is hosted on a mobile device?

NativeScript provides a configuration to allow us to attach the application to a browser and then be able to debug. This behavior allows us to have our debugging in a similar fashion as we would have when running a web application.

The debug command

The NativeScript CLI provides us with a `debug` command that runs the application in debug mode. The command is as shown here:

```
tns debug android
```

This command will install the application on the Android emulator/device and provide a link, as shown in the following screenshot, which can then be used to open the application code in debug mode:

```
# NativeScript Debugger started #
To start debugging, open the following URL in Chrome:
chrome-devtools://devtools/bundled/inspector.html?experiments=true&ws=localhost:40000
```

As we can see in the preceding screenshot, NativeScript hosts the application on port 40000 to debug. Now, if you open the URL in the Chrome browser, you will be presented with the developer tool:

```
Sources   Content scripts   Snippets                    [◀]    homepage.component.ts ×

▶ □ top                                                  1  import { Component, OnInit } from '@angular/core';
▶ ⌂ (no domain)                                          2  import { Router } from '@angular/router';
▼ ⌂ file://                                              3
    ▼ ▓ data/data/org.nativescript.trello/files/app      4  import { Board } from '../models/board';
                                                         5  import { SubTask } from '../models/subtask';
      ▶ ▓ board                                          6  import { Task } from '../models/task';
      ▼ ▓ homepage                                       7  import {TrelloService} from '../services/trello.service';
         ▓ homepage.component.js                         8
         ▓ homepage.component.ts                         9
      ▶ ▓ models                                        10  @Component({
      ▶ ▓ services                                      11    selector: 'app-homepage',
                                                        12    templateUrl: './homepage/homepage.component.html',
                                                        13    styleUrls: ['./homepage/homepage.component.css']
                                                        14  })
```

NativeScript uses WebSockets for the Chrome protocol to allow us to debug. As you can see, this is similar to how you would debug a web application. Here, we can add breakpoints, inspect the values, and add watches, much like in web application debugging.

Developing the Board component

Now, let's finish off our application by adding the Board component. Our Board component will just have one function to be able to display the `Task` and `SubTask` for the Board selected.

So, the code for the `BoardComponent` is fairly simple: we fetch the board ID based on the routing information, and then show the details of the Board on the screen. The code is as follows:

```
@Component({
  selector: 'app-board',
  templateUrl: './board/board.component.html',
  styleUrls: ['./board/board.component.css']
})
export class BoardComponent implements OnInit {
  board: Board = new Board;
  boardId: number;

  constructor(private _route: ActivatedRoute, private _trelloService:
TrelloService) { }

  ngOnInit() {
  this._route.params.subscribe((params) => {
  this.boardId = params["id"];
  });
  console.log(this.boardId);
  this.board = this._trelloService.Boards.find(x => x.id == this.boardId);
  }
}
```

The main difference, as we now know, comes in the HTML file.

Board component template

Let's look at the template code we have for our `Board` component, and then briefly go through the code structure:

```
<StackLayout class="main">
  <label text="Tasks for: {{board.title}}" class="label"></label>
  <ListView [items]="board.task" class="large-spacing">
  <ng-template let-item="item">
  <WrapLayout >
  <Label [text]="item.title" class="task" ></Label>
```

```
<StackLayout orientation="vertical">
<StackLayout class="subTask" *ngFor="let subtask of item.subtask">
<Label [text]="subtask.title" ></Label>
</StackLayout>
</StackLayout>
</WrapLayout>
</ng-template>
</ListView>
</StackLayout>
```

As we learned earlier, in NativeScript we normally use `<StackLayout>` as our wrapper for a template. As we are displaying a list of Tasks and SubTasks, it makes sense to have a `<ListView>` control to show the Tasks associated with the Board.

Inside the Task list, we need another list to display the subtask for which we used the `<StackLayout>` and Angular's `ngFor` directive.

Changes in routing for BoardComponent

The last thing we need to do is add `BoardComponent` in our routing rule so that when a user clicks on any of the Boards, the Angular routing is able to navigate. The final `app.routing` code is as follows:

```
import { HomepageComponent } from "./homepage/homepage.component";
import { BoardComponent } from './board/board.component';
export const appRoutes: any = [
 { path: "", component: HomepageComponent },
 { path: "board/:id", component: BoardComponent }
];
export const appComponents: any = [
 HomepageComponent,
 BoardComponent
];
```

Because we added `BoardComponent` in the `appComponent` array, we do not need to make any changes in the `app.module` file.

Executing the code

With our application completed, let's run the application and see how it behaves on the mobile application.

We again execute the `run` command, which will reload the application on our mobile emulator/device.

Now, if we tap on any of the Boards on the home page, we should be navigated to the Boards page, as shown in the following screenshot:

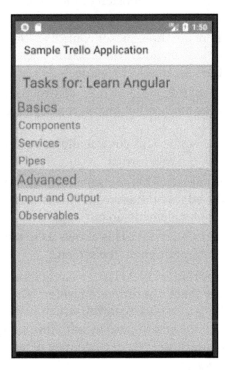

We have not implemented functionalities such as adding a new Task, or adding a new Subtask, which is left for the you to implement to further strengthen their knowledge of NativeScript.

NativeScript UI elements

In our application, we used many of the NativeScript UI elements that replace our existing HTML code. Here, we will go through some of the other UI elements available in the NativeScript framework to help us build a more robust UI:

- **TextField**: The `TextField` control is used as an `Input` field in NativeScript. It has properties such as `hint`, `maxlength`, and `keyboard` type, which allow us to configure the input format on the device.
- **TextView**: This control is an extension of the `TextField` control, wherein it allows users to enter multiline text.
- **Picker controls**: There are three picker controls provided by NativeScript, `DatePicker`, `TimePicker`, and `ListPicker`. These controls provide a form of list view to allow the user to select a value.
- **Layouts**: We have seen the `StackLayout` control used in our application; NativeScript provides many other layout controls to customize our application display:
  - `GridLayout`: This control allows us to place the child UI elements in `row`, `column` format.
  - `DockLayout`: This control allows us to place the child UI elements on the edges of the screen. This is useful if we have some header and footer elements in our application.
  - `AbsoluteLayout`: This allows us to place child elements in an absolute position on the screen.
- **Action bar**: Both Android and iOS have a navigation bar in their applications, but both display and use them in a different fashion. The NativeScript framework provides us with the `ActionBar` control, which works as a wrapper on both the native controls. `ActionBar` provides us with the configuration to allow images, navigation, and styling, and even to customize it based on our needs.

You can find the full list of controls available in NativeScript at `https://docs.nativescript.org/ui/basics`.

Summary

In this chapter, we explored NativeScript and saw how easy it is to modify our web application to be a native mobile application. NativeScript provides us with a framework that allows us to use our web technologies to build a pure native mobile application.

We converted our *Sample Trello* application into a native mobile application using NativeScript, and along the way learned about the fundamental concepts of NativeScript. We looked at how NativeScript uses existing JavaScript/TypeScript code to develop a mobile application using NativeScript modules and NativeScript runtime. We also looked at the multiple configurations with NativeScript CLI to run and debug our application.

In the next chapter, we will look at deploying our web application on the cloud. We will be using Microsoft Azure as our cloud platform, and looking at the steps to deploy our *Sample Trello* application.

10
Deploying Sample Trello on the Cloud Using Microsoft Azure

We have developed our *Sample Trello* application, and in doing so, learned concepts of Angular and TypeScript. We also looked at NativeScript, which helps to convert our web application to a native mobile application. In application development, the last step is deployment.

We have many ways to deploy a web application. We can deploy our application on any of the publicly available hosting servers. If you are working in an organization, then most likely you will have production-based servers available.

Then there is another option: the cloud. The cloud provides us with an exhaustive set of tools to enable the deployment of a web application.

In this chapter, we will do just that. We will cover the following topics:

- We will start by looking at Microsoft Azure as a cloud platform
- Then we will take a brief look at the various options Azure provides to host a web application
- We will focus on the two main options provided by Azure: using FTP and deploying using GitHub.
- While we look at how we deploy using GitHub, we will also look at the continuous integration provided by Azure

Azure Cloud as a deployment platform

In this chapter, we will use Microsoft Azure to deploy our *Sample Trello* application and in doing so will look at some of the features of Azure as a cloud platform.

In Azure, Microsoft has provided its cloud platform, which competes with Amazon's AWS and Google Cloud as one of the premier cloud services. Microsoft Azure provides a host of services under the cloud platform, ranging from virtual machines and web apps to the IoT and functional computing.

The cloud provides a platform to manage and handle all our deployment needs, for any type of application. Applications can be web apps or a database, or even authentication services using Active Directory. This vast variety of services enables the creation of a single unified window into all IT service management needs, providing tremendous benefits.

Benefits of a cloud platform

Having the cloud as the deployment platform over the traditional in-house deployment has many benefits:

- Low maintenance of the hardware
- Increase in speed of deploying the applications to production
- Ability to scale up or out quickly
- Easy monitoring and managing of the production machines

These benefits are one of the main reasons that corporations are rapidly moving toward cloud adoption. In the cloud, you can change your deployment process to be agile and well integrated with your development process, thus providing you with a **continuous integration and deployment (CI/CD)** mechanism. Let's look at these benefits in more detail.

Efficient hosting and deployment

The cloud platform allows us to have a faster deployment cycle. This is mainly because the process of acquiring the required hardware and installing the required software, such as the operating system, database, and so on, no longer takes days or even weeks.

With Microsoft Azure, you can allocate resources on a need basis and have the required software installed on the machines in a matter of minutes. The deployment process in itself is also seamless with Microsoft Azure, with options such as using Azure CLI, the Azure portal, or even in some cases FTP.

Microsoft Azure provides a step-by-step setup process which takes care of all the necessary infrastructure details and lets you focus on deployment. So, for example, if we want to deploy our *Sample Trello* application on a production box, we will have to perform the following steps:

1. First, acquire a box, which can be a Windows- or a Linux-based machine.
2. Then install the operating system with all the required patches.
3. If it's a Windows machine, enable Internet Information Services.
4. If there is a database requirement then either install one on the same box or have a separate box for the database.
5. If we expect high user flow, then we may need more than a single box.
6. With multiple boxes, we would then need a load balancing process set up.
7. And much more

Now, if we want to deploy our application on Microsoft Azure then we need to perform the following steps:

1. If we want to deploy on a virtual machine then spin up a new virtual machine with the required operating system and software.
2. Log in to the virtual machine and deploy.
3. If we want to deploy using Azure as Software as a Service with web apps then create a new web app with the required hardware configuration.
4. Add the deployment setup such as GitHub, Dropbox, FTP, among others, and you are done.

As you can see, all the initial setup is taken care of by Azure, which provides us with more efficiency in deployment.

Scaling

So, your application has more users than it can handle. You will either scale up or scale out. With scale-up, we add more horsepower to our existing production boxes, and with scale-out, we add more production boxes. In both cases, we will have to buy more hardware and then deploy it.

Now, consider the scenario where the increase in the number of users to your website is temporary, such as a holiday season where you expect an exponential increase in user hits. If you buy more hardware then that hardware will not be optimally used post the holiday season.

Microsoft Azure provides a perfect solution for this, with the ability to scale up and/or scale out and then change back to the original configuration when required. This approach helps in making sure we have the best possible hardware configuration when required. And this scaling on the cloud is achieved in minutes, rather than carrying out the whole process of manually setting up new servers. Microsoft Azure also provides automated scaling options, with triggers based on variable factors such as CPU utilization.

Maintenance

Some of the actions that need to be performed regularly to make sure that the business is always up and running are maintaining the servers with the latest patch fixes for the operating system and other installed software, and making sure that the hardware on each box is performing as expected and, in the event of failure, replacing or repairing the hardware.

Microsoft Azure takes care of all these activities and provides default maintenance support for all the services, be it a virtual machine or a web app or even an IoT service.

Monitoring

Monitoring is another aspect where deploying on Azure provides tremendous benefits. We want the ability to monitor application performance and then be able to make decisions based on that. Microsoft Azure provides us with a default set of tools to help us monitor not only application performance but also hardware performance.

We have the ability to monitor functions such as the following:

- HTTP server errors
- Number of requests/responses
- Average response time
- Health checks
- High CPU usage
- High memory usage, which includes physical memory usage, committed memory usage, and page operations

Economy

All the above-mentioned benefits roll into another major benefit of deploying an application in the cloud: cost. The ability to allocate resources on demand, the ability to scale up or out and then back when required, integrated monitoring tools, and easy maintenance all translate into a low cost of operation.

Microsoft Azure provides various plans which are cost-effective and can be catered to the specific requirement. In addition to that, with Microsoft Azure, you have the option to pay per use, wherein you are only charged for the time and resources you use and not for the whole set.

This helps in keeping the cost down and making sure we get a lot of bang for our buck.

Deployment options in Microsoft Azure

At a high level, Microsoft Azure provides two main deployment options for web-based applications: **Platform as a Service (PaaS)**, and **Software as a Service (SaaS)**.

Both these options provide a varying degree of attributes which allow us to deploy web applications seamlessly. On one hand, you have the option to create your own machines, configure your resources, and deploy the application. On the other hand, you use the existing services provided by the Microsoft Azure to deploy your application without worrying about the management of resources.

Platform as a Service (PaaS)

As the name suggests, PaaS is a category of cloud computing where the cloud provider provides a platform, allowing users to build and manage applications. The users are not responsible for infrastructure-related tasks such as network, storage, operating systems, or the required software installation.

The cloud provider manages all the operations of keeping the infrastructure up and running. In Azure, we use virtual machines as a PaaS. Microsoft Azure provides the ability to spin up virtual machines and then use those machines to manage, develop, and deploy any sort of applications. This approach is not only available for web applications but can be used for any service where you want to have specific control of the infrastructure.

Microsoft Azure provides a host of options for virtual machines, as shown in the following screenshot:

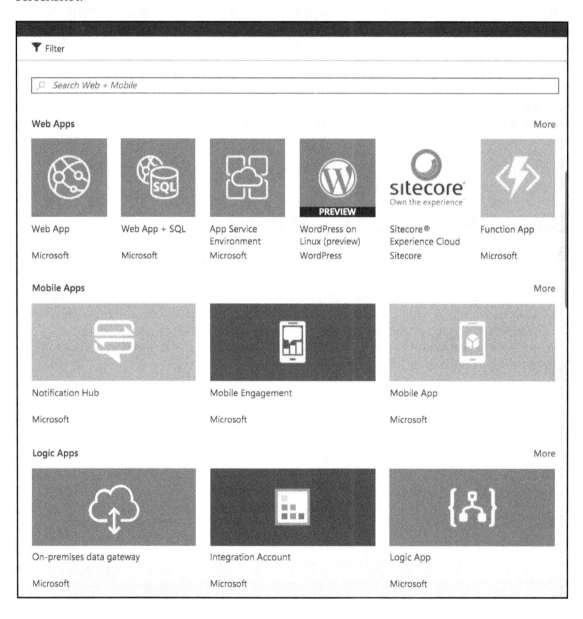

As you can see, there are virtual machines for a Windows-based OS and even a Linux-based OS such as Ubuntu or Red Hat. There are virtual machines with already-set-up software such as SharePoint, MEAN Stack, SQL Server, and much more. In each of these cases, we do not need to worry about the setup of the machine and these bare minimum software and any maintenance activities on these machines. We can use these machines to set up our applications as required.

Software as a Service (SaaS)

In SaaS, the cloud provider provides an on-demand software which is accessed through a web application such as the Azure portal. This software provides users with functionalities that help them manage and deploy their applications.

The main characteristics of SaaS is to provide a common platform for application support through customization and configuration. Using SaaS allows users to focus on the application and not on the infrastructure. Users use SaaS but are not concerned about the physical aspects of the application maintenance, such as how the application is deployed and managed.

Another important advantage of using SaaS as your platform is billing. SaaS is normally billed on per-use basis and not on license fees, as was the case with traditional software. Normally, SaaS is comparatively cheaper than acquiring the dedicated hardware and its management, because of which SaaS has become one of the top cloud platform services.

In Microsoft Azure, there are multiple sets of SaaS available, with varying parameters, as shown in the following screenshot:

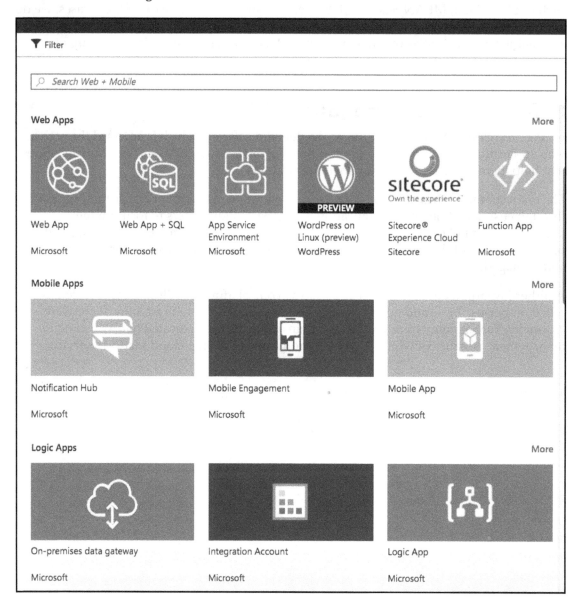

As you can see, a web app is one such example of SaaS, which includes services such as web apps which are used to deploy web applications, function apps which are used to deploy some specific function that can be processed independently or as stitches in a workflow, and much more.

For our application, we will focus on SaaS as our deployment strategy and will showcase the power and simplicity of application deployment and management.

Deploying Sample Trello using a web app service – FTP

We will start with the easiest and fastest option to deploy our web application. Microsoft Azure provides us with the option of web app deployment using FTP, which encompasses the process of creating a specific web app service and then copying your application on the required service.

Azure will then take care of hosting, managing, and monitoring the application. Before we can create a web app service on Azure, we need to create an account on Azure.

Microsoft Azure provides us with the option of a free account with $200 credit for 1 month. You can go to `https://azure.microsoft.com/en-us/` to create your free account.

Once you have your account created, you can navigate to `https://portal.azure.com`, which is where you will have access to all the services of Microsoft Azure, as shown in the following section.

Managing the web app service

The first step in using the web app service as a SaaS for our application is to create a new instance of the web app service.

> For all our demos using the web app service, this step will be same, be it with FTP, local Git, or GitHub.

On your dashboard, select **New** and under **Web + Mobile**, select the **Web App** option as shown in the following screenshot:

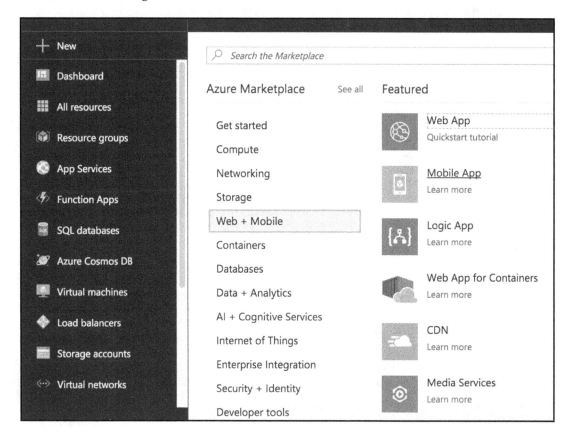

Apart from the **Web + Mobile** services, we can see here the various other services provided by Microsoft Azure, including containers, IoT, database, virtual machines, and much more. Our focus will remain on web apps only.

Creating a web app

Once you select **Web App** on the new services screen shown in the preceding section, you will be presented with a web app form as shown in the following screenshot:

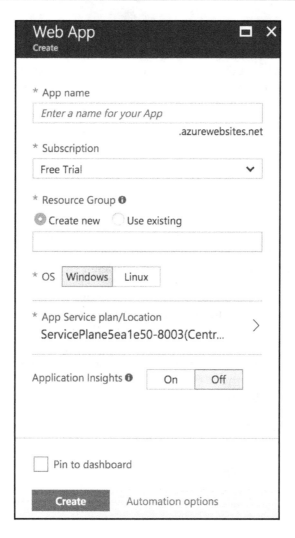

This screen allows us to create a new instance of web app service with a unique name. Enter any name you would like to associate with your web app service. The subscription will be a **Free Trial** as are using the free account from Azure. We have two options for selecting the operating system on which our web application will be deployed. We will here use **Windows** as our OS; you could use **Linux** and the only difference would be the path where the code is copied to be deployed.

Resource group

A **resource group** is a collection of resources which allows us to consolidate different services to have a shared life cycle and policies. If you already have a resource group created earlier, you will have the option to use the existing one or you can create a new resource group.

The best practice is to have separate resource group for different services unless you are looking to have multiple web services linked together.

App service plan

The app service plan allows us to configure the resources which will be required for your application to run. Here, "resources" means the region where you want to deploy the web application, the number of virtual machines, and whether you need shared or dedicated resources. All these configurations let you have a pricing plan to support your application.

The app service plan allows us to plan your scaling strategy, wherein you may want to deploy your application with a minimum set of resources and then increase the resources as and when the application demand increases. Because the app service plan runs on an hourly charge, you are not tied to any specific plan and pricing. Microsoft Azure provides a number of different app service plans with varying cost and we can select one which suits our need. In our case, let's use the S1 Standard plan, which provides 1 core and 1.75 GB RAM and autoscales up to 10 instances.

Once you have filled in all the information and selected the **Create** button, Microsoft Azure creates the new web app service and deploys it.

When creating a web app, I normally select the **Pin to Dashboard** option, which creates a widget on the Azure portal dashboard for easy access.

So now we have created a new web app named `SampleTrello-FTP`, with the same name for our resource group. Once it has been created, you will be navigated to the *SampleTrello-FTP* page on the Azure portal as shown in the following screenshot:

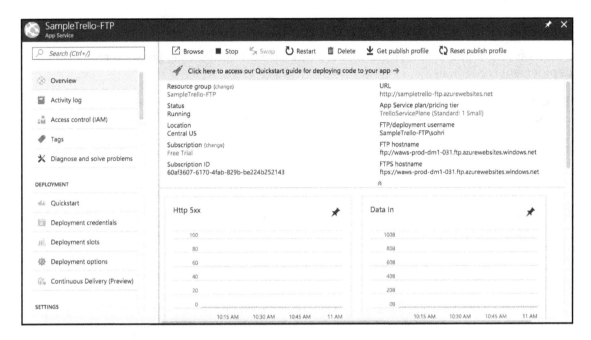

This is like a landing screen for your web app service and contains options for configuration, management, and monitoring of the app server. You can access your web application using the URL tag on the landing screen, which in our case is `http://sampletrello-ftp.azurewebsites.net`. Right now, we have not deployed our *Sample Trello* application on the web app service, hence when you try to navigate to this URL, Azure will show you a default page.

Deploying the Sample Trello application

Now, let's deploy our application on the `SampleTrello-FTP` service. In this case, we will just FTP our code to the `wwwroot` folder, which is the default folder for the Windows OS, and we should have our application up and running.

Before we access our web app service using FTP, it is required to create the deployment credentials which will be used at connection time. These credentials are used for both FTP and local Git deployment options.

You can find the code for this project at `https://github.com/sachinohri/SampleTrello-Azure`.

Creating deployment credentials

Microsoft Azure provides an option on the web app service landing page to create a new deployment credentials.

Select the **Deployment Credentials** option on the left side of the pane and create the new username and password for your web app service as shown in the following screenshot:

This will create new credentials for your web app service, which we will then have to use if we want to FTP to the server.

Deploying the code on the web app

The next step is to deploy our code into the web app service. To be able to do that, we need the FTP URL and the user credentials. We can find these in the profile for our web app service, under the **Get Publish Profile** option.

When we select the **Get Publish Profile** option, Azure provides us with a .publishsettings file which will have details for both FTP and FTPS. For our web app service, the file will have content similar to the following:

```
<publishData><publishProfile profileName="SampleTrello-FTP - Web Deploy"
publishMethod="MSDeploy" publishUrl="sampletrello-
ftp.scm.azurewebsites.net:443" msdeploySite="SampleTrello-FTP"
userName="$SampleTrello-FTP"
userPWD="muHSB0Aqpjgcr9JLfSGzs0m8JEBuxZqh7hr2XrmDtqzZ6jE5D1ljce1hbQkf"
destinationAppUrl="http://sampletrello-ftp.azurewebsites.net"
SQLServerDBConnectionString="" mySQLDBConnectionString=""
hostingProviderForumLink="" controlPanelLink="http://windows.azure.com"
```

```
webSystem="WebSites"><databases /></publishProfile><publishProfile
profileName="SampleTrello-FTP - FTP" publishMethod="FTP"
publishUrl="ftp://waws-prod-dm1-031.ftp.azurewebsites.windows.net/site/wwwr
oot" ftpPassiveMode="True" userName="SampleTrello-FTP\$SampleTrello-FTP"
userPWD="muHSB0Aqpjgcr9JLfSGzs0m8JEBuxZqh7hr2XrmDtqzZ6jE5D1ljce1hbQkf"
destinationAppUrl="http://sampletrello-ftp.azurewebsites.net"
SQLServerDBConnectionString="" mySQLDBConnectionString=""
hostingProviderForumLink="" controlPanelLink="http://windows.azure.com"
webSystem="WebSites"><databases /></publishProfile></publishData>
```

As you can see, this `.publishsettings` file provides us with details such as `publishURL`, which is the address where we do the FTP, and the respective username and password. It also has the destination app URL, which will be the URL of the web application which we deploy.

If the application you deploy has any database dependencies then the database details are available under the connection string settings.

You can use any of the freely available software that allows us to FTP into the server. I use FileZilla for my connection. In our case, the FTP URL will be as follows:

```
ftp://waws-prod-dm1-031.ftp.azurewebsites.windows.net/site/wwwroot
```

The following screenshot shows the FTP connection using FileZilla:

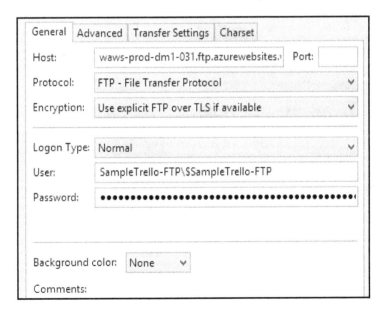

This option is available in **Site Manager** under **File**.

Once connected, you just need to copy the `dist` folder from our *Sample Trello* application. As we learned in `Chapter 8`, *Trello - Using Angular CLI*, Angular CLI provides a `build` command which will build our application and provide the files with the `dist` folder. The command for building the code is as follows:

```
ng build -prod
```

Because our web app is on a Windows machine, we will be copying the `dist` folder under the `site\wwwroot` folder as shown in the following screenshot:

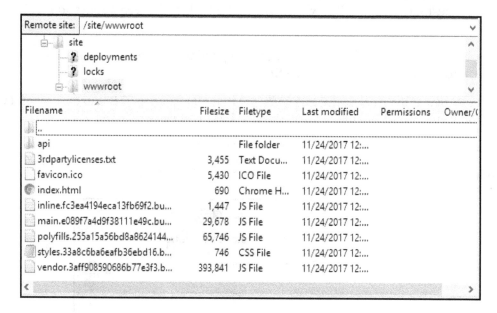

Please note that the preceding screenshot is from FileZilla and the software which you use may have a different outlook.

Now that all files are copied, it's time to run our application. As we saw earlier, on the landing page we had a URL which will point to our application. Earlier, we had copied our code; if we would navigate to the URL, Azure will present us with a sample web page. Now let's see if we have our application running.

Navigate to the URL `http://sampletrello-ftp.azurewebsites.net` and you will be presented with the page shown in the following screenshot:

OK, so our application did load but where are our two existing boards? Let's look at the console of our application. We will see one error as shown in the following line of code:

```
GET http://sampletrello-ftp.azurewebsites.net/api/board/boards.json 404
(Not Found)
```

So, our application was trying to access our `boards.json` file but it cannot find it at the specified path.

web.config file for URL redirection

If you notice, we did copy the `api` folder so why is the application not able to find the JSON file? The reason here is because of how URL routing works on Windows. We need to explicitly define the file extensions which we want our web server to support, or else when the web server encounters any file with an extension it does not understand, the web server is not able to request the file.

To do that, we need to create a `web.config` file and have that file in our `wwwroot` folder. This file will have the mapping for the JSON extension as shown in the following screenshot:

```
<?xml version="1.0"?>

<configuration>
<system.webServer>
<staticContent>
<mimeMap fileExtension=".json" mimeType="application/json" />
</staticContent>
</system.webServer>
</configuration>
```

So, there are two ways to keep this file in our deployment folder. One way is to just create the file and copy to the deployment folder and the other way is to add this file to our project and have it as part of the build process.

The advantage of the second approach is that we will have integrated this file as part of our project and in any further deployments, the `web.config` file will be automatically deployed. Also, if later we want to add other file extensions as well, our file being part of our code folder, we will not have to worry about the different versions of the file.

So, let's add the `web.config` file to our `src` folder and add the reference in our `angularcli.json` file so that at the build, Angular CLI copies this file into our `dist` folder. The following is the change in the `angularcli.json` file:

```
"assets": [
"assets",
"favicon.ico",
"api/board/boards.json",
"web.config"
],
```

As you can see, we have added the reference to `web.config`, under `assets` as this will be treated as a static file by Angular CLI.

Now, when we build our code, we will have `web.config` file copied in our `dist` folder and when we FTP our `dist` folder, the file will be copied on our web server as well as shown in the following screenshot:

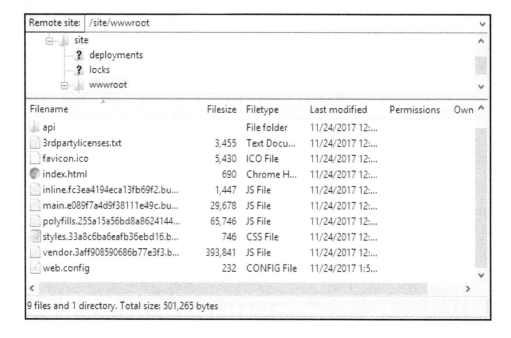

The result

Now, after we have copied the `web.config` file to our deployment folder, we should see our application running correctly as shown in the following screenshot:

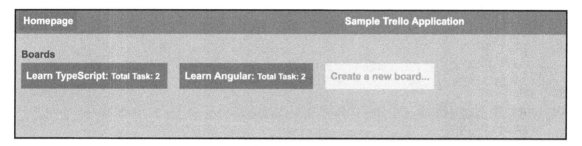

The web server now uses the `web.config` file to understand the request for a JSON file and map it to `application/json`, which allows it to request the file from the server.

Deploying Sample Trello using a web app service – GitHub

In the previous section, we deployed our code on Microsoft Azure using FTP. This approach was simple and we were able to deploy the application in a very few steps.

But, there is one disadvantage to this approach: every time we make a change in our code, and we build and test it, we will have to manually deploy our application on the web server using FTP.

This is fine if you are the only developer on the project and it's a small project. This approach quickly becomes an overhead if you are working on a large-scale project. We need a mechanism to quickly integrate the development process into our deployment so as to automatically deploy the code on the web server every time we check in.

This is where the integration of the deployment process with the central repositories helps. Microsoft Azure provides integration with the following:

- Visual Studio Team Services
- OneDrive
- GitHub
- Local Git
- BitBucket
- Dropbox

We will look at GitHub as our repository and use the code we have for our *Sample Trello* application to configure the deployment process.

Integration with GitHub

When we created the web app service in the last section, we added the deployment credentials which we needed for our FTP. For integrating with central repositories, Azure provides us with **Deployment option** under the **Deployments** section.

Before that, let's create a new web app service similar to what we created for our FTP-based deployment. It's important to understand that for each deployment option, we will need a separate web app service, though we can replace FTP deployment with GitHub deployment on the same web app service.

Here, we will not go through the creation of the web app service as it is already detailed in the previous section.

Once we have the web app service (`SampleTrello-GitHub`) created, we can integrate GitHub into our deployment repository.

Configuring GitHub

To configure a repository, you need to select **Deployment option** from the **Deployment** section in the landing page of the web app. You will be presented with an option to configure your source from a list of all the sources as shown in the following screenshot:

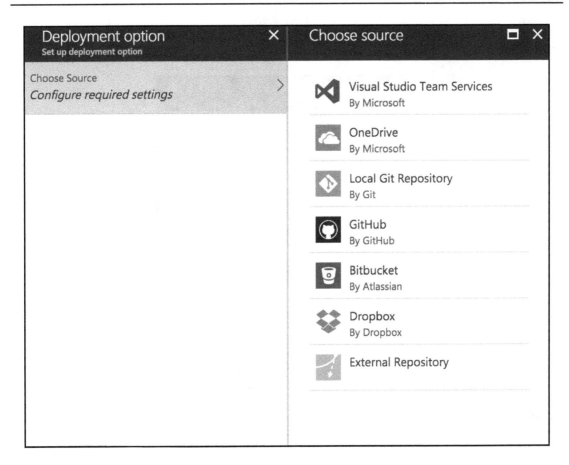

From the list, we will choose **GitHub**; you can choose whichever repository you use for your project and the steps will be similar.

Once you choose GitHub as the source, Azure will ask you for your credentials and then the project options. You may have different branches for your application, with one master being your production branch and others your hotfix or feature branches. Azure allows you to configure which branch you want the code to be deployed from.

Once you have configured all these options, you will have a screen similar to the following screenshot:

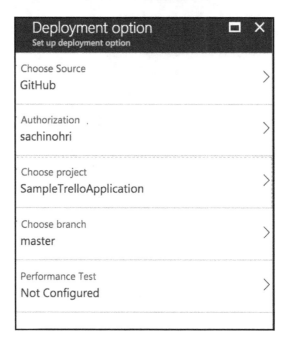

On clicking **OK**, Azure will start the deployment process and copy the code from GitHub to the local folder on the machine where your web app service is running.

Running the application

Once the code is deployed by Azure on the web app, we can try to run the application using the URL, which in our case is `http://sampletrello-github.azurewebsites.net/`.

On running the application, you will see the following error:

```
You do not have permission to view this directory or page.
```

This has happened because when Azure copied the GitHub repository, it copied all the files, which includes our code base. Azure needs the `dist` folder to be able to run the web application.

Adding the dist folder to GitHub

So, we need to check in the `dist` folder as well in our GitHub repository. To be able to do that, you need to change the `.gitignore` file and remove the reference to the `dist` folder. Once done, you should be able to check in the `dist` folder.

Now, Azure will automatically sync the changes from your GitHub repository to the local filesystem where the code is deployed. But, you will still get the same error when trying to run the application. This is because even though now you have the `dist` folder, the web server still does not know where the application is and it has deployed the whole code base.

You can check what code is deployed on the web server by doing an FTP or remote desktop on the server, and checking the content in the `wwwroot` folder.

Azure creates a separate folder with the name `repository`, where it copies all the files from GitHub and then copies the required deployment files to the `wwwroot` folder, as shown in the following screenshot:

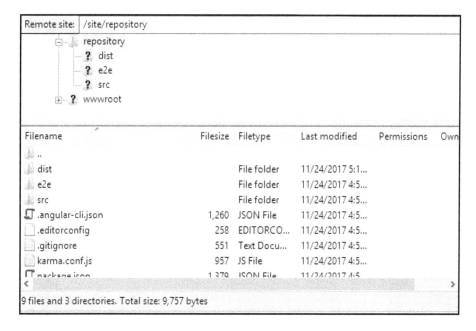

We need to inform the web server of the correct path from where it should copy the code into the `wwwroot` folder. To do that, Azure provides us with an option to add **Application Settings**.

Adding application settings

Under the **Settings** section, we have an option for **App settings**. The web server uses these settings to identify the various configurations required to run the application.

For example, under **App settings**, we have a section for **Default Documents**, which lists all the default documents, such as `default.html`, `index.html`, and much more. The web server searches for any of these files in its `wwwroot` folder, and if it finds one, the web server renders that file.

In our case, that file is `index.html`, so when we request our application using the `http://sampletrello-github.azurewebsites.net` URL, the web server checks for one of the default documents, and renders that.

Similarly, there are other options, such as the .NET Framework version, which will be required if we are deploying a .NET-based web application, or the Java version for Java-based applications. You can even add database connection strings so that the application can determine which database to connect to.

For our application, we need to use the **App settings** section and add the following key-value pair:

```
key: Project
value: ./dist
```

The following is the screenshot of the modified **App settings** for our application:

The key, **Project**, informs the web server to check the web project under the folder defined in the **Value** property. So, here we are informing the web server that the web application is located under the `dist` folder. So, when we save these app settings, Azure will redeploy the code and, this time, will copy the files from the `dist` folder under the `repository` folder in the web server, to the `wwwroot` folder, as shown in the following screenshot:

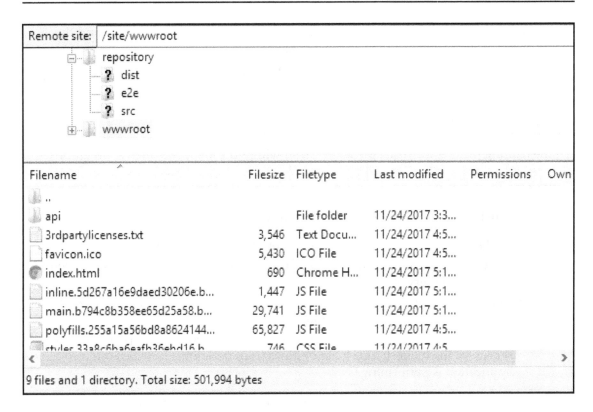

Now, if we run our application, we should be able to see our *Sample Trello* application running successfully.

Continuous deployment and monitoring

The main advantage of having GitHub integrated with our deployment process is the automatic deployment that happens on Azure. So, let's suppose we make a change in our code, probably to fix a bug, and then we run it on the local machine. Once we confirm that our application is working as expected, we check in our code as well as the updated `dist` folder to our GitHub repository.

Azure has a Webhook attached to our GitHub repository which allows Azure to keep track of any changes that happen. As soon as any new changes are reflected on GitHub, Azure triggers a sync process that allows it to pull the latest code from GitHub and redeploy the code on the web server.

This way, we can have our changes automatically deployed on the web server, and the whole deployment process is taken care of by Azure.

Azure also provides an option to initiate a sync manually through the deployment options.

Web application monitoring

On the landing page of the web app service, you will find some of the metrics in graphs. These graphs represent the various different sets of information that can be useful when we want to monitor our application's health.

The default metrics provided by Azure are as follows:

- **HTTP 5xx error**: This tells us the number of server errors reported .
- **Data in/out**: These provide details of the number of bytes that are transferred to and from the server.
- **Request**: This provides the details of the number of requests that have come in for the web application in a period of time.
- **Average response time**: Here, we get information about the response time of our server for the request. This metric allows us to determine how fast our application is performing.

Apart from these metrics, Azure provides us with an option to add **Alerts** to our web server and configure other specific metrics, such as for HTTP 4xx, or Average memory used, or CPU time, and much more. You can configure these from the **MONITORING** section on the landing page, as shown in the following screenshot:

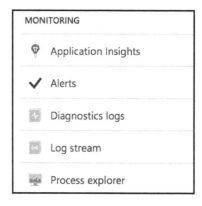

Summary

In this chapter, our focus was on deploying the *Sample Trello* application on Microsoft Azure. We looked at the capabilities of Azure, and of cloud deployment in general. We saw the advantages of using the cloud as our deployment platform in comparison to the traditional in-house deployment.

Then we delved into the deployment of our *Sample Trello* application using a web app service. In web app services, we looked at how we can deploy our application using FTP, and using GitHub as our deployment source. We looked at how to create a new web app service, integrate GitHub with that service, and also how we can manage the app service plan to provide the most economical setup.

In this book, we have focused on learning TypeScript and Angular in depth by developing a couple of applications. This allowed us to not only focus on concepts, but their implementation as well. The next step for everyone is to delve deeper into the concepts of TypeScript and Angular, and develop some amazing applications.

Index